How to Care More

Seven Skills for Personal and Social Change

Miranda Campbell, PhD
Ryerson University

ROWMAN & LITTLEFIELD
Lanham • Boulder • New York • London

Executive Acquisitions Editor: Mark Kerr
Associate Editor: Courtney Packard
Sales and Marketing Inquiries: textbooks@rowman.com

Credits and acknowledgments for material borrowed from other sources, and reproduced with permission, appear on the appropriate pages within the text.

Published by Rowman & Littlefield
An imprint of The Rowman & Littlefield Publishing Group, Inc.
4501 Forbes Boulevard, Suite 200, Lanham, Maryland 20706
www.rowman.com

86-90 Paul Street, London EC2A 4NE

British Library Cataloguing in Publication Information Available

Library of Congress Cataloging-in-Publication Data

Names: Campbell, Miranda, 1981- author.
Title: How to care more : seven skills for personal and social change / Miranda Campbell, PhD, Ryerson University.
Description: Lanham : Rowman & Littlefield, [2022] | Includes bibliographical references and index.
Identifiers: LCCN 2021045541 (print) | LCCN 2021045542 (ebook) | ISBN 9781538145043 (cloth) | ISBN 9781538145050 (paperback) | ISBN 9781538145067 (epub)
Subjects: LCSH: Social change. | Empathy. | Caring. | Justice.
Classification: LCC HM831 .C354 2022 (print) | LCC HM831 (ebook) | DDC 303.4—dc23
LC record available at https://lccn.loc.gov/2021045541
LC ebook record available at https://lccn.loc.gov/2021045542

Contents

Detailed Contents

Introduction

World on Fire

■ ■ ■

It's 2017 and the world is on fire.

At the time, 2017 was the worst year on record for forest fires in British Columbia, Canada, where I am from. I grew up near Vancouver in an area called the Lower Mainland. I remember growing up hearing news of summer wildfires in other parts of British Columbia—in the Okanagan Valley, Salmon Arm, Penticton, places that seemed distant to me. Sometimes the news would be about evacuation, families losing their homes. But this all felt far away, removed, when I was a child.

But in 2017 there was thick smoke in the air from BC wildfires, smoke covering the sun, smoke stretching down to the Lower Mainland, the greater Vancouver area, and farther south to the United States as well, creeping to Seattle, to Colorado—a thick and looming haze. My parents, who live in Surrey, BC, stayed inside because of respiratory distress and other health problems. My mom and dad staying inside, in their air-conditioned house at that, is really a minor brunt of creeping climate change. In his book *The Uninhabitable Earth*, David Wallace-Wells calls out the fallacy of looking at the contemporary rise of natural disasters and a heating planet and thinking, *climate change is here*. He writes, "The devastation we are now seeing all around us is a beyond-best-case scenario for the future of warming and all the climate disasters it will bring."[1] Beyond widespread wildfires in BC and beyond, the contemporary moment has seen record-breaking floods, droughts, and heat waves. In Australia, the 2019–2020 bushfire season became known as the "Black Summer" due to the intensity of the fires, damage to the land, and loss of life. Other record-breaking natural disasters in 2020 include floods in Indonesia, landslides in Brazil, and cyclones in India and Bangladesh. I'm mindful of Wallace-Wells' reminder that it's the Global South that bears and will bear much of the frontline impact of a heating planet and escalating conflict.

So why start this book with this moment from 2017?

I'm starting in 2017 because 2017 was a new phase of my life, a new way of being in the world. My daughter, Elinor, was born November 1, 2016. Welcoming a child into my life and figuring out how to raise her has made me ever more mindful of the future that she will inherit due to the contemporary crises on environmental, economic, social, and political fronts. Unlike when I was a child, none of these challenges seems far away or removed to me anymore: my role as a parent has caused me to reflect on the urgency of these situations—but this urgency was here all along. In the twenty-first century, we've experienced many moments of crisis: the 2008–2009 financial collapse, rising unemployment rates and in particular global youth unemployment, the climate crisis, COVID-19, heightened awareness of systemic racism and the resurgence of the Black Lives Matter movement, and so on.

David Wallace-Wells writes that he's often asked whether it's moral and responsible to have children in this climate, and whether or not it's fair to the planet and to the children. Whether or not to have children is of a course a personal choice, but Wallace-Wells writes that in the course of writing his book, *The Uninhabitable Earth*, he did have a child. I like to think that having children is a hopeful not a destructive act, a commitment to imagining a better future. This book explores many ways to invest ourselves in creating personal and social change, which also invite commitment to creating a better future and to caring more. Wallace-Wells writes that the horrors of climate change are not yet fully scripted. "We are staging them by inaction, and by action we can stop them," he writes.

Through my work and experience as a researcher, teacher, parent, and community member, I've come to see *care* as part of the solution to taking action in our challenging contemporary moment. When we think of care, we might first picture taking care of and raising children, an act that has been historically feminized, and unfortunately devalued in much of Western society. With aging populations, we might also think of care homes, care workers, and care facilities that look after the elderly. With these connotations of care, we picture dependents, children and the elderly, who need assistance managing bodily and physical needs to be able to care for themselves.

This book offers a much more expansive definition of care. When we proclaim we don't care about something, we mean we are not invested and the matter doesn't concern us. This book starts from this place, investigating what small steps and skills can be practiced to reinvest ourselves and concern ourselves with our own wellbeing and the wellbeing of those around us. Think about the common practice of telling someone to "take care," which invites that person to look after themselves. Increasingly, we recognize and have the common language of "self-care." Self-care has become commercialized, and might bring to mind bath bombs, shopping sprees, or other consumer-based indulgences. Shopping might be one way to take care of oneself, but this concept of self-care has much deeper roots. In her essay "A Burst of Light," based in her journals while living with cancer, Black feminist Audre Lorde declared, "Caring for myself is not self-indulgence, it is self-preservation, and that is an act of political warfare."[2] Lorde discusses her experience of racism and marginalization as a Black woman and asserts her right to exist and to care for herself. When women, and in particular women of color, have been directed to care for others, centering yourself and valuing yourself takes on particular salience.

Conversations are increasingly happening about the need to foster care and caring attitudes in light of current societal challenges. For example, in 2018 I presented research at the Care and the Media and Cultural Industries conference at the CAMEo Research Centre in the United Kingdom; the Care Ethics and Precarity conference was also held in 2018 at Portland State University. Meanwhile, grassroots "care collectives" are also on the rise. When the COVID-19 pandemic struck in 2020, many people worldwide were caught off-guard, but also quickly mobilized caring and community-oriented responses, based in mutual aid. In Toronto, the Caremongering-TO Facebook group began with offers to help others get groceries and supplies but expanded to become a wide-ranging vehicle for support, including offers of home office IT assistance and addiction recovery discussions. The PDX Non-Binary Community Effort group, based in Portland, Oregon, circulated a "collective cares" Google Document, including information and resources on topics ranging from how to make a homemade mask to mental health support, child care, and houselessness.[3] Social justice activist and disability justice author Leah Piepzna-Samarasinha circulated the "Half Assed Disabled Prepper Tips for Preparing for a Coronavirus Quarantine" Google Document, similarly sharing information about food, sanitization, health, medical supplies, and mutual aid.[4]

We seem to have a sense that we need to look after ourselves and others, and our current social and economic systems are constraining our ability to do so. But what practical steps can we take to reverse some of the damage? We might look to our leaders or our electoral systems and ask for change, policies, or reform. This is important and needed work but can also feel slow and out of our grasp. This book suggests that we start with ourselves, how we interact with ourselves and others, as one element of social change. Rather than looking for change to come from those in power or in top positions in society, this book profiles young people and grassroots collectives who are already spearheading change, from the bottom up.

When we target personal and social change through how we interact with ourselves and others, we target the realm of what are sometimes referred to as "soft skills." It's perhaps easy to dismiss these skills as a lesser tier of skills, or less valuable than more concrete or "hard skills." You might think that learning a computer program like Photoshop or InDesign is more valuable than something more nebulous like considering how can we better get along.

Concrete, practical skills are of course important, but so too are the skills of responsiveness and reciprocity, targeted here. Authentically learning these skills might be some of the hardest work we do in our lives and is ongoing, reflexive work that is never completely "done." In an episode called "The Death and Rebirth of Soft Skill" of the *Culture First* podcast, host Damien Klotz provides an example of the difference between hard and soft skills through working on an Excel spreadsheet with someone else. He says, "When you think about what makes for a great relationship at work, it's less about, could you sit there and work well on Excel together, and more about, how did you show up for that person, how did you address them, do you address them in a way that comforts them and gives them good feedback?"[5] These qualities of relating to others are more important and more challenging than the technologies, software, or platforms we used to facilitate work and exchange.

We know that soft skills are desired by employers and can influence hiring decisions, alongside hard skills. The employment website LinkedIn's assessment of the most in-demand soft skills for employment in 2020 included creativity, persuasion, collaboration, adaptability, and emotional intelligence.[6] These are some of the skills tackled here, and this book suggests that soft skills are perhaps the most important skills to improve. But the end goal of this book is not to be more employable or to be more in demand on the job market. The purpose of this book is to be able to live well with oneself and others, whether at work, at home, with family, friends, or community groups.

In "The Death and Rebirth of Soft Skills" episode, Klotz interviews human resources specialist Claude Silver about the word *soft* in soft skills. Silver says, "soft connotates mushy. They're not mushy skills. They are necessary life skills. We use them every single day." Silver questions this term, asking, "Why call them soft skills? They are life skills. They are what we need to be human beings. If I'm calling myself soft, I'm taking away my power." Here Silver stresses the necessary and powerful qualities of "soft" skills. In contrast, the podcast also interviews personal and team coach Dara Blumenthal, who is more positive about the word *soft*. Blumenthal says, "I like the 'soft'; it's important that we are able to soften into our experience, to tenderize our environments." The word *soft* is often devalued in our culture, perhaps because it's associated with more feminine or nurturing qualities. Blumenthal suggests recuperating and valuing softness, but "not so that everyone feels good." Having good soft skills might mean having "more difficult, uncomfortable conversations, more often." It means having the skills to address problems and to work toward change, rather than avoiding or assuming everything is okay or will work out fine. Blumenthal suggests that the first step we can take to start doing some of this work on soft skills is with ourselves, and with our self-awareness. This book starts from this place, too, of expanding individual knowledge and capacity through learning and reflection.

A NOTE ON THE ORGANIZATION AND PURPOSE OF THIS BOOK

This book defines care and offers tools that operate as elements of care, including listening, consent, cultivating inclusion, collaboration, love, and resilience. Each chapter is devoted to one of these elements of care and includes practical exercises to foster care. These chapters are not intended as an exhaustive list of all elements of care, but instead they are a starting place for personal and collective reflection and work. This book offers some terms and strategies about how to care more, but ultimately this book is not a prescriptive set of rules. Some definitions and concepts outlined here may evolve over time, but the basic underlying concept that the self exists in relation to others, and care flows from this place, will stay the same.

Because this book covers a lot of ground in its six chapters, it is intended as an entry point into learning and developing an understanding of the topic at hand. For example, you could read a whole book on listening, but that topic here is covered in one chapter. I hope to spark a curiosity for further learning, rather than provide an exhaustive or definitive guide to any one topic. I encourage you to seek out more knowledge from practitioners, activists, artists, and theorists who are working on these issues. Attend workshops or conferences; read more books, pamphlets, essays, and blogs; and talk to your friends, coworkers, neighbors, and family members. This further exploration and further interaction will provide more nuance and insight, but this book will equip you with a solid starting place for your journey.

In each chapter, you will find the following elements:

Definitions of key terms, provided in bold

Profiles of grassroots groups and organizations developing new initiatives to improve a social issue, related to the definitions being discussed in the chapter

Exercises to put your understanding of definitions into practice through hands-on activity, either alone or with others

Questions for Learning and Reflection for developing your own opinions and understanding of key terms, often by applying them to your own life and context

References and Further Reading to provide you with more resources to continue your learning

I hope this book is useful to you and provides you some insight, some understanding, some clarity, some hope, and some inspiration.

Take care,
Miranda

NOTES

1. David Wallace-Wells, *The Uninhabitable Earth: Life after Warming* (New York: Tim Duggan Books, 2019), 18–19.
2. Audre Lorde, "A Burst of Light: Living with Cancer," in *A Burst of Light and Other Essays* (Ithaca, NY: Firebrand Books, 1988), 131.
3. PDX Non-Binary Community Effort, "Collective Cares," n.d., accessed March 16, 2021, https://docs.google.com/document/d/1XBDKJjQsSQOCT64ADuuCaPognKHUTZD7syc_RliGg3o/edit.
4. Leah Lakshmi Piepzna-Samarasinha, "Half Assed Disabled Prepper Tips for Preparing for a Coronavirus Quarantine," March 10, 2020, accessed March 16, 2021, https://docs.google.com/document/d/1rldpKgXeBHbmM3KpB5NfjEBue8YN1MbXhQ7zTOLmSyo/edit.
5. Culture Amp, "Death and Rebirth Life Skills," *Culture First* podcast, season 1, episode 5, February 5, 2020.
6. Bruce M. Anderson, "The Most In-Demand Hard and Soft Skills of 2020," *LinkedIn Talent Blog*, January 9, 2020, accessed May 28, 2021, https://business.linkedin.com/talent-solutions/blog/trends-and-research/2020/most-in-demand-hard-and-soft-skills.

1
Care

■ ■ ■

Environmental, social, political, and cultural events can make us feel unanchored and uncertain about the future. Rather than languish in these feelings, it can be productive to reinvest ourselves in our commitments and communities as a way of building a better future. Which is not to say that we necessarily think, "I am building a better future," every time we collaborate with others or take action. It's easy to get bogged down in the day-to-day logistics of the to-do list, working, and surviving, which makes it challenging to resurface and see how our actions fit into any kind of bigger picture.

I once had the pleasure of seeing Dr. Angela Davis speak, an important figure in the Black Power movement of the 1960s, a movement that fought for Black empowerment and Black civil rights. Davis continues to work and advocate for equality, in particular around the American prison system and the crisis of mass incarceration, which disproportionately affects young Black men in America. During the question period of the lecture I attended, I remember one person asking Dr. Davis about how we continue on and carry a sense of hope, given there are so many different and complex problems to tackle in society. Dr. Davis' response was to start somewhere, with one thing, working with other people, and to trust that this one small thing connects with the bigger picture of other people working on other things elsewhere. We can't tackle everything all at once. One thing is enough, and one thing is a place to start. Starting to think about and work on the "one thing" is also starting to care more.

Take a moment to think about one issue that you find pressing and one small way that you can take action to work on it with other people. For example, you might be troubled by a lack of access to fresh and nutritious food in your area. You might consider volunteering in your local food bank once a week or once a month, or investigate if there is a community garden initiative that supports local people in your area.

Even choosing to educate yourself more about this issue by reading up on it online could be a starting place. There's nothing wrong with common options like donating money or signing petitions as ways to take action, but they can be quick or symbolic gestures that don't really require us to invest ourselves in an issue.

When we start with one thing, we resist the pitfalls of either/or thinking, which might suggest that we need to tackle everything or that we have done nothing—either total social transformation or bust. Another way of describing this either/or way of thinking is called **binary logic**, an overly dualistic way of viewing the world, which has been common in much of Western thinking. You might be familiar with French philosopher René Descartes' famous declaration, "I think, therefore I am." Here, identity is all wrapped up in the mind, in thinking, and we can identify the binary logic of the mind/body split in this declaration. Thinking is being, all or nothing. Instead, we might consider more connected and holistic ways of being and seeing the world, common among feminist and Indigenous thinkers. A more holistic framework allows us to make connections between the small and the big picture, and to pay attention to the in-between parts of working toward a goal. As we'll see below, these in-between parts are the essence of caring.

DEFINING CARE

Recently, I was riding my bike the wrong way up a one-way street. This is illegal, and it's something I know I shouldn't be doing, and I could very well get a ticket for. I turned up this one-way street, and kept biking, because my destination was halfway up the block. The smarter thing would have been to get off my bike and walk it up to where I was trying to go. But, as is often the case, I was in a rush, so I just kept biking. A driver, driving the right way down the one-way street, passed me biking up the wrong way and yelled out the window, "It's a one-way street, stupid!" I was pretty cheesed. So rude, I thought! I'm not stupid, I'm just in a rush. What a jerk. As I locked up my biked, I reflected that I have also said mouthy things to drivers and to other cyclists in the past, and have taken part in my fair share of rude behavior.

The definition of care outlined in this book is based in action and does not suggest merely to be kind, to refrain from saying mouthy things to others, or to follow rules and guidelines that enable safety for everyone. A different definition of care, different than the one outlined here, is being nurturing or warm. Those are lovely personal qualities. But we don't always have to be warm with one another to work toward building a better future. Conflict and differences in collaboration can be a source of creativity. If people feel comfortable speaking up to disagree, this can be a sign of a healthy and caring environment, rather than a toxic one.

Care as Values

Kindness, civility, and politeness can go a long way toward creating a pleasant environment for everyone to inhabit. Based on my anecdote of riding my bike, I can imagine that no one likes being yelled at and told they are stupid. In her book *All About Love*, Black feminist bell hooks highlights values such as friendship, talking together, trust, respect, care, knowledge, and responsibility as "the process of making community wherever we are," which is "unlike other movements for social change that require joining organizations and attending meetings."[1] Here hooks highlights the ways we act toward one another as forms of political action and creating change. Talking with others or taking responsibility for one's actions might at the outset seem very different than other forms of direct political action, like attending a protest. However, hooks suggests that these values create community and might transform our world though meaningful, sustained interpersonal behavior. Similarly, political sociologist Leah Bassel highlights the sphere of "micropolitics," the small or micro spaces where political transformation might take place. She discusses a "reorientation of political practice toward one another, fellow citizens, alongside politics vis-à-vis formal institutions with power."[2] Here Bassel suggests how we act with one another and what our formal political institutions do are both ways of enacting social change. On the whole, this definition of care-as-values that emerges from our interactions with others suggests that individuals can and do have impact in how we shape the world together.

Care as Process

Through the definition of care outlined above, we've started to examine some of the complexities and layers of care. We can further understand some of this complexity through understanding care as a process, not something that is all-or-nothing. In "Toward a Feminist Theory of Caring," Bernice Fisher and Joan Tronto define care as a process made up of four steps.

1. Caring about (paying attention, *attentiveness*)
2. Taking care of (responding, taking *responsibility*)
3. Caregiving (doing the hands-on work, *competence*)
4. Care receiving (the responses of the care receiver to the caring process, *responsiveness*)[3]

In a later book, Tronto adds a further step of care:

5. Caring with (democratic commitments to justice, equality, and freedom for all)[4]

Let's consider these steps through an example of visiting your elderly grandmother. At 4 p.m., you remember it's the usual time that Grandma drinks some tea and has a snack. This is the first step of care, noticing or paying attention. Next, you decide you are going to make some tea and a snack for Grandma. This is the second step, taking care of this need or responding, taking responsibility for it. The third step is actually making the tea and the snack, boiling the water, finding the tea bags, making a sandwich, or putting some cookies on a plate. This third step is doing the hands-on work. Last, the fourth step is Grandma's response. What does she have to say about this tea and this snack? Does she want it? Is it to her liking? Do we need to adjust something based on how we presented it, or is she satisfied? This final step is very important: care is not caring if it is coercive, doing something to someone else that they don't like, or not listening to or disregarding feedback. If there is feedback, this returns us to the first step of care, to pay attention to what is being communicated and adjust accordingly.

When we define care as a multistep process, we can also imagine one person does not have to see this whole cycle through. For example, in the example with Grandma, you might notice that it's 4 p.m. and it's time for Grandma's tea, but you have to go to work. Your brother is also visiting with Grandma, so you ask him if he can make the tea. This is still the process of care: you have paid attention and responded, and your brother does the hands-on work and listens to the responses from Grandma.

Fisher and Tronto outline four factors that impact the capacity to deliver care:

1. Time
2. Material resources
3. Knowledge
4. Skill[5]

Let's return again to Grandma and her tea. Above, we considered the example that you might notice it's Grandma's teatime, but you don't have the *time* to make her tea. Likewise, Grandma might be on a fixed income, and maybe there's no tea in her cupboard for you to make, so the *material resources* are not available for you to make her anything. Maybe you love Grandma, but your life has not allowed you to be present in the ways you would have liked, and you lack the *knowledge* about her schedule and don't even know it's her teatime. Finally, maybe Grandma likes her tea made in a traditional British kind of way that involves all kinds of steps, like warming the pot before putting boiling water in, and you don't have the *skill* to make tea in the kind of way she likes. This example is relatively simple, but we can think about these factors in a broader sense, about how care is organized in society, beyond individuals and individual choices and capacities. Much care to the elderly is delivered through facilities that might have profit rather than care as their primary motive, and staff in these facilities can often be poorly paid with poor working conditions, limiting their capacity to be caring. This is why Tronto's fifth step of care is important, caring with. Tronto asserts that the work of democracy is to equip all citizens to have the capacity to care, in the pursuit of justice, freedom, and equality. Not all people have the same access to time, material resources, knowledge, and skill, and access impacts individuals' capacities. In Tronto's argument, the project of democracy is to identify and reduce barriers and obstacles to caring.

Care as Relational Action

What is care? To begin, care can start from a place of situating yourself in relation to others. Who do you care for, and who cares for you? When we start thinking this way, we notice that care is relational, meaning it flows between two or more people. The concept of **relationality**, being embedded in a web of relations, differs from a binary logic of a divided, either/or self. Let's begin an exploration of relationality with the concept of relationships. Philosophy professor Anthony Weston notes the importance of relationships for people:

> We are social beings as well as individuals. We are born to other humans, grow up in families, and take on traditions and heritages and communities. And we all live, in turn, in deep interrelation with the larger-than-human natural world. Values central to relationship are caring, participation, and community. Recognizing how much our communities make us who we are also calls forth not only gratefulness but also a responsibility to protect, sustain and attend to them.[6]

Here we can see caring as emerging from relationships and as a central value in relationships. We can also note a relational concept of the self, with humans being defined as social beings. Even if we identify as individuals, Weston reminds us of all the social structures, like families, communities, and institutions, that impact how we develop a sense of self.

For feminist philosopher Nel Noddings, an ethics of care is based in relational ethics, meaning care is based in relationships and the ethics of how individuals relate to one another. She underscores a **relational ontology** for an ethic of care, meaning a theory of self that is relational rather than isolated or autonomous. In her book *Caring: A Relational Approach to Ethics and Moral Education*, Noddings suggests that caring is "rooted in receptivity, relatedness, and responsiveness."[7] With this foundation, "our efforts must, then, be directed to the maintenance of conditions that will permit caring to flourish."[8] If humans are relational beings, care emerges from these relations. Care can further be developed by creating supportive conditions for care to flourish. Similarly, psychologist Carol Gilligan proposes an ethic of care in her book *In a Different Voice*. Gilligan's work addresses a gender gap in theorizing ethics, suggesting that, historically, philosophy has focused on ways of being that are coded as masculine. Caring has historically and continues to be coded as feminine, and like Noddings, Gilligan seeks to recuperate and restore the value of care. In a 2011 interview, Gilligan defined care as

> an ethic grounded in voice and relationships, in the importance of everyone having a voice, being listened to carefully (in their own right and on their own terms) and heard with respect. An ethics of care directs our attention to the need for responsiveness in relationships (paying attention, listening, responding) and to the costs of losing connection with oneself or with others.[9]

Even though care is based in the relational nature of the self, this does not suggest a loss of individuality: here care is described as an element that allows everyone to have a voice and to connect with themselves, based in relations with others. In this book, we'll explore different ways of paying attention, listening, and responding as ways of enacting care. As much as we will define care as relational and responsive, based in reciprocity, we want to avoid a concept of care as transactional. A transactional definition is much narrower—I'll do something for you, if you do something for me: a system known as quid pro quo, or a favor for a favor. This quid pro quo idea is the basis of fair contracts and exchange, but instead of defining care as a contractual, transactional value, we instead want to cultivate a sense of being in it together. This sense of caring is a bit murkier than a simple idea of you scratch my back, I'll scratch yours, so we'll spend some time here exploring definitions of care.

Indigenous scholar Robin Wall Kimmerer, author of the book *Braiding Sweetgrass: Indigenous Wisdom, Scientific Knowledge, and the Teaching of Plants*, provides an expansive overview of the importance of paying attention in reciprocal, nontransactional ways in her essay "Returning the Gift."

> Paying attention is an ongoing act of reciprocity, the gift that keeps on giving, in which attention generates wonder, which generates more attention—and more joy. Paying attention to the more-than-human world doesn't lead only to amazement; it leads also to acknowledgment of pain. Open and attentive, we see and feel equally the beauty and the wounds, the old growth and the clear-cut, the mountain and the mine. Paying attention to suffering sharpens our ability to respond. To be responsible. This, too, is a gift, for when we fall in love with the living world, we cannot be bystanders to its destruction. Attention becomes intention, which coalesces itself to action.[10]

Kimmerer outlines the joy and challenges of paying attention to the world, as the world is both full of wonder and suffering. It can be a challenge to be responsive to this mixed context of being in the world, but Kimmerer outlines this reflexivity and responsiveness as a gift that can catalyze personal and social change. Paying attention, responsibility, intention, and action can all be part of a definition of an ethics of care.

Here I suggest two overlapping definitions of care: one as a personal value (care as values), and one as a process (care as process). Taking action emerges in the space between these two definitions (care as relational action) and is the main definition of care for this book (see figure 1.1). Each chapter in this book focuses on one aspect of care as relational action

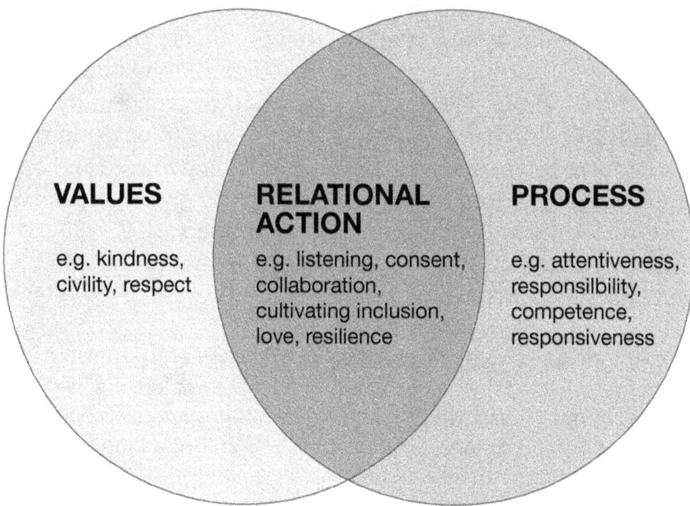

Figure 1.1 Defining Care

(listening, consent, collaboration, cultivating inclusion, love, and resilience). These chapters are not intended as a definitive or all-encompassing definition of care. Rather, these chapters, each focused on an elements of care as relational action, are offered in this book as a starting point for your own personal journey for discovering your own caring pathway as a way of being, relating, and responding to the world.

In "Toward a Feminist Theory of Caring," Fisher and Tronto define care expansively, as "a species activity that includes everything that we do to maintain, continue, and repair our 'world' so that we can live in it as well as possible."[11] Maintaining, continuing, and repairing suggest investment in the often behind-the-scenes work that makes society operate. Care might most readily suggest caring for dependents, like children and the elderly, but Fisher and Tronto's definition expands past this context of dependent care. Fisher and Tronto's broad definition is also an active one, including "everything" we do that allows us to live as well as possible in the world. Within this expansive, active definition of care, we might include both a commitment to values and a commitment to process.

Activity 1.1: Pod Mapping Our Relational Selves

This activity is adapted with permission from the "Pods and Pod Mapping Worksheet," written by Mia Mingus for the Bay Area Transformative Justice Collective (BATJC).[12] BATJC is a community group based in Oakland, California, working to build and support transformative justice. This approach to harm works toward repair with affected individuals without relying on intervention from the police and the state, such as prisons, given the oppressive role these institutions play in the lives of marginalized people. The BATJC developed the concept of "pods" in relation to transformative justice to enable people to envision their support networks in a concrete way. Here we are going to use this concept of pods and the BATJC's pod mapping worksheet to investigate the concept of a relational self and caring connections to others.

The BATJC explains that the concept of "community" can be vague and sometimes too open:

> We found that, not surprisingly, many people do not feel connected to a "community" and, even more so, most people did not know what "community" meant or had wildly different definitions and understandings of "community." For some, "community" was an overarching term that encompassed huge numbers of people based on identity (e.g. "the feminist community"); while for others "community," referred to a specific

> set of arbitrary values, practices and/or relationships (e.g. "I don't know them well, but we're in community with each other"); or some defined "community" simply by geographic location, regardless of relationship or identity (e.g. "the Bay Area community"). We found that people romanticized community; or though they felt connected to a community at large, they only had significant and trustworthy relationships with very few actual people who may or may not be part of that community. For example, someone might feel connected to "the queer community," but when asked who from that "queer community" they felt they could trust to show up for them in times of crisis, vulnerability or violence, they could only name 2 or 3 people.

Community is still an appropriate term in many contexts and a term that the BATJC uses. But *pod* refers to a specific, limited, and nameable number of people that you can call on for support. As the BATJC says, "in general, pod people are often those you have relationship and trust with, though everyone has different criteria for their pods." People can have multiple pods for different contexts and different purposes: people they rely on and people who rely on them. The BATJC notes that often people only have a few dependable relationships in their lives, so having a pod with one or two people is normal. This is because our broader Western, capitalistic system drives us toward competitive individualism rather than cooperative and community care.

In this activity, we will explore the concept of the pod in practical terms to underscore that idea of the relational self, that we exist in relation to other people around us. Who are those people, specifically? Who do you care for, and who cares for you? The BATJC uses this pod mapping worksheet to develop mutual support and accountability through times of crisis and harm, but here we will use this worksheet in a broader sense, to investigate who we care for and who cares for us, to also start thinking about expanding and nurturing our relationships and our relational selves.

1. Write your name in the middle grey circle.
2. The surrounding bold-outlined circles are your pod. Write the names of the people who are in your pod. We encourage people to write the names of actual individuals, instead of things such as "my church group" or "my neighbors."
3. The dotted lines surrounding your pod are people who are "movable." They are people that *could be moved* into your pod but need a little more work. For example, you might need to build more relationship or trust with them.

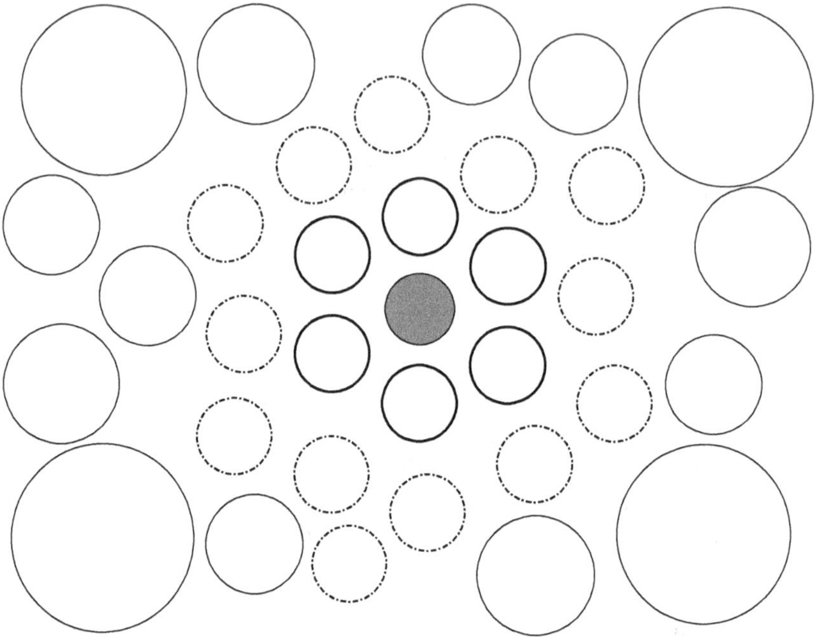

Figure 1.2 BATJC Pod Mapping Worksheet

Written by Mia Mingus for the Bay Area Transformative Justice Collective (BATJC)

4. The larger circles at the edge of the page are for networks, communities, or groups that could be resources for you. It could be your local domestic violence direct service organization, or your cohort in nursing school, or your youth group, or a transformative justice group.
5. Are there other people, networks, or groups you would like to bring into your pod? How might you foster those connections? You can also write in names of desired connections that you would like to develop for your pod.

According to the BATJC, your pod(s) may shift over time, as your needs or relationships shift or as people's geographic locations shift. Growing one's pod is not easy and may take time. In pod work, we measure our successes by the quality of our relationships with one another, and we invest the time it takes to build things like trust, respect, vulnerability, accountability, care, and love.

For information about the BATJC and for more information about the "pod" concept, visit https://batjc.wordpress.com/pods-and-pod-mapping-worksheet/.

CARE MORE

When you see something you identify as a glaring problem in society, what can you do, besides continuing on with your normal life with a feeling of being bogged down? In the following profile, reflect on what aspects of care as values, care as a process, and care as relational action you can identify.

Care More was started in 2014 by Mercedes Smith, who hails from Brooklyn, New York, after she finished her university degree at Bloomsburg University of Pennsylvania. When she returned home to New York City in 2014, she was struck by the level of visibility of homeless people in the streets. She reached out to her friend Joseph Moore to talk about passing these people every day on her way to work, saying no one stops to ask these people how they are doing, and expressed her desire to do something. Joseph suggested that they start something, saying, "People need to care more about each other."[13] This conversation was the genesis of Care More as an organization.

To start, Mercedes decided to go to the drugstore and buy toiletries to give out to homeless people in her daily travels. This was the first action of Care More as an organization, which has grown from one person with toiletries in her purse to a nonprofit organization also active in Philadelphia and New Jersey, integrating hundreds of volunteers. Speaking up and doing something about problems she notices is something that Mercedes has done her whole life. When she was fourteen, Mercedes was struck by the conflict in Sudan and the lack of news coverage about the Darfur genocide. So she emailed an editor at Newsday.com, pointing out this problem, prompting the news organization to cover the crisis and to send a news crew and photographers to Darfur. Noticing and taking initiative can led to change, and these values are a cornerstone of Care More as an organization. Care More's vision statement outlines that "we believe that every act of caring counts. Small deeds can often go unacknowledged and unrewarded but we hope to show the world that every ounce of kindness and generosity can help others become more compassionate—and in turn help make our world a better place."[14]

Today, it's not only Mercedes giving out needed items to homeless people. Through word of mouth and social media, volunteers help in the Care More cause of restoring a sense of humanity and dignity in interactions with homeless people. The organization started with local parks in New York City, involving volunteers to expand the distribution of needed items to the homeless. Care More advocates for a caring approach through interacting with homeless people as human beings with individual stories, talking the time to talk to these individuals as people, not only distributing them stuff as passive recipients of charity.

To help reach their objectives, Care More collaborates with other organizations, like Boys & Girls Clubs and YMCAs. The organization does "pop-up care give backs," collecting and distributing items in different spaces and places. Care More also collects clothing through bins at these organizations and through their volunteers. Care More then creates pop-up shopping experiences, with clothing donations hung up neatly for homeless people to select what they want, rather than clothing just being bagged up and given.

In 2015, the Afropunk Music Festival contacted Care More to coordinate an outreach give back, giving the people who volunteer with Care Moore free tickets to the festival. Care More cofounder Joseph Moore says the goal of the organization is "to make giving back part of a lifestyle, not something you dread."[15] Their hope is that young people integrate caring into the ways they live their lives, and collaborations with festivals like Afropunk help promote caring as vital and engaging, not something dreadful or shameful.

Longer term, Care More hopes to reduce homelessness while also teaching children to be kind and give back to their communities. In a TEDx Talk titled "The Artful Gift of Care," Mercedes acknowledges that delivering care packages is not in itself going to end homelessness. Still, she thinks this type of work can increase awareness, and "communication can knock down barriers."[16] For Care More, this type of social change starts on a human level with positive values, starting with people themselves, and endeavoring to make sure all people feel dignity and worthy of living.

For more information about Care More, visit https://www.letscaremore.com/.

DEVALUATION OF CARE AND REEVALUATION OF CARE

As we saw above, Fisher and Tronto define care expansively, as a species activity. All people give and receive care, but this is not the way that care has historically been and continues to be commonly defined and perceived. Care is often gendered, with women being viewed as caretakers of both children and the elderly. But these divides of who is assigned the work of caring in society go much deeper than gender. Tronto writes that care has been "historically relegated as the concerns of women, working-class people, and racial and ethnic minorities."[17] Social marginalization and historical devaluation and oppression have also required some communities to develop systems to care for themselves, in the absence of social and state provisioning. For example, we can examine the actions and responses of LGTBQ+ communities in the face of the AIDS epidemic of the 1980s. In this era, government inaction and lack of response to this crisis stemmed from homophobic attitudes and denigration of the lives of LGTBQ+ individuals.[18] This lack of response can be analyzed as a failure of democracy under Tronto's definition of "caring with," or "democratic commitments to justice, equality, and freedom for all." In the absence of state-provided care, LGTBQ+ communities learned to share knowledge, resources, and medicine and to care for one another through the formation of care collectives, as has been depicted in films like *Dallas Buyers Club* and plays like *Angels in America* and *The Normal Heart*.

Indigenous scholar Leanne Betasamosake Simpson's work traces the impact of colonialism on care work and on the creation of gendered roles of who performs care. She states the "colonial gender binary . . . sets out two sets of rigidly defined roles based on colonial concepts of femininity and masculinity. It then places colonial concepts of maleness and masculinity as more important than female and femininity."[19] In opposition to a colonial gender binary of male versus female, Simpson identifies a more integrated Indigenous theory of self that comprises traits that came to be coded as either "masculine" or "feminine." She writes, "If I am to be able to take care of myself on the land, I need to have a proficiency in hunting, fishing, gathering, making shelter, traveling, ceremony, warmth, light, and feeding and clothing myself and those reliant upon me. I cannot restrict myself to an exclusively gendered workload and just expect to survive."[20] All of the tasks that Simpson names here can relate to an expansive definition of care, taking care of the self, others, and the world. Simpson outlines that tasks that have now been coded as "female" and as "caring" work, like cooking, sewing, and looking after children, were performed by people of all genders prior to colonization.

When the work of caring is divided and assigned to particular genders, it is also devalued and not seen as "work." When some types of care work are not defined as work, they also become invisible. **Invisible labor** refers to behind-the-scenes, logistical work that is necessary for tasks to be completed but is often not seen, celebrated, or defined as work. Conducted by psychology researchers Lucia Ciciolla and Suniya S. Luthar in 2019, the "Invisible Household Labor" study assessed the work women do in household management when living in heterosexual married/partnered relationships with children. Despite some advances in gender equality, women reported that they alone assumed responsibility for coordinating household management, including household routines, schedules, and order in the household.[21] These types of tasks are examples of invisible labor, which is often gendered and devalued. In their outline of care as a process, Fisher and Tronto outline the complexities and contradictions of care emerging from "the lack of integration between phases of caring," in that those who are most often responsible for doing the hands-on work of caring lack power and resources to execute caring well, leading to fragmentation and alienation from care work. Not being recognized or valued for care work can also lead to feeling alienated by this work. Despite these challenges, Fisher and Tronto hope to develop "new visions of a society in which caring is a central value and institutions truly facilitate caring."[22]

Disability justice activist Leah Lakshmi Piepzna-Samarasinha identifies the invisible labor of care work and the systemic social divides in who is expected to perform this invisible care labor, writing that "the thing about being a working-class or poor and/or disabled and/or parenting and/or Black, Indigenous or brown femme is that people are going to ask you to do stuff for them. Oh, are they ever."[23] While care work is often divided and asked of people from these communities, Piepzna-Samarasinha writes, "I don't think that only femme or feminine people offer care labor, or can. I know femmes who suck at this stuff. And I know many masculine and other-gendered people who do care labor, and I want all genders of people to be receiving and providing that labor in our communities." The solution to invisible care work is not to outsource it, shun it, or think we are not recipients of it. Instead, we might celebrate and value this work *as* important work. Piepzna-Samarasinha writes that care labor should be a choice, not an automatic delegation, but should also be celebrated and recognized as "next-level genius skill. . . . This is skilled labor!"[24]

Take a moment to reflect on your own values and background. Who did the care work and invisible labor in your household when you were growing up? Were different types of tasks equally valued and celebrated, or were some tasks invisible and devalued? Has this background and experience influenced your own understanding of care and who you think should perform this type of work?

FACTORS THAT IMPACT ABILITY TO CARE

Above, four factors that impact the capacity to deliver care were outlined (time, material resources, knowledge, and skill). Another way to conceptualize these four factors is through an understanding of power. Ability to care can be impacted by our social location and our relative amount of power in society. If care is impacted by power, how do we define power?

Power

Power is a slippery term to define because it's both everywhere in society and is also often unspoken. French philosopher Michel Foucault asserts,

"Power is everywhere, not because it embraces everything, but because it comes from everywhere."[25] This definition is important, because it locates power as not only coming from those in positions of power, like elected officials or those in leadership positions, but also from "everywhere." Power has potent impacts on our lived experience. Foucault also suggests that "power produces; it produces reality; it produces domains of objects and rituals of truth."[26] In this definition, we can see that power influences how we see the world, including what and who is valued. Power produces our definitions and what we see to be true or not true. Applying this understanding of power to a definition and understanding of care, we can see that power influences whether or not care is valued or seen as skilled labor, or is invisible and not celebrated.

Power can be understood to impact access to resources and *agency* or the ability to act and influence our own realities. Power can influence whether or not we are able to care for ourselves and for others fully and meaningfully and in the ways that we might most desire. As will be discussed below through the concept of intersectionality, power also has structural components, meaning structural factors impact the relative power that individuals and groups have in society. For example, we can assume that all people want the best for their children, but not everyone has *access* to choices for their children's education, depending on where they live and their level of income. Historical and present-day factors impact structural access, for example, the history of racially segregated schools in the United States and residential schools for Indigenous children in Canada. To return to our definition of care as a process, not everyone has access to time, material resources, knowledge, or skill, and power impacts access to these four factors that influence capacity for caring.

Similarly, agency or the ability to take action can be minimized by our relative amount of power in society. Feminist theorists have made interventions in this understanding of power to suggest that even if we are not in a powerful position in society, we might still be able to exert agency, especially in commanding our own reality. bell hooks states that "women need to know that they can reject the powerful's definition of their reality—that they can do so even if they are poor, exploited, or trapped in oppressive circumstances. They need to know that the exercise of this basic personal power is an act of resistance and strength."[27] hooks' definition of personal power is equally important for other historically marginalized groups, not only women. For Hannah Arendt, power is defined as "the human ability not just to act but to act in concert."[28] In this definition, power is a "human ability," not only for those in elevated positions of power in society. Arendt suggests that "acting in concert," or the ability to work collaboratively, might be a true definition of power.

This definition might also best correspond with a relational definition of self: we exert power through relations with others—working with others can be a way to take action as a form of power to enact caring social transformation. This again returns us to a question of access: who has access to making connections and collaborating with others, and who is isolated and devalued in society?

Privilege

Related to the concept of power and the capacity to act and care is the term *privilege*. Privilege is also a sticky concept, because it is sometimes difficult to acknowledge the ways that we carry privilege in the world. One way to look at **privilege** is the difference between ascribed status and achieved status. **Ascribed status** refers to the status we carry in the world by virtue of our social location, including gender, race, social class, sexuality, ability/disability, age, and so on. In a meritocratic society, we tend to believe that our social mobility and success stem exclusively from our achievements, or our **achieved status**. It can be difficult to see that social location can contribute to our social standing, as we want to be celebrated and seen for our merits and efforts alone.

In 1989, white social justice educator Peggy McIntosh published the essay and toolkit "White Privilege: Unpacking the Invisible Knapsack." Using the metaphor of the knapsack, McIntosh defines privilege as "an invisible package of unearned assets which one can count on cashing in each and every day, but about which one is largely oblivious."[29] Though McIntosh's essay popularized the concept of privilege and brought it into public conversation and consciousness, this concept has been discussed by racialized scholars and writers prior to McIntosh's essay. For example, in his 1935 book *Black Reconstruction in America, 1860–1880*, Black sociologist and writer W. E. B. Du Bois discussed the privilege that poor white people carried in comparison to poor Black people, commenting that "the white group of laborers, while they received a low wage, were compensated in part by a sort of public and psychological wage."[30] This "psychological wage" can be seen as accruing the benefits of white privilege. Focusing on race and the privilege that white people have in society, McIntosh outlines fifty areas of privilege in her essay, including access to housing, employment, and legal and medical help, but also agency in choice of clothing and ways of speaking. Some of the areas of McIntosh's outline of privilege are subtle, like feeling welcomed and included, and some suggest freedom from harm and violence, like lack of scrutiny from police and other authorities.

Let's return to my opening example, of being called stupid while riding my bike the wrong way up a one-way street. Here we can also see the privilege I carry in the world as a white woman: disregarding and feeling entitled to break rules, like traffic laws, not fearing scrutiny from police, and feeling indignation when being called out about the wrongfulness of my actions. With reflection, this privilege comes into focus for me, which suggests the ongoing work that needs to be done to recognize and acknowledge white privilege.

A focus on privilege suggests a nuanced understanding of the subtle and not-so-subtle ways race privilege and racism are maintained, beyond acts of overt and explicit hate. McIntosh writes, "I was taught to see racism only in individual acts of meanness, not in invisible systems conferring dominance on my group." This dominance can also be known as white supremacy. In her book *Me and White Supremacy*, Layla Saad defines **white supremacy** as "a racist ideology that is based on the belief that white people are superior in many ways to people of other races and that therefore, white people should be dominant over other races."[31] Understanding white supremacy means examining broader systems of power and racial dominance that individuals are embedded in. White supremacy encompasses more than explicit acts of hate and also includes racial dominance being maintained through privilege and power in broad areas of society, such as leadership positions, beauty standards, visibility, surveillance, access, and fair treatment.

One way that white supremacy materializes beyond explicit racism or through "individual meanness" is through **unconscious bias**, or automatic preference for some things over others. Unconscious bias can surface problematically "when you allow unconscious biases—or blind spots—to influence your behavior and the way you treat others," states Tiffany Jana, coauthor of *Overcoming Bias: Building Authentic Relationships across Difference*.[32] In other words, unconscious bias becomes a problem when we have automatic, implicit, negative associations with minority groups, and these biases guide our beliefs and interactions. These implicit and unconscious biases are deep-seated, reinforced by media representations, both in terms of who is visible and who is not in the media, alongside how different groups are portrayed. Unconscious bias is also reinforced through our institutions and institutional cultures, like school, family, and work. Diversity educators suggest that a first step in overcoming biases is awareness, shifting from our unconscious to our conscious mind when encountering people who are different from us, to move from implicit social cognition to active awareness. In 1998, Project Implicit researchers at Harvard University developed online "implicit association tests" (IAT) for individuals to learn about their unconscious biases in different areas, such as race, gender, disability, and so on. Taking one of these tests can be a starting point for the work of addressing unconscious bias. Acknowledging bias, recognizing it when it emerges, and unlearning bias is vital and ongoing, lifelong work. Resources at the end of this chapter can help guide this work. There is a wealth of antiracist education and literature available beyond those suggested at the end of this chapter: aim to seek out and center BIPOC (Black, Indigenous, and People of Color) thinkers and speakers in your journey of learning about and unlearning white supremacy.

This work of checking privilege, being aware of unconscious bias, and unlearning white supremacy is a form of care. Returning to Fisher and Tronto's definition of care as "repair[ing] our 'world' so that we can live in it as well as possible," we can notice the emphasis on *we*, that we live in the world together. Discussing the work of unlearning and dismantling white supremacy, Saad writes,

> We are living in challenging times. There is much work to be done. And it begins with getting honest with yourself, getting educated, becoming more conscious of what is really going on (and how you are complicit in it), and getting uncomfortable as you question your core paradigms about race. If you are willing to do that, and if we are committed to doing the work that is ours to do, we have a chance of creating a world and way of living that are closer to what we all desire for ourselves and one another.[33]

Striving for conditions of equality means investigating who we are and how we show up in our interactions with others, including how dominant systems of power impact our identities as individuals and our interactions with others.

In 1970, Black writer James Baldwin and white anthropologist Margaret Mead met for a public conversation in New York City on race, identity, power, and privilege. The transcript of this conversation was published in a book called *A Rap on Race*. Baldwin and Mead talk through their responses to painful American history, including colonialism, slavery, and continued racial injustice. One response to this painful history might be a sense of guilt. Indeed, Baldwin suggests that there might be some forms of "useful guilt." Mead suggests instead the term *responsibility*: "it is saying I am going to make an effort to have things changed." While guilt looks to the errors of the past, responsibility is aware of the errors of the past and focuses on action in the present toward a better future. Mead says, "It's what we do this week that matters."[34] Similarly, care is forward looking, striving for social transformation, while being aware of barriers and inequality.

Intersectionality

Peggy McIntosh's interventions on privilege focused on race based in her lived experiences as a white woman. In additional to racial privilege, we can identify other forms of privilege, including male privilege, heterosexual privilege, able-bodied privilege, and so on. To identify overlapping forms of privilege or oppression, **intersectionality** is a useful tool. Black writer and poet Audre Lorde famously stated, "There is no such thing as a single-issue struggle, because we do not live single-issue lives."[35] Intersectionality is a concept to access this complexity of the overlapping issues that make up our lived experience. This concept comes from the interventions and responses of Black feminists in the feminist movement and organizing work of the 1960s–1980s, which was largely led by white and middle-/upper-class women. Key focuses for the feminist movement of this time, often referred to as the "second wave" of feminism, were access to employment outside of the home, equal career opportunities, and access to reproductive choice and sexual freedom. This second-wave feminist focus on employment outside of the home or career opportunities through the lens of gender inequality did not acknowledge the experiences of Black and racialized women or poor women, who might already be working to support themselves and their families. The white middle-class female experience of feeling oppressed or trapped in their households and lives is far from universal and does not capture experiences of racial inequality and discrimination.

An enlarged framework is needed to access these complexities and intersections of gender, race, class, disability, and so on. The term *intersectionality* was coined by Black feminist Kimberlé Crenshaw in 1989. Following from Crenshaw's work, intersectional feminists question that gender is the primary or exclusive category that explains women's experiences and suggest that gender needs to be understood as intersecting with other social categories. In her 1989 essay, Crenshaw writes:

> I argue that Black women are sometimes excluded from feminist theory and antiracist policy discourse because both are predicated on a discrete set of experiences that often does not accurately reflect the interaction of race and gender. These problems of exclusion cannot be solved simply by including Black women within an already established analytical structure. Because the intersectional experience is greater than the sum of racism and sexism, any analysis that does not take intersectionality

into account cannot sufficiently address the particular manner in which Black women are subordinated.[36]

In addition to an analysis of the need to include multiple and overlapping categories of identity to understand human experience, intersectionality is also used as an analytic tool to understand broader social systems and how they impact lived experience. In their overview of intersectionality, Patricia Hill Collins and Sirma Bilge state that an intersectional analysis includes six areas of understanding (table 1.1).[37]

To conclude, let's return to the definition of care as relational action. An intersectional analysis of care asks what factors impact care, including power, privilege, and social context. This understanding of care is grounded in relationality and complexity and works toward social justice.

Table 1.1 Elements of Intersectionality

Element	*Explanation*
Social Inequality	Multiple factors, like race and class, cause social inequality in society
Power	Lives and identities are shaped by and across different domains of power, including • interpersonal: how people relate to each other • disciplinary: rules and policies that enables some activities and constrict others • structural: organizational frameworks that shape flows of activities • cultural: societal meanings and values, including what is valued and what is not
Relationality	Emphasis on interconnections, using a holistic, both/and framework instead of an either/or framework
Social Context	Historical, intellectual, and political contexts that shape what we think and do
Complexity	Seeing multiple factors as intertwined when thinking analytically
Social Justice	Understanding that our contemporary status quo has not achieved equality or fairness for all, and striving to achieve these goals

Adapted from Collins and Bilge, *Intersectionality*, 25–30.

Activity 1.2: Intersectional Card Game

In this activity, you'll take time to reflect on aspects of your intersectional self. Use this activity as an opportunity to reflect on your identity, so that you can further reflect on how you relate to others and their intersectional identities.

I learned this activity from community artist and program coordinator Naty Tremblay during a volunteer training at SKETCH Working Arts. This activity was facilitated by Naty Tremblay and was cocreated for Courage Labs Toronto.

Required materials: four sheets of different colored paper (in this example, blue, pink, yellow, and green, but any colors are fine) and a pen.

Step 1: Cut your colored paper into small squares. You should have about five to ten squares in each color of paper before you start. These squares are your "intersectionality cards."

Step 2: Fill out your cards.

- Blue: Communities or groups you are part of, either online or in person. This could be extracurricular activities, subcultures, and the like. For example, you might be part of a snorkeling community, a church group or religious community, a LGBTQ+ community, an artist community, or a student group on campus. Write down one community you are a part of on each of your blue cards.
- Pink: Skills you have. Often we think about our skills in public-facing and professional ways, like what you would put on a résumé. These could be the skills you write down here, but they can also be other, more personal skills you have, like climbing trees, cooking, resolving arguments—things you may or may not list on your résumé. Write down one skill you have on each of your pink cards.
- Yellow: Experiences that have marked you. These experiences could be from your childhood or growing up, from your work experience, from your relationships, from traveling, and so on. Write down one experience on each of your yellow cards.
- Green: Identifiers, parts of your identity that can be visible or invisible. For example, your gender, your race, your family identity, your job, your religion, and the like. Write down one identifier on each of your green cards.

Step 3: Now we are going to assemble different "tableaus" or arrangements of cards based on what aspects of your intersectional self materialize in different situations. Assemble the cards for each of the situations in A–F in front of you, and clear them aside and start a new tableau for each situation.

A. When you go for a job interview, which of your cards do you lead with? Bring together the relevant blue, pink, yellow, or green cards that "show up" in this situation.
B. When you are with your family, friends, or chosen family, the people you feel most comfortable with, what cards do you lead with? Bring together the relevant blue, pink, yellow, or green cards that "show up" in this situation.
C. When you are in a conflict, which cards do you draw on? Bring together the relevant blue, pink, yellow, or green cards that "show up" in this situation.
D. When you are on a date, which cards do you lead with? Bring together the relevant blue, pink, yellow, or green cards that "show up" in this situation.
E. When you are at school or at work, which cards do you draw on? Bring together the relevant blue, pink, yellow, or green cards that "show up" in this situation.
F. When you are on public transit and people see you, what cards of yours do you think people see? Bring together the relevant blue, pink, yellow, or green cards that "show up" in this situation.

Step 4: Reflection: What cards got used most often and which got used less in this activity? In which situations could you bring more of the various aspects of yourself forward? What did you learn or what are your broader takeaway points from this activity? How does this activity relate to the concept of intersectionality? How might this activity influence your understanding of intersectionality in defining care and in how we relate to one another?

QUESTIONS FOR LEARNING AND REFLECTION

1. Defining Care: In this chapter, we've seen definitions of care as values, care as process, and care as relational action. Which of these definitions resonates most with you and why? In a few sentences, write your own personal definition of care.
2. Starting Somewhere: This chapter encourages small, consistent actions as a basis for caring social transformation. Identify one issue

in society that concerns you and identify one, small way you might start taking action related to this issue, in collaboration with others.

3. Care Deficits: Gather background information on any recent controversies you've heard reported about in the media. Analyze these controversies from the perspective of care as a process. In which of Fisher and Tronto's four stages of care was there a deficit or lack of care? Then analyze the factors impacting capacity to care (time, material resources, knowledge, and skill) to determine if any of these areas were lacking in your identified controversy.
4. Privilege Inventory: Our relative amount of privilege depends on our social location. Peggy McIntosh suggests that people are "largely oblivious" to their privilege, but a first step is moving toward awareness. McIntosh's exercise asks individuals to reflect on their racial identity and on whiteness, but an intersectional approach involves reflecting on multiple categories of identity, and understanding how identity can be shifting according to context.

   For this privilege inventory, reflect on

   a. Race
   b. Gender
   c. Social class
   d. Sexuality
   e. Ability/disability
   f. Any other categories of identity

   Next, reflect on different contexts, including your

   a. Home
   b. School/work
   c. Neighborhood
   d. Community and leisure spaces

   In which of these areas do you feel you carry privilege? How does this privilege show up or not show up in different contexts of your life in terms of your access and opportunities? How might you take responsibility for this privilege and commit to action?

NOTES

1. bell hooks, *All About Love: New Visions* (New York: Harper Perennial, 2000), 143.
2. Leah Bassel, *The Politics of Listening: Politics and Challenges for Democratic Life* (London: Palgrave Pivot, 2017), 11.

3. Bernice Fisher and Joan Tronto, "Toward a Feminist Theory of Caring," in *Circles of Care*, ed. Emily Abel and Margaret Nelson (Albany, NY: SUNY Press, 1990), 36–54.

4. Joan Tronto, *Caring Democracy: Markets, Equality and Justice* (New York: New York University Press, 2013).

5. Fisher and Tronto, "Toward a Feminist Theory."

6. Anthony Weston, *A 21st Century Ethical Toolbox*, 2nd ed. (New York: Oxford University Press, 2008), 107.

7. Nel Noddings, *Caring: A Relational Approach to Ethics and Moral Education*, 2nd ed. (Berkeley: University of California Press, 2013), 3.

8. Noddings, *Caring*, 5.

9. Ethics of Care, "Carol Gilligan," July 16, 2011, accessed October 19, 2020, https://ethicsofcare.org/carol-gilligan/.

10. Robin Wall Kimmerer, "Returning the Gift," *Minding Nature* 7, no. 2 (2014): 20.

11. Fisher and Tronto, "Toward a Feminist Theory of Caring," 40.

12. Mia Mingus, "Pods and Pod Mapping Worksheet," Bay Area Transformative Justice Collective, June 2016, accessed June 29, 2021, https://batjc.wordpress.com/resources/pods-and-pod-mapping-worksheet/.

13. Joseph Moore, personal interview, November 15, 2019.

14. Care More, "Our Vision," accessed October 21, 2020, https://www.letscaremore.com/.

15. Joseph Moore, personal interview, November 15, 2019.

16. Mercedes Smith, "The Artful Gift of Care," TEDx Lincoln University, YouTube.com, February 3, 2020, https://www.youtube.com/watch?v=wIDJyVYHQ1w.

17. Tronto, *Caring Democracy*, 143.

18. Marty Fink, *Forget Burial: HIV Kinship, Disability, and Queer/Trans Narratives of Care* (New Brunswick, NJ: Rutgers University Press, 2021).

19. Leanne Betasamosake Simpson, *As We Have Always Done: Indigenous Resurgence through Radical Resistance* (Minneapolis: University of Minnesota Press, 2017), 123.

20. Simpson, *As We Have Always Done*, 128.

21. Lucia Ciciolla and Suniya S. Luthar, "Invisible Household Labor and Ramifications for Adjustment: Mothers as Captains of Households," *Sex Roles* 81 (2019): 467–86.

22. Fisher and Tronto, "Toward a Feminist Theory," 56.

23. Leah Lakshmi Piepzna-Samarasinha, *Care Work: Dreaming Disability Justice* (Vancouver: Arsenal Pulp Press, 2018), 136.

24. Piepzna-Samarasinha, *Care Work*, 141.

25. Michel Foucault, *The History of Sexuality: An Introduction*, vol. 1, trans. Robert Hurley (New York: Pantheon Books, 1978), 98.

26. Michel Foucault, *Discipline and Punish: The Birth of the Prison*, trans. Robert Sheridan (New York: Pantheon Books, 1977), 194.

27. bell hooks, *Feminist Theory: From Margin to Center*, 3rd ed. (New York: Routledge, 2014), 92.

28. Hannah Arendt, *On Violence* (Boston: Houghton Mifflin Harcourt, 1970), 44.

29. Peggy McIntosh, "White Privilege: Unpacking the Invisible Knapsack," National Seed Project, originally published 1989, accessed October 21, 2020, https://nationalseedproject.org/Key-SEED-Texts/white-privilege-unpacking-the-invisible-knapsack.

30. Joshua Rothman, "The Origins of Privilege," *New Yorker*, May 14, 2014, accessed October 21, 2020, https://www.newyorker.com/books/page-turner/the-origins-of-privilege; W. E. B. Du Bois, *Black Reconstruction in America, 1860–1880* (1935; repr., New York: Free Press, 1998), 700.

31. Layla F. Saad, *Me and White Supremacy: Combat Racism, Change the World, and Become a Better Ancestor* (Naperville, IL: Sourcebooks, 2020), 12.

32. Liz Alexander, "What Millennials Learned about Bias from This Harvard Test," *Psychology Today*, May 8, 2017, accessed October 21, 2020, https://www.psychologytoday.com/us/blog/preparing-the-unpredictable/201705/what-millennials-learned-about-bias-harvard-test.

33. Saad, *Me and White Supremacy*, 5.

34. James Baldwin and Margaret Mead, *A Rap on Race* (Philadelphia: J. B. Lippincott & Co., 1971), 59–61.

35. Audre Lorde, "Learnings from the 60s (1982)," Black Past, August 12, 2012, accessed October 20, 2021, https://www.blackpast.org/african-american-history/1982-audre-lorde-learning-60s/.

36. Kimberlé Crenshaw, "Demarginalizing the Intersection of Race and Sex: A Black Feminist Critique of Antidiscrimination Doctrine, Feminist Theory and Antiracist Politics," *University of Chicago Legal Forum* 1 (1989): 139–67.

37. Patricia Hill Collins and Sirma Bilge, *Intersectionality* (Cambridge: Polity Press, 2016).

REFERENCES AND FURTHER READING

Tiffany Jana and Matthew Freeman, *Overcoming Bias: Building Authentic Relationships Across Difference* (Oakland, CA: Berrett-Koehler Publishers, 2016). Focusing on individuals' relationships with others, Jana and Freeman provide definitions, context, and exercises and activities for readers to do the work of recognizing, addressing, and overcoming bias.

Leah Lakshmi Piepzna-Samarasinha, *Care Work: Dreaming Disability Justice* (Vancouver: Arsenal Pulp Press, 2018). What is the impact of ableism in social justice movements? Leah Lakshmi Piepzna-Samarasinha argues for "collective access" and a politics of inclusion in community spaces as a radical form of love and care, highlighting how we can create a better and more joyful future together.

Layla F. Saad, *Me and White Supremacy: Combat Racism, Change the World, and Become a Better Ancestor* (Naperville, IL: Sourcebooks, 2020). In 2018, Saad ran a thirty-day #meandwhitesupremacy challenge on Instagram, guiding people to identify and understand white supremacy. Her Instagram challenge became an international cultural phenomenon, galvanizing a discussion about how to reduce the harm of white supremacy in our ways of being and interacting with others. In this book, Saad guides readers through the internal work of locating the impact of white supremacy and white privilege in the ways that they see themselves, the world, and others.

Nel Noddings, *Caring: A Relational Approach to Ethics and Moral Education* (Berkeley: University of California Press, 2013). This book was first published in 1986 and intervenes into a masculine tradition of philosophy of ethics that emphasizes rationality and reasoning in morality, or questions of right or wrong. Noddings introduces questions of feeling and care, which have traditionally been coded as feminine, in how we guide our actions. Focusing on education, Noddings discusses providing care and receiving care, alongside caring for animals, plants, things, and ideas.

Leanne Betasamosake Simpson, *As We Have Always Done: Indigenous Resurgence through Radical Resistance* (Minneapolis: University of Minnesota Press, 2017). Simpson provides an insightful overview of the destructive impact of colonialism on Indigenous ways of being and doing. She advocates for Indigenous resistance and resurgence, rooted in Indigenous knowledge and theorizing, including holistic and integrated theories of identity, belonging, and caring.

2
Listen

■ ■ ■

If you've ever gone to a yoga class or done meditation, you're likely familiar with the idea that breathing and breath work is a skill and a practice that we can develop. Yes, we are all breathing if we are alive, but focusing on inhaling and exhaling can quickly calm agitation, reduce an elevated heart rate, and produce a sense of relaxation. Like breathing, listening can happen whether or not we are actively aware that we are doing it, but focusing on listening can produce better results and improve our personal relationships, our work lives, and our sense of wellbeing. We can create a more caring culture by listening to people around us in our everyday lives. Better listening asks that we actively tune in to people and care about what they have to say.

In chapter 1, we defined care as relational action, impacted by power and privilege. In chapter 2, we examine the role of listening as an active process, full of complexities, and as one element of a caring "toolkit." We might think listening is an innate ability (if we are not deaf or hearing impaired), but we might better conceptualize listening as a skill that can be continually improved. Research shows that the average person only retains a small fraction of what they hear.[1] Sociologists studying listening suggest that this is not merely an individual problem but is connected to broader societal trends. In her book *The Politics of Listening*, Leah Bassel highlights listening as a "social and political process that can create responsibility to change roles of speakers and listeners and thereby disrupt power and privilege."[2] Key here is the idea of taking turns and changing roles, disrupting dominant patterns of who is most often heard and given a platform in society. In her discussion of the politics of listening, Bassel draws on sociologist Les Back and political scientist Susan Bickford's analyses of how speaking and listening are differently valued. Back states that "our culture is one that speaks rather than listens."[3] While our culture places a lot of emphasis on speaking and expressing ourselves, we might also recognize the interdependence of speaking and listening as joined parts of engaging with and caring for others. It's important to recognize these broader social and political considerations as part of democratic exchange. Bickford suggests that opportunities to exchange roles of speaking and listening as interdependent peers are declining in our contemporary political moment. She asserts that even as careful listeners, we can never truly "inhabit others' perspectives or hold their perspectives as they do, we are still travelers coming from somewhere else." Nonetheless, we can still endeavor to mutually engage with others by creating "a path as we travel" together.[4] Listening can be one part of creating this path for mutual exchange.

Sociologist Hartmut Rosa stresses the economic conditions that lessen these possibilities for mutual exchange in our society. For Rosa, our contemporary moment is one of acceleration, or living in a sped-up reality, where more and more demands are made on our time. For Rosa, the antidote to acceleration is resonance. Turning to the Latin etymology of the word *resonance*, Rosa suggests resonance is to resound, a characteristic of relationships between "two vibrating bodies whereby the vibration of one body prompts the other to itself vibrate in turn." Though "two bodies in a resonant relationship each speak 'with their own voice,' the vibrations of two bodies in a resonant relationship can mutually reinforce each other, their amplitudes growing ever larger."[5] This definition of resonance has implications for the important skill of listening to others. When we listen to others fully, we can mutually amplify our individual frequencies. This does not mean that we lose ourselves when we listen and consider the perspectives of others. Rather, in a mutually supportive relationship of listening, each individual resonates louder and closer to their true self.

These philosophic underpinnings to the concept of listening are important as they open broad considerations about the importance and the challenges of listening to one another in a democratic society. In this chapter, listening is targeted as a practical skill that can lead to improved outcomes as we create a path by traveling with others. What would the world look like if we focused more attention on others, and more people listened and remembered the information they received? What impact could this have on our relationships and our capacity to care for ourselves and one another?

WHAT IS ACTIVE LISTENING?

Active listening is a way of showing interest in a speaker while developing a fuller understanding of their experience. This is a particular type of listening and asks particular kinds of things of the listener. Keep in mind that active listening is not something that we need to be doing all the time: we can all learn to better listen, but this type of listening is one of many and might not be appropriate for all occasions.

In short, active listening might be best described as listening without an agenda. It asks that we listen without adding our own thoughts and feelings on top of the speaker's. Instead, we listen, clarify if our understanding of the speaker's thoughts is accurate, and support and validate the speaker's thoughts and expressed ideas or feelings. Active listening means temporarily suspending our own preconceived notions about what someone else means or is saying, and instead listening "to what is actually being said" and listening "for the unexpected and surprising."[6]

We live in a culture in which the need to be pithy and to foreground our own selves is high. In a limited number of characters, Twitter asks us to be sharp and clever. Facebook asks us, "What's on your mind?" Instagram offers us a parade of perfectly posed selfies. It's easy to feel the natural instinct to want to be noticed and to be validated. But pushed to the extreme, this instinct can make conversation sometimes feel like a game of one-upmanship, where someone says something that reminds us of our own experience, and we want to share our own similar story. Sharing our experiences is a way to build connections and to relate to others, but as discussed above, we are living through social, economic, and political times that sometimes put extreme emphasis on competitive individualism, which not only hinders our capacities for care and for mutual engagement but also impacts our sense of wellbeing. Active listening asks us to put this competitive individualism aside for a few minutes, and instead only focus on the person who is speaking. Simply put: it's not about you.

We've all likely felt misunderstood or that we haven't been listened to, but this experience takes a deeper dimension if we consider the experiences of marginalized people and groups. At a broader, societal level, consider the ways that marginalized groups haven't been listened to or haven't had their thoughts and experiences heard and validated as important. Marginalized voices have been devalued. We can also consider the implications of power and distribution of resources, which limits which voices can be heard in our public arena. These problems are pervasive and can't be easily corrected with one simple fix, but one meaningful place to start is by more actively listening to those around us on a regular basis.

ELEMENTS OF ACTIVE LISTENING

Active listening can be broken down into four parts:

Stop Talking: While active listening, we notice and pause our impulse to interrupt to share our own stories and experience. Instead, in this kind of listening, the talking we are going to do is to ask probing questions to get the speaker to keep going. Examples of probing questions are "How long did that go on for?," "How did that make you feel?," or "Can you tell me more about that?" We don't need to be constantly probing, though: this is another way of taking up airtime! Allow the speaker to talk fully, and get comfortable with pauses and silences. Stay present. It's normal to get distracted or lose your focus when someone else is talking. When you notice your mind wandering, return your attention to the speaker. It's also okay to ask the speaker to repeat, saying, "I'm sorry, I missed that. Can you say that again?" Or you might say, "I'm sorry I interrupted you there. Please continue."

Validate: The goal of active listening is not to add to or to question the speaker's story. The goal is to make them feel heard. Verbal and nonverbal affirmations go a long way to signal that we are attentively listening. Refrain from looking at your phone or your watch. It's not necessary to fix your gaze on the speaker continuously, but work on maintaining eye contact and demonstrating that you are listening by nodding your head, or with other vocal cues, like "Hmm," "I see," "Oh no," or "That's great," where and if appropriate.

Verify: Have you accurately heard what you think you have? As active listeners, we can ask questions about the speaker's story to make sure we have understood. Avoid telling the speaker how they feel with statements like, "That must have been very difficult for you." Instead, ask questions or check your understanding with statements like, "That sounds very hard" or "How did you feel about that?" Typically, in normal conversations, instead of verifying, we add to what the speaker has said by sharing our own story or experience. While normal, this impulse can derail active listening and change the focus of what is being discussed. Keep your focus on the speaker.

Affirm: The goal of active listening is not to critique, judge, or offer unsolicited advice. It's also normal to want to try to be helpful. Often, though, our unsolicited advice is not helpful and can feel to others like we are telling them what to do, or that we are suggesting we know better. Trying to be hopeful can also sometime be dismissive and discount the speaker's experience. "Things will get better" and "It's not that bad" are examples of statements to try to avoid, as they might not come across as affirming. Check this impulse and return to your verifying statements. For example, try "That sounds very stressful" instead of "Don't worry too much about it." Remember, the goal of active listening is to allow the speaker to fully share their experience. Rather than offering suggestions, affirm the person and what you've heard. "It sounds like you are trying hard" and "I'm sorry that happened to you" are examples of affirming statements.

Though active listening can be conceived as having these four components of stop talking, validate, verify, and affirm, we don't need to think of active listening as a mechanical or linear process that needs to be always used as a four-part sequence. These four components are useful reminders and tools to practice to be more attentive and attuned to others whenever, wherever. In conversations, you might reflect, "Do I need to stop talking?" or "Have I really understood what I think I have?" Rather than chastising yourself, focus on hearing others and celebrating their stories.

CALL YOUR GIRLFRIEND PODCAST: FRIENDSHIP AND FUN OVER THE PHONE

Active listening means paying attention to others and understanding and appreciating them. In the following profile of the *Call Your Girlfriend* podcast, consider the fun of friendships that are mutually supportive through actively listening to one another and affirming each other's experiences. At first glance, active listening might sound boring or sterile, but listening to this podcast quickly shows us the fun and joy of paying attention to others, and of listening as part of caring. How might you create the kind of atmosphere found in *Call Your Girlfriend* in your own immediate environment?

Ann Friedman and Aminatou Sow are best friends. They first met at a *Gossip Girl* viewing party in Washington, DC, but soon found themselves spread across the United States, with Friedman living in California and Sow living in New York. Like many best friends, they kept in touch via regular phone calls, but these two also created an agenda of what they would talk about when they planned to talk, including current events, and that's where the concept for their podcast was born. Released every Friday since 2014, the *Call Your Girlfriend* podcast features Friedman and Sow chatting about popular culture, politics, and their everyday lives, all via their regular Skype conversations across the country.

In their book *Big Friendship: How We Keep Each Other Close*, Sow and Friedman write that their friendship has evolved over the years, including growing apart and then working to figure out "how to stay centered in each other's lives."[7] But when you listen to the podcast, Friedman and Sow's long friendship is front and center, and it's clear that they listen to and support each other, above all. According to Sow, "We are real friends and we do enjoy each other. It doesn't feel like work."[8] This enjoyment is clear from the frequent chuckles and cheering in the podcast.

"I'm actually laughing when Amina says something funny," Friedman says. "I'm laughing because she's hilarious, not because the show needed a laugh at that moment."[9]

What if we all lived in a world where we affirmed one another, celebrated each other's successes, and sought to lift each other up, not tear each other down? For Sow and Friedman, this affirmation connects to what they call "shine theory," and this is particularly important for women and other marginalized people. They say, "We believe that when one of us shines, we all do. Our default is collaboration, not competition." In *Big Friendship*, Sow and Friedman write, "Shine Theory often takes the form of sharing resources, contacts, and opportunities." They describe it as long-term investment in helping friends and collaborators, and "relying on their help in return." This doesn't mean that if you try to practice shine theory that you will never feel jealousy about others' success. But Sow and Friedman suggest that shine theory can help how you respond to those feelings too, allowing you to "move on so you're not just stewing in your own resentment."[10]

We can hear shine theory definitely at play in the *Call Your Girlfriend* podcast in its focus on listening to the stories and experiences of women and celebrating and validating these experiences rather than questioning or criticizing them, or picking apart or resenting someone's success. Sow and Friedman also model this philosophy in how they talk to each other. The podcast is plenty sassy, with witty banter flying back and forth, but the two women genuinely care and check in on one another. In the very first episode of the podcast, Friedman mentions that Sow was recently featured on the *Forbes* 30 Under 30 list. This doesn't sound forced—it sounds like one friend being proud of another.

Another feature of the podcast is interviews with famous guests, like writer Zadie Smith, actress/politician Cynthia Nixon, philanthropist Melinda Gates, celebrity chef Samin Nosrat, and Black Lives Matter cofounder Alicia Garza, among many others. "We highlight women who are agents, creators, movers, and shakers who have smart, interesting things to say," says the podcast website.[11] On *Call Your Girlfriend*, Friedman and Sow call these VIP guests "power ladies" and "sheroes." But the questions the hosts ask these boss lady guests often angle toward navigating everyday realities with dignity and empowerment rather than the ins and outs of being in the public eye. For example, Garza shares her tips for refraining from unloading right away in situations of conflict. She says that in these situations, she writes what is on her mind in the Notes feature on her phone, saves it, and comes back to her notes if necessary if further provoked by the same individual at a later time.

The *Call Your Girlfriend* podcast doesn't suggest that famous women are the be-all and end-all of who we need to listen to, though. The podcast also features a healthy dose of reality and ordinary experiences of women. One episode, "Thank You for Being a Friend," is about the early days of friendships and features voice mail clips of listeners narrating how they met their future best friends. The podcast is sure to highlight the behind-the-scenes support from producer Gina Delvac, who was the friend who encouraged Friedman and Sow to start taping their weekly conversations in the first place.

Friedman and Sow also hope that more women get into podcasting, and they devoted one episode of their show to teaching their listeners how to make their own podcasts. "If audio would get easier to do, there would be more people in podcasting," says Sow.[12] Beyond making your own podcast, listening to *Call Your Girlfriend* might remind us to get on the phone and listen to what our friends have to say. In our era of digital connection, it's sometimes easier to send a text or message a friend online. But picking up the phone to talk means making time and space to listen and support the people who are dear to us.

For more information and to access the *Call Your Girlfriend* podcast, visit https://www.callyourgirlfriend.com/.

AMPLIFYING THE VOICES OF OTHERS

The process of affirming or echoing others' statements is one part of active listening, but in this section we will focus on the broader implications of affirming and amplifying others' stories. In her passionate commencement speech to the 2018 graduating class of Barnard College, soccer Olympic Gold medalist and FIFA World Cup champion Abby Wambach told the young female graduates that "change is here." Women no longer have to resign themselves to feeling grateful for whatever they have. They can feel grateful, while also demanding more, and asking for what they deserve. In her speech, Wambach outlines strategies for how to accomplish this:

> Amplify each others' voices. Demand seats for women, people of color and all marginalized people at every table where decisions are made. Call out each other's wins and just like we do on the field: claim the success of one woman, as a collective success for all women. Joy. Success. Power. These are not pies where a bigger slice for her means a smaller slice for you. These are infinite. In any revolution, the way to make something true starts with believing it is. Let's claim infinite joy, success, and power—together.[13]

In her speech, Wambach emphasizes collaboration, not competition, as a pathway to success, based in supporting and amplifying others.

Amplifying each other's voices, or the concept of amplification, went viral in 2016 when this become known in the media as a strategy developed by female White House staffers during the Barack Obama administration. Even if Obama was a self-identified feminist, his staff was still dominated by men, and female staffers found themselves talked over when they managed to be invited to important meetings. Research shows this is a common reality everywhere: women are more interrupted than men when they speak and are given less credit for their ideas. To counter these tendencies, female White House staffers decided to repeat the ideas of other women and credit the idea to the woman who spoke. One female staffer said, "We just started doing it, and made a purpose of doing it. It was an everyday thing."[14] This staffer said this strategy had an impact, and President Obama starting calling on women more often to share their ideas. In Obama's second term as president, his inner circle of top aides was gender balanced.[15]

Amplification is a tool to counter the tendency to talk over and silence people from marginalized groups by making a conscious effort to notice these patterns and to verbally affirm people who are talked over. For amplification to take place, we need to start by more deeply tuning in and listening. In our group conversations, in meetings at work, in social gatherings, but also in the media and in our broader culture, who gets to speak and who is interrupted, talked over, or has their experience called into question and invalidated? When you notice someone getting continually interrupted, you can intervene. You don't have to be the boss or the team leader at your job to notice these dynamics and work on meaningfully changing the culture. Remember, as Abby Wambach says, change is here. You are the change. When someone is interrupted, redirect the conversation when you can back to the person who was speaking. When someone is not credited for their idea or contribution, credit them. When someone's experience is dismissed, affirm it.

Amplification can also take place through our social media feeds. Return to your principles of active listening: your social media feeds do not have to be all about you. How can you demonstrate that you are listening and affirming the experience of others, especially those from marginalized groups? Be intentional about what content you post and share. You don't necessarily have to announce what you are doing, though there's nothing wrong with drawing attention to the identity of the content creator either. But simply sharing the articles, videos, clips, art, or other creations of people from marginalized groups is an act of amplification. Cumulatively, these acts can have a big impact and shift the patterns of whose voices are heard in our society.

Reflection on whose voices are championed and whose are silenced means tuning into subtleties and nuances, beyond overt racist, sexist, or homophobic statements, or other kinds hateful statements toward marginalized people's identities. Coined in 1978 by Harvard University professor Chester M. Pierce, the term *microaggression* has come into public consciousness through psychologist Derald Sue's books on this topic. **Microaggressions** are statements that invalidate, question, or dismiss marginalized people's experiences of marginalization. Microaggressions can be verbal or physical cues, like ignoring someone, avoiding eye contact, or crossing the street. Imagine a woman sharing her experience of feeling like she was interrupted and talked over in a business meeting, or a racialized person sharing their experience of being racially profiled by the police. Examples of microaggressions in response to these experiences could include these people being told, directly or indirectly, "Why don't you just get over it" or "It's not really that bad" or "That's not really what's happening." Microaggressions can also invalidate the marginalized person's experience when a more privileged person tries to suggest that the experience is universal and not connected to marginalization. Return to the example of a woman sharing her experience that she feels like she was interrupted or talked over in a business meeting. A male colleague suggesting that this used to happen to him until he just learned to speak up more is also an example of a microaggression, as it denies the particularity of the woman's experience as a woman. Microaggressions can also sometimes almost be mistaken for a compliment, like telling a person of color that they "speak really good English" or are "very articulate." While different than, for example, yelling a racial slur at someone, these statements still cause harm. Research shows that the experience of microaggressions has negative impact on mental and physical health. In one research project, microaggressions were shown to result in decreased trust with health and service providers, when marginalized people experienced microaggressions from these providers.[16]

On the other hand, **microaffirmations** can help intervene into microaggressions. When we notice that a microaggression has occurred, we don't need to be mere bystanders, even if we are not directly involved in the conversation. It's not always safe, appropriate, or timely to directly question and curtail problematic statements, though this is important work to do when possible. Microaffirmations are one type of amplification strategy. For example, if you hear a racialized person being told something to the effect of "It's not really that bad" when they are sharing a difficult experience that stems from their identity as a racialized person, you might respond with an affirming statement like, "I'm sorry that happened to you."

Microaffirmations don't only have to intervene in problematic situations. A microaffirmation can also be a small gesture, like smiling, making eye contact, nodding, and lingering to spend time or ask how someone is doing. To this end, one definition of microaffirmations from a team of science researchers led by Mica Estrada suggests that microaffirmations "are subtle or ambiguous kindness cues that can include tone of voice, space left between people when interacting, subtle mimicry, and actions that convey vulnerability." This research on microaffirmations suggests they can cultivate an environment that results in a greater sense of belonging and resilience.[17]

CALLING OUT AND CALLING IN

Active listening asks that we refrain from speaking and instead focus our attention on the speaker. But careful listening doesn't mean that silence is always needed or even appropriate. When we hear something that we find prejudiced or objectionable, we could feel that it's necessary to speak up. **Calling out** is the practice of naming prejudiced behavior and calling attention to the objectionable nature of a speaker's statements. When you call out someone, you plainly name what you see as a problem. Examples of calling out might include saying something like "I find your behavior to be sexist" or "That's homophobic."

Increasingly, in our digitized and networked society, calling out happens online. High-profile individuals might be called out through social media by having their behavior or remarks posted and shared for the world to see. Individuals might also have their past histories or social media content reposted as examples of past prejudiced or problematic behavior. This type of calling out sometimes happens when high-profile individuals are receiving accolades or recognition. This online call-out culture means that the stakes online are higher, and no one can reasonably expect anonymity for their prejudice in our contemporary digital arena.

Call-out culture might also make for a tense online environment, where we might fear our offhand remarks can spiral out of control. Robyn Doolittle comments that call-out culture sometimes results in an atmosphere where "those who violate the codes of acceptable thought and behavior are banished to the digital pillory for a mass public shaming. . . . This trend began years ago, thanks to social media, and the result is that people refrain from thoughtful discussions out of fear of saying the wrong thing and being branded 'unwoke.'"[18] What Doolittle suggests here is that the stakes online have become so high that people can fear saying the wrong thing and then be "canceled," and so refrain from sharing their thoughts at all. As such, the extreme version of call-out culture is sometimes known as cancel culture, where being "canceled" or written off can result in being fired, boycotted, or simply no longer getting support from others.

In *Time* magazine, journalist Sarah Hagi discusses the extreme version of call-out culture, **cancel culture**: "The idea is that if you do something that others deem problematic, you automatically lose all your currency. Your voice is silenced. You're done." However, Hagi responds that this perspective about cancel culture "isn't real, at least not in the way people believe it is." Instead, Hagi's analysis suggests that people in power are receiving criticism or facing consequences and accountability for their actions, which they are not used to, and then complaining about being "canceled."[19] Hagi comments that "because of social media, marginalized people like myself can express ourselves in a way that was not possible before. That means racist, sexist, and bigoted behavior or remarks don't fly like they used to." Complaining about being "canceled" or that "cancel culture" has gotten out of hand can be a way to avoid criticism and to avoid accountability for one's words and actions. This debate about whether or not cancel culture is "real" points to two things: the need to identify and stop problematic and harmful behavior from continuing, and the need to find ways to engage in difficult conversations.

What if we don't want to have a public discussion with someone about their prejudice, or if we feel like someone who has said something prejudiced might benefit from being educated about why what they said was offensive? **Calling in** is the practice of speaking to someone privately about their prejudiced behavior and explaining why it is problematic. This practice steps away from the public arena of the online space, which can result in shaming and ostracizing of offenders. Defining "calling in" as "a less disposable way of holding each other accountable," Ngọc Loan Trần suggests that calling in is a process of recognizing that mistakes can be made, reflecting on the importance of your relationship with the person who has made a mistake, choosing to engage in a conversation, and then "talk[ing] about it together, like people who genuinely care about each other."[20]

Calling out and calling in both must be undertaken with care. Returning to the factors that impact capacity to care from chapter 1, you might consider if the person whose behavior or remarks you found problematic lacked time, material resources, knowledge, or skill. If you find this might have been the case, calling in, a strategy of working with others to offer education, may be the best road forward. Calling in requires time, energy, and emotional labor. It can be difficult to have uncomfortable conversations with people who don't recognize that their behavior or speech is harming others. If your intention is to change this person's ways, calling in might be a more effective strategy that creates more dialogue and discussion. Be aware that these conversations often require patience and persistence. There are times when calling out remains an effective and useful tactic to draw attention to problematic behavior.

In her book *We Will Not Cancel Us*, adrienne maree brown discusses the "social destruction of call outs and/or cancelations." She acknowledges that call outs have a long history and continued effectiveness as a strategy of speaking truth to power: "call outs have been a way to bring collective pressure to bear on corporations, institutions, and abusers on behalf of individuals or oppressed peoples who cannot stop the injustice and get accountability on their own." brown names power imbalances, and call outs can be deployed as an effective tactic for those with less power to call attention to injustice. At the same time, brown notes a proliferation of call outs being used "not just as a necessary consequence for those wielding power to cause harm or enact abuse, but to shame and humiliate people in the wake of misunderstandings, contradictions, conflicts, and mistakes."[21] In short, call outs can be effective with those using power to cause harm and abuse, but can also be overused in cases of conflict and mistakes.

brown suggests that people learn and gain clarity and discernment about differences between conflict and abuse, alongside developing skills at having difficult conversations about misunderstandings, conflicts, and harm. In the age of social media, it can sometimes be easier to jump online to call someone out than to engage with that person in a conversation. In those circumstances, call outs can result in destruction rather than more justice. It is beyond the scope of this book to dive into all of these intricacies that brown outlines with sophistication in her book (check it out in the "References and Further Readings" section below). To conclude this section, I return to the overarching goal of creating a more caring culture, and invite you to reflect on what circumstances allow call outs to create more care, and in what circumstances call outs can destroy bonds, create isolation, or fail to work toward more justice.

ALLYSHIP

Allyship is the process of using privilege to support marginalized people in seeking fair treatment and justice. PeerNetBC defines allyship as "an active, consistent, and arduous practice of unlearning and re-evaluating, in which a person in a position of privilege and power seeks to operate in solidarity with a marginalized group."[22] What this support looks like in practice can take many forms. Implementing the tools from this chapter is a good starting place to begin an ongoing practice of allyship. Active listening, amplification, microaffirmations, and calling in and calling out oppressive speech or behavior can all be examples of allyship. We might also consider the process of **bystander intervention:** when we are not directly affected by oppressive behavior, but witness something uncomfortable or objectionable taking place, we might intervene, when it is safe and appropriate, to challenge this dynamic. In bystander intervention, we want to be cautious about escalating a situation or making a targeted person feel unsafe. Sometimes a better strategy is to engage with the person being adversely affected by the oppressive behavior. If you witness a marginalized person being demeaned or verbally attacked, is it possible to engage with this person to affirm their wellbeing?

We can think of bystander intervention more broadly, not only as a tool for interrupting an attack on a marginalized person in the moment, but as part of an ongoing broader strategy for developing allyship. If we are people who have privilege in the world, can we take initiative and consider issues that don't directly affect us? For example, you might support LGBTQ+ rights or disabled people's rights, even if you are not a member of these groups. At the same time, a practice of allyship is conscious of not taking over, not speaking on behalf of marginalized groups, and not seeing oneself as a savior. Instead of speaking on behalf of a marginalized group, we can better use the practice of amplification and use our privileged position to amplify the voices of others. This sometimes involves making space for others and reflecting on our role. Are we taking over the conversation and talking too much? If this is the case, we might need to return to a place of active listening.

We can listen by paying attention when people are talking to us, but we can also listen more broadly by tuning in to the issues affecting marginalized people and seeking to learn. A process of allyship engages in ongoing self-education. Rather than asking marginalized people to educate you, you can instead read about the issues, keep on top of current events, watch films and documentaries, and engage with the creative expressions of artists from marginalized communities. We have never learned too much, and learning is never complete. Be wary of calling yourself an ally: this is not a label or identity marker to give yourself, and allyship is not one fixed "thing." It's better to think of allyship as a lifelong process and practice of learning and supporting. Be aware that you might think of yourself as engaging in a practice of allyship but might nonetheless be called out or called in for objectionable behavior or speech. This might result in an experience of cognitive dissonance, where you are being told something that contradicts your self-image. This can be difficult, but refrain from reacting defensively. Return to the practice of active listening, respond appropriately, and consider a genuine apology. Being called out might be painful, but can also be an opportunity for further growth and learning.

Activity 2.1: Active Listening Exercises

We can practice more actively listening in our day-to-day lives, but taking time out to hone these skills can further allow us to deepen our capacity to listen.

In a group of three, decide who will be the speaker, the listener, and the observer. Rotate through each of these roles so that everyone has a chance to perform the different roles in each of these exercises.

1. Listening Without Talking: In this exercise, the speaker will choose a topic that is important to them and that they can comfortably speak about at length. This topic might be something from their professional, student, or family life or be something they value. The observer will also be the timekeeper. Set a timer for three minutes. The speaker will speak about their topic for three minutes. The listener will demonstrate they are listening through nonverbal communication. The observer will observe the listener's listening and record their behavior. This could be their verbal interjections, their body posture, their eye contact, their nonverbal utterances, and more. Try to record as many things as possible. After the three minutes are up, each person in the exercise will share their experience. Was it difficult or uncomfortable to speak or listen for three minutes? What types of listening behaviors were observed?
2. Questions and Verification: In this exercise, the speaker will choose a topic that is a real concern to them. This might be a social, cultural, or political issue. Again, the observer will be the timekeeper. Set a timer for three minutes. The speaker should share both factual information and personal feelings, or how they feel about this issue. The listener will ask questions to probe further and verify that they understand what the speaker is saying. The listener should ask a variety of open-ended and closed questions (an open-ended question asks for more information, and a closed question produces a fixed or specific answer, like

yes or no). The listener will summarize and reflect back what they hear the speaker saying and ask if their understanding is accurate. The observer will keep track of the listener's responses and the types of questions they ask. Note if the questions are open-ended or closed, and if the questions seem to accurately reflect what the speaker is focusing on. After the three minutes are up, each person in the exercise will share their experience. The speaker will comment on whether or not they felt their main point was understood, the listener will comment on whether or not it was challenging to focus on verifying questions, and the observer will comment on the types of questions asked.

3. Validation and Affirmation: In this exercise, the speaker will share a difficult experience or a challenge from the past. Choose an experience that feels comfortable to talk about: you may or may not want to share your most personal and private challenges. The observer will be the timekeeper. Set a timer for three minutes. The speaker will speak about their experience. The listener will demonstrate they are listening through verbal and nonverbal communication. In this exercise, the listener can both verify that what they heard is accurate and then validate and affirm this experience. Focus on validating through echoing the challenges shared rather than offering advice or hope. The goal of this exercise is to offer affirmation rather than to probe further, but affirmation might require some further verification of understanding. The observer will record the listener's statements and categorize them as either verifying, affirming, or other. After the three minutes are up, each person in the exercise will share their experience. The speaker will comment on whether or not they felt validated and which comments they found the most affirming. The listener will comment on whether or not they felt the urge to offer advice or commiserate by adding in their own experience. The observer will comment on the types of comments recorded and assess whether they were more of a verifying or more of an affirming nature.

Keep in mind that these exercises are just that: exercises. They will feel artificial, as they are not the same thing as following the flow of a regular conversation. Think of engaging in these activities as the same thing as going to the gym to train your muscles: doing reps at the gym is how we improve strength and agility. Similarly, more consciously engaging in listening through exercises is how we can improve our capacity to engage and care for others.

Further Listening Activities

If you don't have access to a small group you can practice with, you can reflect on listening through watching a variety of different types of dialogue online or on television. Try to find clips of political debates, late-night or daytime talk show interviews, and in-depth journalistic interviews. Obviously, these different formats have different purposes, and active listening might not be the main goal. We can still reflect on the type of listening that is or is not happening. As you review these clips, ask yourself: How often are speakers interrupted? Do the listeners seem to understand the speakers' main points? What types of questions are asked? Are the experiences that speakers share affirmed or denied by the listeners? Summarize your findings across the clips that you watch.

QUESTIONS FOR LEARNING AND REFLECTION

1. Group Meeting: The next time you are in a group setting, whether it is with family or friends, at work, or in a community setting, sit back and observe the group dynamics. Who speaks the most and who is the quietest? Do any members of the group interrupt, speak over, or take credit for the ideas of others? How might you practice amplification or microaffirmation in this group setting?
2. Social Media Amplification: Consider the context of historical and present-day marginalization. Which groups or people receive less attention in our contemporary media environment? How might you intervene in this dynamic? Identify key individuals or groups that you feel merit more broad attention, and engage in a campaign of social media amplification. Retweet, share, or repost the content that you feel is most valuable or most lacking in contemporary public discourse.
3. Calling Out versus Calling In: Research examples of people who have been called out online. Though you might not have access to behind-the-scenes information or prior conversations, are there examples of people being called out where you think calling in would have been more appropriate? Draft sample agendas or talking points for any difficult conversations you might think would have been worthwhile in these calling out scenarios. Alternatively, why do you think the call out was warranted?

NOTES

1. Ralph G. Nichols and Leonard A. Stevens, "Listening to People," *Harvard Business Review*, September 1957, https://hbr.org/1957/09/listening-to-people.

2. Bassel, *Politics of Listening*, 3.

3. Cited in Bassel, *Politics of Listening*, 4.

4. Cited in Bassel, *Politics of Listening*, 8.

5. Hartmut Rosa, *Resonance: A Sociology of Our Relationship to the World*, trans. James C. Wagner (Cambridge: Polity Press, 2019), 165.

6. Andrew Dobson, *Listening for Democracy* (Oxford: Oxford University Press, 2014), 173.

7. Aminatou Sow and Ann Friedman, *Big Friendship: How We Keep Each Other Close* (New York: Simon & Schuster, 2020), xviii.

8. Melissa Locker, "Call Your Girlfriend: Podcast Dishes on Everything from Benghazi to Bieber," *Guardian*, March 5, 2016, accessed June 11, 2021, https://www.theguardian.com/culture/2016/mar/05/call-your-girlfriend-podcast-politics-pop-culture.

9. Locker, "Call Your Girlfriend."

10. Sow and Friedman, *Big Friendship*, 76, 70, 74.

11. Call Your Girlfriend, "About Us," accessed June 22, 2021, https://www.callyourgirlfriend.com/about.

12. Call Your Girlfriend, "About Us."

13. Abby Wambach, "Remarks as Delivered: Commencement 2018," Barnard College, accessed November 11, 2020, https://barnard.edu/commencement/archives/2018/abby-wambach-remarks.

14. Susan Chira, "The Universal Phenomenon of Men Interrupting Women," *New York Times*, June 14, 2017, accessed November 11, 2020, https://www.nytimes.com/2017/06/14/business/women-sexism-work-huffington-kamala-harris.html.

15. Claire Landsbaum, "Obama's Female Staffers Came up with a Genius Strategy to Make Sure Their Voices Were Heard," *The Cut*, September 13, 2016, https://www.thecut.com/2016/09/heres-how-obamas-female-staffers-made-their-voices-heard.html.

16. Gina Torino, "How Racism and Microaggressions Lead to Worse Health," Center for Health Journalism, USC Annenberg, November 10, 2017, accessed November 12, 2020, https://centerforhealthjournalism.org/2017/11/08/how-racism-and-microaggressions-lead-worse-health.

17. Mica Estrada et al., "The Influence of Microaffirmations on Undergraduate Persistence in Science Career Pathways," *CBE Life Sciences Education* 18 (2019): ar40.

18. Robyn Doolittle, *Had It Coming: What's Fair in the Age of #MeToo?* (Toronto: Penguin Random House, 2019), 12.

19. Sarah Hagi, "Cancel Culture Is Not Real—At Least Not in the Way People Think," *Time*, November 21, 2019, accessed November 13, 2020, https://time.com/5735403/cancel-culture-is-not-real/.

20. Ngọc Loan Trần, "Calling In: A Less Disposable Way of Holding Each Other Accountable," in *The Solidarity Struggle: How People of Color Succeed and Fail at Showing Up for Each Other in the Fight for Freedom*, ed. Mia McKenzie (Oakland: BDG Press, 2016), 61.

21. adrienne maree brown, *We Will Not Cancel Us: And Other Dreams of Transformative Justice* (Chico, CA: AK Press, 2020), 40–41.

22. Anti-Oppression Network, "Allyship," accessed November 13, 2020, https://theantioppressionnetwork.com/allyship/.

REFERENCES AND FURTHER READING

adrienne maree brown, *We Will Not Cancel Us: And Other Dreams of Transformative Justice* (Chico, CA: AK Press, 2020). This short book, which brown calls a leaflet, offers an expanded version and discussion of a viral blog post that brown wrote in the summer of 2020 about call-out culture. brown puts call-out culture in the context of social justice movements and transformative justice, which brown articulates as "the work of addressing harm at the root, outside the mechanisms of the state, so that we can grow in right relationship with each other." brown suggests that in this context, call outs are sometimes not helpful in moving toward this overarching goal of more justice, as they can sometimes be both punitive and performative. brown invites readers to reflect on how individuals can both be harmed and be harmful, and how generative conflict can be useful to work toward healing, but this type of conflict needs skills, time, and the capacity to sometimes lean into discomfort. *We Will Not Cancel Us* concludes with a useful list of resources, including books, podcasts, articles, and networks that define and engage with transformative justice.

Montreal Urban Aboriginal Community Strategy Network, "Indigenous Ally Toolkit," March 2019, https://reseaumtlnetwork.com/wp-content/uploads/2019/04/Ally_March.pdf. This toolkit provides a step-by-step guide toward being an ally to Indigenous people, including things not to say, terminology, and dos and don'ts.

Anti-Oppression Network, "Allyship," https://theantioppressionnetwork.com/allyship/. PeerNet, which developed this resource, is a not-for-profit organization dedicated to fostering peer support and community involvement. This resource gives a detailed overview of the definition and practice of being an ally.

Derald Wing Sue, *Microaggressions in Everyday Life: Race, Gender, and Sexual Orientation* (Hoboken, NJ: Wiley, 2010). In this book, Columbia professor and psychologist Derald Sue gives an overview of the psychological impact of microaggressions and develops solutions to interrupt bias, prejudice, and discrimination.

Mia McKenzie, ed., *The Solidarity Struggle: How People of Color Succeed and Fail at Showing Up for Each Other in the Fight for Freedom* (Oakland, CA: BDG Press, 2016). Addressed to Black people, Indigenous people, and people of color, this book addresses the successes and challenges of finding common ground in allyship for collective gains.

3

Consent

■ ■ ■

THE #METOO MOVEMENT

On October 17, 2017, Black feminist and social activist Tarana Burke tweeted, "It's beyond a hashtag. It's the start of a larger conversation and a movement for radical community healing. Join us. #metoo."[1] The #MeToo movement, focusing on sexual violence, enabled a moment of reckoning and much needed conversation about the principle of consent not being adhered to in our society. On October 15, 2017, the phrase "me too," which was coined by Tarana Burke in 2006, was tweeted by actress Alyssa Milano: "If you've been sexually harassed or assaulted write 'me too' as a reply to this tweet," igniting what we now call the #MeToo movement.[2] The #MeToo hashtag prompted an outpouring of sharing of experiences of sexual violence on social media, first from other actresses and celebrities like Viola Davis and Lady Gaga. But the #MeToo movement saw women from all walks of life sharing their experiences, posting #MeToo on their social media feeds to signal solidarity and their own experiences of sexual violence.

The viral spread of the #MeToo hashtag and this movement of consciousness raising in 2017 was enabled by decades of prior feminist work and organizing. Tarana Burke started using the phrase "me too" in 2006, on social media platform Myspace, to spread solidarity among survivors of sexual violence. Burke says she developed the phrase "me too" after a disquieting experience of having a young teen survivor of sexual violence disclose her experience of being assaulted. Upon reflecting on not knowing what to say in this moment to console this survivor, Burke says she wishes she had the courage to say, "me too." In addition to coining the phrase, Burke also works toward what she terms **empowerment empathy**, where survivors of sexual violence feel empowered to share their experience, rather than feeling shame, stigma, or silenced, and survivors instead empathize, validate, and support each other's experiences.[3]

To further do this work, Tarana Burke founded an organization called Just Be Inc. Formed to support teen and preteen girls, Just Be Inc. acknowledges the role of "media, music and pop culture that increasingly diminish the importance, worth, and esteem of girls and women, particularly women of color." Just Be Inc. develops programs that "center around empowerment and guidance for girls as they grow and begin to define themselves." For example, the Jewels program, for girls aged twelve to eighteen, targets life skills, conflict resolution, self-development, goal setting, leadership development, and life mapping, depending on the ages and levels of the girls attending. The organization also offers workshops for girls of color aged twelve to eighteen in schools and community settings, including "You and 'the Bae': Navigating Romantic Relationships" and "'Me Too': Exploring Sexual Abuse, Assault and Exploitation in our Community."[4] Burke's work showcases that survivors of sexual violence have long worked to create support networks for each other, in the absence of a broader culture that supports and believes their experiences.

In 2017, the outpouring of women and other marginalized people coming forward to speak about their experience of sexual violence, in the entertainment industries and beyond, caused many commentators to describe the moment as a "watershed" or "tipping point" in acknowledging inequities in these industries. *Time* magazine named "The Silence Breakers," or the women coming forward to discuss sexual violence in their workplaces, as the Person of the Year.[5] Once these floodgates were opened, critical questions were raised about workplace safety, gender roles, power, and agency, but not only in the entertainment industries—these questions affect us all, inside and outside of our workplaces. How can we shift from a culture where the experience of sexual violence is widespread to a culture of consent?

The #MeToo movement in 2017 was first ushered in through numerous women reporting experiences of sexual violence with Hollywood film producer Harvey Weinstein. This story was publicized in the press through the investigative reporting of two journalists working at the *New York Times*, Jodi Kantor and Megan Twohey, whose article "Harvey Weinstein Paid Off Sexual Harassment Accusers for Decades" was published on October 5, 2017, after several years of investigation. At the end of October 2017, *USA Today* compiled a list of women coming forward with allegations against Weinstein, from "inappropriate" to "criminal" behavior, ranging from requests for massages, to intimidating sexual advances, to rape. *USA Today* kept an ongoing tally of these reports, totalling more than eighty women by June 2018.[6] In 2020, Weinstein was sentenced to twenty-three years in person after being convicted of rape in the third degree and a criminal sexual act.

In their book *She Said: Breaking the Sexual Harassment Story That Helped Ignite a Movement*, Kantor and Twohey discuss the process of their journalistic investigation and the difficulty of getting women to speak about their experiences on the record. They showcase that the settlement agreements that many of these women received from Harvey Weinstein, offering financial compensation for their hardship, effectively muzzled them, as the terms of their settlements prevented them from speaking about their experiences. These legal terms amplified a broader culture of shame, stigma, and disbelief of women's experiences, and this culture silences women's stories. The #MeToo movement began to chip away at these societal stigmas, moving toward more widespread acknowledgment and support for women's experiences of sexual violence.

A NOTE ON TERMINOLOGY: SEXUAL VIOLENCE

Definitions of sexual violence, including assault, abuse, and harassment, can vary in different contexts. These terms also have different legal definitions in different legal jurisdictions.

To cover a range of unwanted sexual behavior, the grassroots advocacy group called #AfterMeToo, discussed below, uses the broad, non-legal term sexual violence to cover both sexual harassment (unwanted sexualization or sexual comments) and sexual assault (unwanted sexual touching or sexual activity).[7] Similarly, the #MeToo movement also uses the term sexual misconduct to highlight a wide range of unwanted sexual behaviors. The University of Iowa defines sexual misconduct as a "broad term encompassing any unwelcome behavior of a sexual nature that is committed without consent or by force, intimidation, coercion, or manipulation. The term includes sexual assault, sexual harassment, sexual exploitation, and sexual intimidation."[8] For example, comedian Louis C.K.'s problematic behavior in the workplace surfaced in 2017, with assistants reporting that C.K. frequently masturbated in front of them or during phone meetings. This behavior might not meet a common definition of sexual assault, involving unwanted sexual touching, but nonetheless demonstrated a violation of the right to a fair, respectful, and safe workplace. Key in both of these terms, sexual violence and sexual misconduct, is a lack of consent.

Different terms are used to describe individuals who experience sexual violence. The term *survivor* has commonly been used to suggest a sense of power and strength in recovery from sexual violence. RAINN, the Rape, Abuse & Incest National Network, the largest anti-sexual-violence organization in the United States, states that the term *victim* can be used "when referring to someone who has recently been affected by sexual violence, and the term *survivor* can be used to "refer to someone who has gone through the recovery process, or when discussing the short- or long-term effects of sexual violence."[9] It's important to note that individuals who have experienced sexual violence can be in different states of their recovery process. RAINN suggests "some people identify as a victim, while others prefer the term survivor. The best way to be respectful is to ask for their preference." This in itself is an important element of consent: calling people what they want to be called.

Through the #MeToo movement that started in 2017, a flood of high-profile sexual violence stories appeared, but some of these stories had long roots. For example, on April 26, 2018, actor Bill Cosby was found guilty of three counts of aggravated indecent assault. This guilty verdict came after decades of complaints about Cosby, some dating back to the 1960s, and dozens of women making complaints about nonconsensual sex with Cosby, often having been unknowingly sedated by Cosby with the drug methaqualone, commonly known as Quaaludes. In 2021, Cosby's criminal conviction was overturned due to legal technicalities and a previous nonprosecution agreement, but our purpose in this chapter is not to delve into legal proceedings but rather to understand the widespread problem of lack of consent in order to care more and do better. Similarly, in 2019, musician R. Kelly was charged with eighteen counts of child sexual exploitation. For many years, news about R. Kelly's sexual relationships with young teenage girls circulated, with a story first appearing in the *Chicago Sun Times* in 2002. The *Surviving R. Kelly* documentary, released in early 2019, shed further light on these sexual abuse allegations in a thorough and comprehensive manner, including many detailed interviews with survivors. In 2021, Kelly was found guilty on charges of racketeering, sexual exploitation of a child, kidnapping, bribery, and sex trafficking.

These high-profile celebrity cases reveal an abuse of power, where powerful men have been enabled to behave in reprehensible ways, often for decades. In the *Surviving R. Kelly* documentary, Kelly's ex-wife Drea Kelly discusses the restrictive and abusive conditions of her marriage to Kelly. At one moment, she ponders why Kelly was able to continue his abusive behavior for so many years, and proclaims, "The reason why he could do it was because he has people helping him."[10] The film also highlights a culture of disregard and neglect of Kelly's victims, who were Black girls and women. In *Vox* magazine, Feminista Jones writes, "Black women have been calling out R. Kelly for years. Nobody listened."[11]

This attention to high-profile cases of sexual violence in the #MeToo movement also revealed the need for conversation and awareness around what constitutes consent and what constitutes a violation. In 2018, an anonymous woman's experience with comedian Aziz Ansari was published in an article titled "I Went on a Date with Aziz Ansari. It Turned into the Worst Night of My Life." The woman, who uses the pseudonym Grace in the article, describes a date with Ansari that ended at his apartment. Grace says she repeatedly felt pressured to have sex and felt uncomfortable with a quick escalation of sexual activity. She says she physically was "giving off cues that [she] wasn't interested" and verbally repeated the phrase "next time." Through the evening, Ansari continued to initiate sexual encounters through a variety of suggestions. Eventually, Grace decided to leave and ended the evening with crying on her way home.[12] Responses to the Aziz Ansari story were mixed, with some commentators suggesting that this story deflected attention from the #MeToo movement and the widespread experience of sexual violence in the workplace. Other commentators felt this story highlighted broader issues around normative gender roles and consent, including questions of why men feel entitled to sex, and why women lack agency or do not feel empowered to directly and clearly communicate their wants and desires with regard to sex.

For sexual consent educators, this Ansari incident might be a teaching tool to discuss the concept of **sexual scripts**. Sociologists John Gagnon and William Simon first developed this concept in their book *Sexual Conduct*, published in 1973. The concept of sexual scripts suggests that individuals do have agency, or the capacity to make their own decisions, but the way that we make these choices is guided by scripts, or what is expected in certain situations. In many contemporary sexual encounters, conventional sexual scripts suggest that an intimate encounter is defined by a man and woman engaging in penetrative sex. Feminist, queer, and disability studies scholars have made interventions into how intimate encounters are defined, suggesting that these encounters are also defined by people of different genders, engaging in an array of different intimate acts. In *Sexual Conduct*, Gagnon and Simon suggest that sexual scripts, the conventions of what is expected in sex, are guided by cultural, historical, and social conditions. This approach differs from a biological understanding of sex as a reproductive imperative. Instead, a sociological approach suggests that what takes place in intimate encounters is also socially constructed by norms and values in society. In the context of consent, what we individually do or do not consent to can also be guided by scripts of what is expected in certain situations.[13]

If the principle of consent is often violated and is sometimes also unclear, how can we create conditions where all individuals feel that they have agency to speak, are respected when they refuse to participate in things they don't want, and feel empowered to ask for what they do want? These high-profile cases and the #MeToo movement focused on sexual violence, but as we will explore further below, consent is not a precondition only for sexual encounters but also applies in a wide array of interactions.

#AFTERMETOO

The #MeToo movement first publicized the issues of sexual violence and consent in Hollywood, and spread out worldwide. These issues of sexual violence are not only a Hollywood problem, and responses and solutions are being developed at the grassroots level in a variety of places. #AfterMeToo is an organization that is working to create change in the entertainment industries and beyond, fostering solidarity to counter sexual violence while working to develop better systems of support and accountability for all types of precarious workers.

#AfterMeToo was founded by three Canadian women working in the entertainment industries, actresses Freya Ravensbergen and Mia Kirshner and director Aisling Chin-Yee. After the #MeToo story broke in 2017, Ravensbergen, Kirshner, and Chin-Yee quickly came together to proactively develop a response to this outpouring of women's experiences of sexual violence. In December 2017, they partnered with the Canadian newspaper the *Globe and Mail* to hold a symposium, called #AfterMeToo, to examine workplace sexual violence in the entertainment industries and to create change. This symposium provided a forum for participants to share their experiences and also developed recommendations for new systems of accountability. The group says they used the word *After* in their title because "we want to move beyond recognition and towards actual system, culture and policy changes that protect us from workplace sexual violence."[14]

The #AfterMeToo symposium was directed toward this goal of change, with nearly fifty attendees developing recommendations through roundtable discussions and a public forum. Participants included actors, directors, crew, agents, union representatives, human rights lawyers, employment lawyers, criminal lawyers, psychologists, advocates for survivors of sexual violence, technology innovators, and experts on organizational change. Many of these participants were survivors of sexual violence. At the symposium, ten roundtable discussions were recorded and made publicly accessible through #AfterMeToo's website, with topics ranging from the role of casting directors and agents; issues with the criminal justice system; and trauma, memory, and the psychological effects of sexual violence. After the symposium, an advisory committee of experts researched international best practices and produced a report containing nine recommendations and action items, including the following:

- Increasing funding for survivors of sexual violence
- Creating an independent national organization to combat sexual violence in the entertainment industries
- Investigating past cases of sexual violence in the entertainment industries
- Employers and unions imposing substantial consequences for perpetrators of sexual violence
- Creating a "safety fund" to support counseling and legal advice for survivors
- Prohibiting sexual violence in contracts, collective agreements, and workplace policies
- Mandatory sexual violence prevention training for all
- Creating technology to support survivors to report their experiences
- Demanding leadership accountability

Since the release of this report, #AfterMeToo has also worked to put these recommendations into action and create change, recognizing that there is often lip service and surface-level policy changes around issues of harassment and safety in organizations, but the widespread experience of sexual violence persists, even with the heightened awareness about the problem through the #MeToo movement. To further document this problem, in 2021 #AfterMeToo conducted a national survey of arts and culture workers, polling more than one thousand arts and culture workers in Canada, finding that 92 percent of the respondents had experienced or witnessed sexual violence. Key changes that these survey respondents noted they would like to see are the creation of an independent body to handle reports of workplace sexual harassment in the performing arts, film, and television industries; better training and accountability; and cultivating more inclusive, equitable cultures in these industries.

With funding from the federal Canadian government, #AfterMeToo partnered with the Canadian Women's Foundation to create a digital platform to support survivors of sexual violence, given that information online about how to report an experience of sexual violence can be overwhelming, and the process of reporting and retelling an experience of sexual violence can be traumatizing and triggering. The #AfterMeToo platform offers legal advice in plain language and other information about laws, judicial systems, mental health supports, and reporting options across Canada for those who experience or see workplace sexual harassment. #AfterMeToo cofounder Freya Ravensbergen calls this platform a "one-stop shop for survivors. When they really don't know what to do with what's just happened to them, this is a place where they can go. They can get information, they can get guidance on what their options are and guidance as to what option might be better suited to them."[15] Beyond providing better supports to survivors of sexual violence, Ravensbergen hopes to see broader cultural shifts around attitudes toward consent and sexual violence, with more women in leadership positions, better education for children about consent, and better representations of women and traditionally marginalized people in the media, seeing women, Black people, Indigenous people, and people of color in empowered roles in film, television, and advertising.

RAPE CULTURE VERSUS CONSENT CULTURE

If we understand sexual violence as a widespread problem that needs to be addressed, how do we define consent? Feminists developed the term **rape culture** not only to discuss incidents of sexual violence but also to point to the broader cultural acceptance of unwanted acts and behaviors. In their book *Transforming a Rape Culture*, Emilie Buchwald, Pamela Fletcher, and Martha Roth write, "In a rape culture, women perceive a continuum of threatened violence that ranges from sexual remarks to sexual touching to rape itself."[16] Important to note here is the gradient of unwanted sexual behavior: rape culture includes rape but also a range of smaller and often everyday acts. The term *rape culture* refers to the culture that normalizes and condones these types of acts. In her book *Sexual Consent*, Milena Popova discusses rape culture as "a cultural environment (a set of beliefs, practices, and attitudes) that enables sexual violence to thrive. Elements of rape culture may include rape myths and victim blaming as well as more subtle and insidious practices and beliefs."[17]

The 11th Principle: Consent! community group was formed in response to issues of sexual violence at the Burning Man festival, held annually in the desert in Nevada. This group, now incorporated as a nonprofit organization called Enthusiastic Consent, uses a pyramid diagram to visualize the continuum of rape culture (see figure 3.1). At the tip of this pyramid is the most egregious example of sexual violation: rape itself. If rape is the most egregious outcome of rape culture, rape culture is the broader system that not only produces this act but also normalizes it through silencing women or not believing their experiences. This pyramid shows that assault is at the apex of rape culture but is enabled by degradation and normalization. Examples of normalization behaviors at the bottom of the rape culture pyramid include "sexist attitudes" and "unwanted non-sexual touch." The prevalence of these types of unwanted behaviors suggests that rape culture is not only sexual and

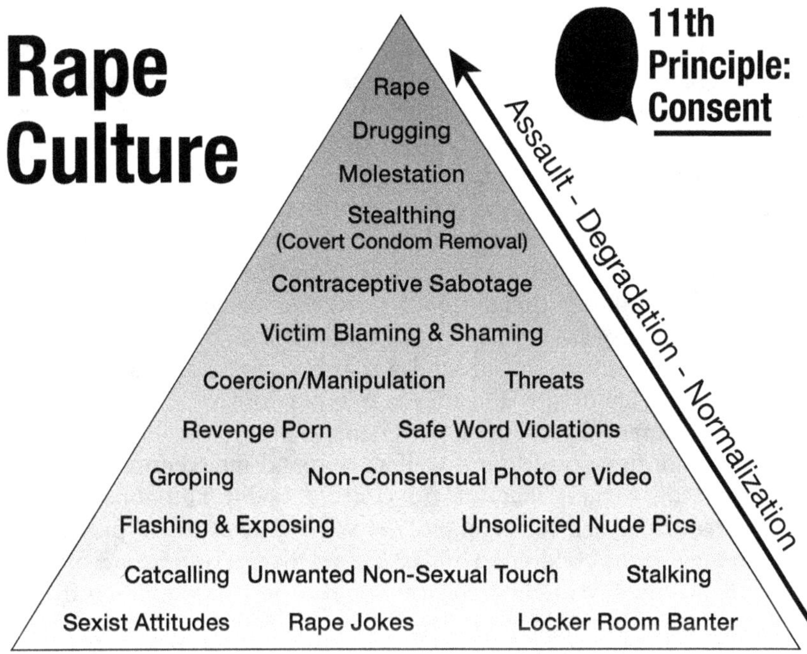

Figure 3.1 Rape Culture Pyramid

sexual violation. It is also broader cultural norms that devalue women and deny them agency and respect. Enthusiastic Consent explains, "Tolerance of the behaviors at the bottom supports or excuses those at the top. To change outcomes, we must change culture."[18] Fostering a consent culture involves all individuals thinking about the ways we relate to one another, our boundaries, and the boundaries of others.

Bodies Matter

One part of fostering a culture of consent is respecting your own bodily autonomy and the bodies of others. **Bodily autonomy** is defined as "the right to self governance over one's own body without external influence or coercion."[19] Key is the ability to make decisions about one's own body, for oneself, without others influencing these decisions. For consent educators, bodily autonomy "is generally considered to be a fundamental human right."[20] Sexual violence violates this basic human right. Consent educators suggest that the principle of bodily autonomy applies in sexual encounters but is more expansive than this. Consider the example of young children. In some cases, children are not able to fully decide for themselves what to do with their own bodies, as parents and caregivers intervene to ensure the health and welfare of children, for example, ensuring that children wear warm clothing during winter months, or ensuring that children attend school or receive medical attention when they are sick. There are moral as well as legal obligations for parents and caregivers to ensure the health and welfare of children, which in some cases constricts children's capacities to freely choose for themselves what they can or cannot do with their own bodies.

Alongside these health and welfare parental interventions, consent educators still suggest that the principle of bodily autonomy applies to children. Consider, for example, the somewhat common practice of encouraging young children to hug or kiss relatives. From the perspective of bodily autonomy of children, we would instead ask children if they want to give or receive hugs or kisses, and respect the decision to say no, if this is what a child wants. Consent educators suggest that influencing a child to provide or receive physical affection against their will teaches them early on that they lack agency when it comes to consent, and that the consent and bodily autonomy of others doesn't matter. We can see in this example how the principle of bodily autonomy is much more expansive than only sexual intimacy. What other examples can you think of where the principle of bodily autonomy has or has not been respected, in contemporary or historical circumstances? What factors allow or prevent different groups from having full bodily autonomy?

From "No Means No" to "Yes Means Yes" and Beyond

A cultural shift from rape culture, where sexual violence is widespread, toward a culture of consent requires thinking about what consent means and what it looks like in practice. The last few decades have seen different models of consent, developed by sex education and consent educators and activist and student groups. Often, these models are developed and deployed at colleges and universities, as these places are often where young people become sexually active and navigate the boundaries of sexual consent.

In the 1990s, the Canadian Federation of Students, a national organization for postsecondary students, created the No Means No campaign.

This phrase, "no means no," became popularized as a slogan and way of understanding the right to refuse to engage in sexual activity, and the importance of listening to women when they say no or decline to participate in sex. This campaign and approach to consent was important, as it validated the right to decline, refuse, or withdraw consent.[21] However, this **no means no** approach to consent also became critiqued as it has certain limits. There are many reasons why an individual may not utter the word *no* to decline to participate in sex. Sexual assault can occur when a person is unconscious, asleep, inebriated, or drugged and is unable to give consent or say no. Returning to the concept of sexual scripts, there are other, social reasons why it is sometimes difficult for women to clearly, verbally articulate a no in response to sex. In her article "Navigating Consent: Debunking the 'Gray Area' Myth," Sara Alcid critiques this "no means no" model as perpetuating uneven power dynamics, even as it tries to accord women agency and respect. Alcid writes that this model "positions men as the gatekeepers of consent and sets up a power dynamic that undermines consent as an ongoing conversation between two partners." Key here is the phrase "ongoing conversation," rather than a yes/no, either/or model of consenting to or refusing sex.

Alcid also draws attention to other situations where consent is incorrectly assumed to be implied. She writes, "Many people in relationships assume that their relationship status translates into a permanent state of consenting to sex."[22] In the past, these assumptions were reflected in legal structures, where sex within marriage was regarded as a right of a spouse. In 1993, the United Nations Declaration on the Elimination of Violence against Women stated that marital rape was a human rights violation. Through the late twentieth century, legal structures began to change in many jurisdictions, with the recognition of marital rape or spousal rape as a crime and punishable offence.[23]

While the No Means No campaign might have intended to succinctly put emphasis on respecting the right to refuse, in practice it may have put too much emphasis on the word *no*. There are multiple verbal and nonverbal ways to refuse or withdraw consent, and there are many conditions in which a person may not be comfortable to freely give or withdraw consent, including unequal power relations. For these reasons, consent educators also advocate for the principle of **affirmative consent**, meaning that consent should be informed, enthusiastic, and ongoing. This approach to sexual consent was first developed in 1990 at Antioch College in Ohio in a document called "Sexual Offense Prevention Policy." At the time, this approach was widely ridiculed and critiqued as overly restrictive, in that it asked for verbal consent for each step of a sexual encounter. Many of these critiques suggested this step-by-step approach to verify that both parties were consenting to participate in a sexual encounter was unnecessary and counter to common modes of romance and sexual seduction. However, advocates of this affirmative consent model suggest that it is not punitive but rather is sex-positive, involving active negotiation of sexual encounters. One student enrolled at Antioch College, Iris Olson, profiled in the *New York Times* article "The Reinvention of Consent," states, "Those discussions are what make sex wonderful. You have more control of the situation."[24] A variation of affirmative consent, **enthusiastic consent** is a model that suggests that consent means "you shouldn't do anything that your partner isn't actively excited about (or at least excited to try)."[25] This model has also been critiqued as individuals may express consent in a variety of ways, and what excitement looks like may vary across individuals.

This active negotiation of consent goes beyond sexual encounters to being respectful of people's bodies and boundaries in other ways. Asking for consent could seem like every encounter becomes a minefield or check box to complete. Instead, we might think about consent as an element of care, thinking about others, and being responsive to their feedback. Are we being mindful about other people's wants, needs, and capacities, or are we imposing our will or assuming without verifying that we understand others' desires?

In the context of sexual encounters, a 2019 study of 615 college students in the United States and Canada examined how individuals refused sex and whether or not gender or relationship status influence how individuals indicate refusal or lack of consent to engage in sexual activity.[26] The study found that many individuals refused sex without saying the word *no*, including using excuses or nonverbal cues. The researchers conducting this study, Tiffany Marcantonio and Kristen Jozkowski, conclude that sexual assault prevention and consent education needs to be more expansive and include thinking about "the variety of refusal cues," including direct verbal, direct nonverbal, and indirect nonverbal. Examples of these refusal cues include saying no, creating physical distance, using body language, and withdrawing attention. This complexity in refusal cues suggests the importance of paying attention to nuance while mobilizing our active listening skills, and being receptive and responsive to both verbal and nonverbal cues.

CULTURAL APPROPRIATION

Consent and respect for bodily autonomy also relates to respect for cultural autonomy and sovereignty. This respect for cultural autonomy is often violated in what is known as cultural appropriation. For example, outdoor music festivals can sometimes be a place to get away from the confines of everyday life, to enjoy music but also to relax and take a break from it all. But in the early 2010s, the Coachella music festival in California become infamously known for its festivalgoers wearing Indigenous headdresses or war bonnets, in what become called the "hipster headdress." Due to controversies over the popularization of festivalgoers wearing these traditional Indigenous items at festivals, several music festivals decided to respond by banning the wearing of these items at their events. In Indigenous cultures, these war bonnets are designated for sacred ceremonial, not fashion, purposes, to be worn only by chiefs who have earned this privilege in their communities.[27] Musical festivals are of course not the only or prime places where issues of cultural appropriation emerge, but this incident at Coachella illuminates broader issues of power, privilege, and respect as they relate to consent and cultural appropriation in many contexts.

A NOTE ON TERMINOLOGY: INDIGENEITY

Indigenous peoples worldwide have been called and use various terms to describe themselves. This is an ongoing discussion, with no clear, single "right answer."

The term *Indian* is a misnomer, given to Indigenous people in America after colonization. That said, many organizations that represent Indigenous people still have *Indian* in their names, for example, the National Congress of American Indians (NCAI) and the American Indian Movement (AIM). However, this term is not commonly accepted to be used by non-Indigenous people as it has been used with racist and disparaging intent. For example, after a resurgence of public protest in 2020, the Cleveland Indians baseball team announced it would drop *Indian* from its name.

The term *Native*, as in Native American, was popularized in response to the inaccuracies of the term *Indian*. Native is often still commonly in use, but also is seen as overly broad and generic. The term *Indigenous* is used to describe First Peoples worldwide, including and outside of North America, and is the term selected to be used in this book. For example, the United Nations has a Declaration on the Rights of Indigenous Peoples. The term *Aboriginal* is often commonly used, especially in Canada and Australia. This term is also quite broad, referring to original people of the land. A different approach to these broad terms is to aim to use the name of the particular nation or group that an Indigenous person belongs to, to respect difference and diversity, and not treat Indigenous peoples as a monolithic whole.

Bob Joseph, the founder of Indigenous Corporate Training Inc. and member of the Gwawaenuk Nation, says, "One of the key messages I give in my workshops and training: 'Go with what they are calling themselves.'" Joseph states this is not a matter of personal preference of what you would like to call others: "It's not about your comfort level—it's about showing respect and using the term that individuals and organizations have chosen for themselves."[28]

In her article "But Why Can't I Wear a Hipster Headdress," Cherokee scholar Adrienne Keene, who is an assistant professor in American studies and ethnic studies at Brown University, responds to this issue of the "hipster headdress," outlining four main reasons why non-Indigenous people wearing traditional Indigenous regalia is a problem, including perpetuating stereotypes, lack of awareness of spiritual significance, similarities to Blackface, and the history of genocide and colonialism. Keene explains the problem of costuming oneself in another race with stereotypical representations: "You are pretending to be a race that you are not, and are drawing upon stereotypes to do so. . . . You're collapsing distinct cultures, and in doing so, you're asserting your power over them." Wearing an Indigenous war bonnet as a fashion item contributes to "dismissing and minimizing the continued subordination and oppression of Natives."[29]

A broad takeaway point from the "hipster headdress" or war bonnet discussion is to exercise caution with taking the cultural expressions of other cultures, especially those that have lived through and continue to live through subordination and oppression. But this does not mean that we should necessarily stop engaging with the cultural forms of other cultures wholesale. Engaging in **cultural appreciation** can mean respectfully engaging with the cultural expressions of other cultures, reflecting on the meaning and context of how these cultural expressions are intended to be used. In the case of Indigenous cultural expressions, many Indigenous creators would suggest making sure to purchase art and cultural forms from Indigenous creators directly and supporting their businesses, rather than supporting knockoffs or other products that have been produced without the participation or consent of Indigenous peoples. Here education and listening are key to make sure you understand the purpose and significance of the cultural form you are appreciating, including whether or not and how the cultural form is intended to be used by those outside of the community.

The "Think Before You Appropriate" guide, created by the Intellectual Property Issues in Cultural Heritage Project, defines **cultural appropriation** as "to take something that belongs to someone else for one's own use . . . appropriation happens when a cultural element is taken from its cultural context and used in another."[30] This process of borrowing cultural elements can be quite common in our contemporary culture, which borrows and remixes references from a multitude of places to assemble together a new whole. The "Think Before You Appropriate" guide opens by acknowledging this common process of cultural borrowing and blending: "people and cultures have always exchanged and borrowed ideas from each other to create new forms of art and symbolic expression. Whether intentionally or not, most if not all human creations reflect varied sources of inspiration."[31] For example, popular television shows like *The Simpsons* commonly make references and riff on other works of popular culture. In the documentary film *RiP! A Remix Manifesto*, filmmaker Brett Gaylor outlines a "Remixer's Manifesto," which contains the following elements:

1. Culture always builds on the past.
2. The past always tries to control the future.
3. Our future is becoming less free.
4. To build free societies you must limit the control of the past.[32]

This definition of a remix culture differs from a definition of cultural appropriation, as all cultural borrowing is not equal. Returning to an intersectional framework, introduced in chapter 1, we can ask questions about power and privilege. What factors enable or prevent different groups in society to participate in their own cultural traditions? Is there an equal playing field for cultural remixing, or have some groups profited from the "borrowing" of culture, to the detriment of others? When does "borrowing" become theft? Who has the power to control the use of the past? In the context of Indigenous people and the traditional war bonnet, we might be mindful of the context of colonialism, where Indigenous people were often forcibly prevented from practicing their own cultural traditions or had their cultural traditions removed from them and face ongoing injustices in the present day.

WE'RE A CULTURE, NOT A COSTUME CAMPAIGN

Ohio University's S.T.A.R.S. (Students Teaching About Racism in Society) is a student group dedicated to the prevention of racism through education and awareness. This group was founded in 1988, through a course that was being run at Ohio University. Now S.T.A.R.S. runs peer-to-peer diversity training with the goal of facilitating discussions about diversity and discrimination through the principle of "each one teach one," or shared learning through individuals educating their peers.

One of S.T.A.R.S.' most successful campaigns, which received international attention and exposure, is the We're a Culture, Not a Costume campaign, focusing on racially insensitive Halloween costumes and cultural appropriation. Starting in 2013, this campaign developed a series of posters, released online and promoted through social media, that depicted a student from a minority or racialized group next to someone dressed as a caricature of that minority or racialized group in a Halloween costume. Placing students from a cultural group next to a costumed version of that cultural group helps communicate the human and harmful impact of these racially insensitive depictions in a personal way. The slogan for these posters reads, "This is not who I am, and this is not okay."

The campaign slogan, We're a Culture, Not a Costume, helps explain the limited, stereotypical, and negative portrayal of cultural groups through costumes. Halloween is a fun event, but this fun should be carried out without racism and harm. Subsequent versions of the We're a Culture, Not a Costume campaign have amplified the lasting repercussions of these stereotypical costumes that a person might wear for their one fun night. "You wear the costume for one night. I wear the stigma for life," reads another poster tagline.

For more information about S.T.A.R.S. or to view their poster campaign gallery, visit https://www.ohio.edu/orgs/stars/Home.html.

Debates around what constitutes cultural appropriation are increasingly happening in the public arena. For example, many pop stars, including Miley Cyrus, Taylor Swift, Justin Bieber, and others, have been called to account for their appropriation of Black cultural expressions for their own benefit. Discussing the all-too-common practice of appropriation of Black culture in music and fashion, Johanna Yaovi, the founder of the Curl Project, defines **Blackfishing** as "picking and choosing common black traits and characteristics for one's benefit . . . while we continue to face discrimination on a day to day basis."[33] Blackfishing results in limited and often stereotypical tropes of Blackness becoming appropriated and commodified, revealing anti-Black racism at play.

One example of these discussions of cultural appropriation comes from 2016, when actress Amy Schumer was under scrutiny for releasing a parody video of Beyoncé's "Formation" video. Schumer, a white woman, was criticized for her version of this song and video, as Beyoncé's music and imagery celebrated Black culture alongside voicing the experiences and marginalization of Black people in the United States. For example, Beyoncé's video features an image of a sinking police car in New Orleans, thought to be a critique of the slow intervention and response to the devastation of Hurricane Katrina in 2005, which overwhelmingly affected Black residents in New Orleans, resulting in the deaths of more than a thousand people. The "Formation" video ends with a young Black boy wearing a hoodie standing in front of a wall that says "stop shooting us," also thought to be a commentary on police violence and killings of Black people. In contrast, Schumer's version of the video features her singing and dancing jokingly with three other actresses, Goldie Hawn, Wanda Skyes, and Joan Cusack. In her response to the criticism that her video was misguided, racially insensitive, and a form of cultural appropriation, Schumer released an essay, "Information about My 'Formation,'" in which she states her video was not a parody but a tribute based in respect, which was authorized: "Of course I had Beyoncé and Jay Z's approval. They released it on Tidal [their streaming platform] exclusively for the first 24 hours," suggesting that consent was sought and given for this version of the video.[34] Nonetheless, this incident raises broader questions about entitlement, access, use, and reuse of others' cultural expressions removed from their original context and meaning, especially with regard to cultural expressions from historically marginalized people and communities.

To clarify this problem of harm and an uneven playing field in cultural appropriation, the "Think Before You Appropriate" guide introduces the term **cultural misappropriation**, "a one-sided process where one entity benefits from another group's culture without permission and without giving something in return."[35] Key in this definition is a lack of consent and a lack of reciprocity. Cultural misappropriation means taking something from another group, without permission, for one's own benefit.

There is no fixed checklist to follow to know if your behavior falls under cultural appreciation, cultural appropriation, or cultural misappropriation. Instead of a checklist, follow the principles of consent and reciprocity. Are you asking permission? Are you giving something back to affected communities in exchange for what you are using, or do you solely benefit? Are there contemporary or historical factors that create an uneven playing field for this act of cultural "borrowing"? In the *Huffington Post*, journalist Julia Brucculieri acknowledges the complexity of these issues, titling her article "The Difference between Cultural Appropriation and Appreciation Is Tricky." Some of this trickiness is because we are constantly surrounded by sources of inspiration. Especially in the context of inspiration from historically marginalized and underrepresented communities, "designers should be transparent about their inspirations from the get-go," writes Brucculieri.[36] Beyond acknowledgment, creators can compensate communities that they are drawing from, as well as working with principles of collaboration instead of appropriation. In her article, Brucculieri quotes Rhon Manigault-Bryant, associate professor of Africana studies at Williams College, who says, "Giving credit is one thing,

Table 3.1 Five Principles of Responsible Creative Collaboration

Free Prior and Informed Consent	• Goals of the collaboration are presented to potential partners • Individuals who are approached are in a position to give consent on behalf of the community
Shared Control over Process and Product	• Partners are comfortable with their respective amount of input and control over goals, approach, and final outcomes of the collaboration • History of appropriation and colonialism might mean that relationship and trust building is a lengthy process
Acknowledgment and Attribution	• Clearly identify all collaborators and the nature of their contribution to the work
Respect for Cultural Differences	• What are the worldviews, beliefs, and customs of those you are seeking to collaborate with? • Is the proposed collaborative project at odds with these worldviews?
Reciprocity and Benefit Sharing	• Discuss appropriate balance between what you are receiving and what you are giving to the collaboration. This includes financial and nonfinancial benefits

Adapted from the "Think Before You Appropriate" guide

but being included from the onset is also important." Rather than asking permission to give tribute or to use inspiration, creators instead can seek to partner or collaborate with those they are inspired by. Below, in Activity 3.1, you will have the opportunity to think about how to ethically partner with other cultures and communities in business arrangements. Table 3.1 gives some guidelines from the "Think Before You Appropriate" guide to help you develop responsible partnership strategies in this activity and beyond.

DECOLONIZING CULTURE

Beyond the problems of cultural misappropriation, what steps are possible to move toward more ethical or consensual relationships with historically marginalized and underrepresented groups? The "Think Before You Appropriate" guide's elements of responsible collaboration offer one way to move in this direction, a move toward **decolonizing culture**. Educator, scholar, and member of Skwah First Nation Bill Mussell defines decolonization as "a process where a colonized people reclaim their traditional culture, redefine themselves as a people and reassert their distinct identity."[37] Many contemporary cultural institutions are grappling with their legacies of cultural misappropriation and determining how they can move forward on a path toward decolonization. Museum scholars John Giblin, Imma Ramos, and Nikki Grout note that "many of the collections [in art museums] made during and since the colonial era are unique and powerful reflections of this [colonial] history." For example, the British Museum in London, England, contains many artifacts gained through Britain's colonial conquests, including the Parthenon Marbles from Greece, the Rosetta Stone from Egypt, and the Gweagal shield from Aboriginal people in Australia.[38]

The process of decolonization is not only focused on repatriating objects; it also targets perspectives and worldviews. Decolonization has particular salience in art and cultural institutions, as these institutions were often developed through centering a white and Eurocentric perspective on art, culture, and the world. In the context of art museums, Rachel Hatzipanagos in the *Washington Post* defines decolonization as "a process that institutions undergo to expand the perspectives they portray beyond those of the dominant cultural group, particularly white colonizers."[39] Artist and curator Shaheen Kasmani states that decolonization is "the upfront challenge of white supremacy, de-centers the Eurocentric view, values narrative of that has been made Other. It dismantles systems of thoughts [that place] the straight white man as standard."[40] This means both reckoning with the past and creating a more expansive space for different and diverse views and cultural expressions in the present.

Artists and art institutions have deployed various strategies to move toward decolonizing their cultural legacies. For example, when Susan Goldberg become the editor-in-chief of *National Geographic* magazine in 2018, she chose to commission an external assessment of the representation of race in the magazine, noting that *National Geographic* "did little to push its readers beyond the stereotypes ingrained in white American culture until 1970."[41] In a further example of working to decolonize culture, in 2018 the Field Museum of Natural History in Chicago decided to close and renovate its Native North American Hall to better reflect and partner with Indigenous groups to represent Indigenous art and culture. In a press release, Jaap Hoogstraten, director of exhibition, says, "The Field Museum has established a new collaborative process that will allow the exhibition to be informed by Native American scholarship. The exhibits will always be co-curated by Native American scholars and community members, so visitors will encounter unique perspectives and learn from multiple knowledge streams about the history of Native Americans and contemporary concerns and ways of life." Patty Loew, an Ojibwe advisory committee member, says, "For too long, our histories have been interpreted though an outsider's lens. This renovation, in which Indigenous people are participating, provides an important and long-overdue opportunity for us to tell our own stories."[42] Loew's words here reflect a decolonial approach to culture: moving away from an outsider lens to a position that centers the stories of underrepresented and historically marginalized communities, and creating opportunities for these stories to be told. In short, decolonizing culture means moving away from the dominance of white and Eurocentric views, so that diverse stories and cultural expressions can be shared by representative creators, on their terms. In the context of care and consent, here we can see consent moving past merely acceptable or tolerable relationships and moving toward more just and mutually beneficial, relational partnerships.

Activity 3.1: Cultural Misappropriation Versus Cultural Appreciation Case Study: Relationship and Business Building Strategy

Overview and Background on Case

In 2012, the Navajo Nation, an Indigenous territory spanning the regions of Arizona, Utah, and New Mexico, filed a lawsuit against the clothing retailer Urban Outfitters. Though Navajo-style prints are distinctive and recognizable, craft and design are not typically covered by intellectual property laws. However, the Navajo Nation registered and trademarked their name in 1943.

In 2011, Urban Outfitters launched a Navajo line of products, including underwear, a drinking flask, jewelry, and T-shirts. The release of this product line was met with dismay and displeasure from members of the Navajo community. Sasha Houston Brown of the Santee Sioux Nation wrote an open letter to Urban Outfitters to outline the nature of the problem with its "Navajo" products: "There is nothing honorable or historically appreciative in selling items such as the Navajo Print Fabric Wrapped Flask, Peace Treaty Feather Necklace, Staring at Stars Skull Native Headdress T-shirt or the Navajo Hipster Panty," she wrote. "These and the dozens of other tacky products you are currently selling referencing Native America make a mockery of our identity and unique cultures."[43]

Initially, Urban Outfitters continued to sell its Navajo product line. Urban Outfitters' PR director, Ed Looram, commented, "The Native American-inspired trend and specifically the term 'Navajo' have been cycling thru [*sic*] fashion, fine art and design for the last few years. We currently have no plans to modify or discontinue any of these products."[44]

In addition to infringement of the trademarked Navajo name, the lawsuit filed by the Navajo Nation in 2012 also cited the 1990 Federal Indian Arts and Crafts Act in the United States, which made it illegal to "offer or display for sale, or sell any art or craft product in a manner that falsely suggests it is Indian produced, an Indian product, or the product of a particular Indian or Indian Tribe or Indian arts and crafts organization."

In 2016, this court case concluded with a settlement. This settlement included financial compensation for the Navajo Nation, as well as a "supply and license agreement" for collaboration on a jewelry line.

Activity

Review the elements of responsible creative collaboration from the "Think Before You Appropriate" guide, cited above. Before Urban Outfitters released its product line in 2011, what steps could the company have taken to develop a responsible collaboration? When members of the Navajo Nation expressed their displeasure with the product line in 2011, what would a more appropriate response have been from Urban Outfitters? What steps or measures could Urban Outfitters implement to avoid these kinds of clashes and lawsuits in the future? What broader lessons about consent and cultural appropriation can be learned from this case study? What would a decolonial approach to business look like for Urban Outfitters? What would you hope to see from the "supply and license" collaboration on the jewelry line?

QUESTIONS FOR LEARNING AND REFLECTION

1. Consent Culture Spectrum: This chapter has given an overview of the differences between rape culture and consent culture. Draw a horizontal line and write the most extreme examples of forms of rape culture and consent culture at either end. Then, fill out the line with your own examples of different forms of rape culture or consent culture, on a gradient between these two extremes. If a horizontal line does not seem like the most appropriate shape, develop a different shape of your own.
2. Cultural Appropriation Spectrum: This chapter has given an overview of the difference between cultural appreciation, cultural

appropriation, and cultural misappropriation. Think of a cultural form or cultural product that you enjoy that does not come from your own cultural background. Draw a horizontal line and put an example of the most extreme form of cultural misappropriation of this product at one end. Then, put an example of a form of cultural appreciation at the other end of this horizontal line. Fill out the line with other examples of cultural appreciation to cultural misappropriation, on a gradient between these two extremes. Again, if a horizontal line does not seem like the most appropriate shape, develop a different shape of your own. After completing this diagram and the one above, consider what factors or conditions make you put your examples on one side (consent/appreciation) or the other (rape culture/cultural misappropriation).

NOTES

1. Tarana Burke, Twitter post, October 17, 2017, https://twitter.com/taranaburke/status/919704949751255040?lang=en.
2. Alyssa Milano, Twitter post, October 15, 2017, https://twitter.com/alyssa_milano/status/919659438700670976?lang=en.
3. Me Too, "Tarana Burke, Founder," accessed October 26, 2020, https://metoomvmt.org/get-to-know-us/tarana-burke-founder/.
4. Just Be Inc., "About Us," accessed November 24, 2020, https://justbeinc.wixsite.com/justbeinc/purpose-mission-and-vision.
5. Stephanie Zacharek, Eliana Dockterman, and Haley Sweetland Edwards, "The Silence Breakers," *Time.com*, December 8, 2017, accessed October 26, 2020, http://time.com/time-person-of-the-year-2017-silence-breakers/.
6. Sara Moniuszko and Cara Kelly, "Harvey Weinstein Scandal: A Complete List of the 87 Accusers," *USAToday.com*, June 1, 2018, accessed October 26, 2020, https://www.usatoday.com/story/life/people/2017/10/27/weinstein-scandal-complete-list-accusers/804663001/.
7. David Butt and Chi Nguyen, "AfterMeToo Report," #AfterMeToo, March 6, 2018, accessed November 26, 2020, https://a085d11e-6d13-4974-83f0-d75131b04e1c.filesusr.com/ugd/1766c7_398ee90fdbb047af951203f20a5f3db3.pdf.
8. University of Iowa, Office of Sexual Misconduct Response Coordinator, "Sexual Misconduct," accessed November 26, 2020, https://osmrc.uiowa.edu/policy/sexual-misconduct.
9. RAINN, "Key Terms and Phrases," accessed November 26, 2020, https://www.rainn.org/articles/key-terms-and-phrases.

10. Tamra Simmons, Dream Hampton, Jesse Daniels, Joel Karsberg, Jessica Everleth, and Maria Pepin, executive producers, *Surviving R. Kelly* (Lifetime, 2019).

11. Feminista Jones, "Black Women Have Been Calling Out R. Kelly for Years. Nobody Listened," *Vox*, January 9, 2019, accessed June 9, 2021, https://www.vox.com/first-person/2017/7/21/16008230/r-kelly-surviving-sex-cult-abuse-john-legend-chance-the-rapper.

12. Katie Way, "'I Went on a Date with Aziz Ansari. It Turned into the Worst Night of My Life," *Babe*, January 13, 2018, accessed November 24, 2020, https://babe.net/2018/01/13/aziz-ansari-28355.

13. John H. Gagnon and William Simon, *Sexual Conduct: The Social Sources of Human Sexuality* (Chicago: Aldine Books, 1973).

14. Butt and Nguyen, "AfterMeToo Report," 3.

15. Canadian Press, "AfterMeToo Group Creating Digital Centre for Survivors of Workplace Violence," CBC News, October 14, 2018, https://www.cbc.ca/news/entertainment/aftermetoo-digital-centre-survivors-1.4862446.

16. Emilie Buchwald, Pamela Fletcher, and Martha Roth, eds., *Transforming a Rape Culture* (Minneapolis: Milkweed Editions, 1994), vii.

17. Milena Popova, *Sexual Consent* (Cambridge, MA: MIT Press, 2019), 182.

18. 11th Principle: Consent!, "Rape Culture Pyramid," https://www.11thprincipleconsent.org/consent-propaganda/rape-culture-pyramid/.

19. SexInfo Online, "Bodily Autonomy," November 1, 2018, accessed November 26, 2020, https://sexinfoonline.com/bodily-autonomy/.

20. SexInfo Online, "Bodily Autonomy."

21. Canadian Federation of Students, "Gender-Based Violence," accessed November 26, 2020, https://cfsontario.ca/campaigns/gender-based-violence/.

22. Sara Alcid, "Navigating Consent: Debunking the 'Gray Area' Myth," *Everyday Feminism*, January 4, 2013, accessed November 26, 2020, https://everydayfeminism.com/2013/01/navigating-consent-debunking-the-grey-area-myth/.

23. United Nations, Office of the Human Rights for High Commissioner, "Declaration on the Elimination of Violence against Women," General Assembly resolution 48/104, December 20, 1993, accessed November 26, 2020, https://www.ohchr.org/EN/ProfessionalInterest/Pages/ViolenceAgainstWomen.aspx.

24. Katherine Rosman, "The Reinvention of Consent," *New York Times*, February 24, 2018, accessed November 26, 2020, https://www.nytimes.com/2018/02/24/style/antioch-college-sexual-offense-prevention-policy.html.

25. Jaclyn Friedman, "'Yes Means Yes' and Enthusiastic Consent," Our Bodies Ourselves, October 15, 2011, accessed November 26, 2020, https://www.ourbodiesourselves.org/book-excerpts/health-article/yes-means-yes-enthusiastic-consent/.

26. Tiffany L. Marcantonio and Kristen N. Jozkowski, "Assessing How Gender, Relationship Status, and Item Wording Influence Cues Used by College Students to Decline Different Sexual Behaviors," *Journal of Sex Research* 57, no. 2 (2020): 260–72.

27. Calum Marsh, "Osheaga's Headress Ban Shows Festival's Zero Tolerance for Cultural Appropriation," *Guardian*, July 17, 2015, accessed December 15, 2020, https://www.theguardian.com/culture/2015/jul/17/osheaga-music-festival-headdress-cultural-appropriation; Dorian Lynskey, "This Means War: Why the Fashion Headdress Must Be Stopped," *Guardian*, July 30, 2014, accessed December 15, 2020, https://www.theguardian.com/fashion/2014/jul/30/why-the-fashion-headdress-must-be-stopped.

28. Bob Joseph, "Indigenous or Aboriginal: Which Is Correct?," CBC News, September 21, 2016, accessed December 16, 2020, https://www.cbc.ca/news/indigenous/indigenous-aboriginal-which-is-correct-1.3771433.

29. Adrienne Keene, "But Why Can't I Wear a Hipster Headdress," *Native Appropriations*, April 17, 2010, accessed December 16, 2020, http://nativeappropriations.com/2010/04/but-why-cant-i-wear-a-hipster-headdress.html.

30. Intellectual Property Issues in Cultural Heritage Project, "Think Before You Appropriate: Things to Know and Questions to Ask in Order to Avoid Misappropriating Indigenous Cultural Heritage," Simon Fraser University, 2015, 2.

31. Intellectual Property Issues, "Think Before You Appropriate," 2.

32. Wikipedia, "*RiP!: A Remix Manifesto*," accessed December 15, 2020, https://en.wikipedia.org/wiki/RiP!:_A_Remix_Manifesto.

33. Priya Elan, "Blackfishing: 'Black Is Cool, Unless You're Actually Black,'" *Guardian*, April 14, 2020, accessed March 15, 2021, https://www.theguardian.com/fashion/2020/apr/14/blackfishing-black-is-cool-unless-youre-actually-black.

34. Amy Schumer, "Information about My 'Formation,'" *Medium*, October 27, 2016, accessed December 15, 2020, https://medium.com/@amyschumer/information-about-my-formation-b416d2adfc71#.ot3a3gptr.

35. Intellectual Property Issues, "Think Before You Appropriate," 3.

36. Julia Brucculieri, "The Difference between Cultural Appropriation and Appreciation Is Tricky. Here's a Primer," *Huffington Post*, July 2, 2018, accessed December 15, 2020, https://www.huffingtonpost.ca/entry/cultural-appropriation-vs-appreciation_n_5a78d13ee4b0164659c72fb3.

37. Bill Mussell, "Cultural Pathways for Decolonization," *Visions Journal* 5 (2008): 4–5, https://www.heretohelp.bc.ca/visions/aboriginal-people-vol5/cultural-pathways-for-decolonization.

38. John Giblin, Imma Ramos, and Nikki Grout, "Dismantling the Master's House: Thoughts on Representing Empire and Decolonising Museums and Public Space in Practice; An Introduction," *Third Text* 33, nos. 4–5 (2019): 471–86.

39. Rachel Hatzipanagos, "The 'Decolonization' of the American Museum," *Washington Post*, October 11, 2018, accessed December 16,

2020, https://www.washingtonpost.com/nation/2018/10/12/decolonization-american-museum/.

40. Shaheen Kasmani, "How Can You Decolonise Museums?," *Museum Next*, June 2, 2020, https://www.museumnext.com/article/decolonising-museums/.

41. Olga Viso, "Decolonizing the Art Museum: The Next Wave," *New York Times*, May 1, 2018, accessed June 24, 2021, https://www.nytimes.com/2018/05/01/opinion/decolonizing-art-museums.html.

42. Field Museum, "Field Museum to Renovate Native North America Hall, to Open 2021," October 29, 2018, accessed June 24, 2021, https://www.fieldmuseum.org/about/press/field-museum-renovate-native-north-america-hall-open-2021.

43. Nicky Woolf, "Urban Outfitters Settles with Navajo Nation after Illegally Using Tribe's Name," *Guardian*, November 19, 2016.

44. Jenna Sauers, "Urban Outfitters and the Navajo Nation: What Does the Law Say?," *Jezebel*, October 13, 2011, accessed June 24, 2021, https://jezebel.com/urban-outfitters-and-the-navajo-nation-what-does-the-l-5849637.

REFERENCES AND FURTHER READING

Milena Popova, *Sexual Consent* (Cambridge, MA: MIT Press, 2019). This accessible text gives a thorough overview of the issues of sexual consent, including a glossary, different approaches to thinking about consent, and next steps for action.

Intellectual Property Issues in Cultural Heritage Project, "Think Before You Appropriate: Things to Know and Questions to Ask in Order to Avoid Misappropriating Indigenous Cultural Heritage" (Simon Fraser University, 2015). This guide, cited throughout this chapter, provides definitions and guidelines, specifically for creators and designers, to ethically partner with Indigenous peoples to represent Indigenous cultures through collaboration.

Native Appropriations blog, http://nativeappropriations.com/. Run by Cherokee Nation member Adrienne Keene, "Native Appropriations is a forum for discussing representations of Native peoples, including stereotypes, cultural appropriation, news, activism, and more." This blog offers accessible and insightful discussion of these issues from an expert with lived experience.

Indigenous Corporate Training Inc., *Indigenous Peoples: A Guide to Terminology*, https://www.ictinc.ca/indigenous-peoples-a-guide-to-terminology. This free ebook, available online, gives an overview of terminology relating to Indigenous peoples, including explanations of forty-three different terms in use today.

Anuradha Vikram, *Decolonizing Culture: Essays on the Intersection of Art and Politics* (San Francisco: Art Practical Books and Sming Sming Books,

2017). This book is a collection of seventeen essays written by Anuradha Vikram between 2013 and 2017 and published online on the website *Daily Serving*'s #Hashtags column. These essays address the topics of race, gender, and colonialism in current events in contemporary art, both in the United States and internationally.

4

Collaborate

■ ■ ■

"Sharing is caring" is a common phrase that even preschool-aged children know to say when playing with others. Though we can easily recite this refrain, the work of meaningfully committing to collaborating with others is much more challenging. "Teamwork makes the dream work" is another common phrase about collaborative endeavors—but working in a team setting can sometimes be a nightmare rather than a beautiful meeting of energies. How can we best work with others toward mutually beneficial goals or shared outcomes?

From the rise of coworking spaces to the so-called sharing economy, *collaboration* is a term that is valued in our contemporary culture, but it is also often used in hollow and celebratory ways. In this chapter, we will draw on some of the best practices from the research literature on creative collaboration. *Creative* here doesn't mean that all collaborations have to do with artistic work or creative expression. Rather, we'll focus on how collaboration, when it's working well, can be the source of new ideas and innovation. We'll learn from artistic and creative industries settings that working with others can be both some of the most challenging work we do and also the most necessary to create social change and grow and flourish as individuals.

In their book *Collaborative Production in the Creative Industries*, James Graham and Alessandro Gandini state that "from the artisanal workshops of the Renaissance masters to the globally networked start-ups of the twenty-first century, the character, context and consequences of creative collaboration have been mythologised and mystified in equal measure."[1] Creative collaborations are often admired and romanticized; we can think of famous examples of collaborations, like between musicians John Lennon and Paul McCartney, visual artists Andy Warhol and Jean-Michel Basquiat, industrial designers Charles and Ray Eames, or comedians Ilana Glazer and Abbi Jacobson, where the sum has been greater than the parts.

While the outputs of famous creative collaborations are well-loved and celebrated products of creativity, the idea of serendipity and finding your creative soul mate is not a practical strategy for improving the quality and capacity of working with others. Behind many of these famous examples of creative collaboration are mountains of logistical work and unsung heroes. Still, we have the idea that collaborating with others is part of being a creative and successful person. In their book, Graham and Gandini reference the 2014 BuzzFeed article "10 Habits of Highly Creative People." The fourth item on this list, after physical activity, napping, and daydreaming, is collaborating. This article highlights another famous example of setting the stage for collaboration, from 1999, when Steve Jobs designed the Pixar Studios campus: "his first priority was encouraging creative collaboration. He tossed aside the original design—which called for three separate buildings, dividing the computer scientists, the animators, and the directors and editors—in favor of one large, central space with just two bathrooms where encounters among different specialists would be inevitable."[2]

This BuzzFeed article might be somewhat tongue-in-cheek, but it still reveals contemporary values and trends, including the need to collaborate well with others. Pixar is much celebrated for box office and critical and creative success with animated films like *Toy Story* and *Finding Nemo*. Some of the framework for collaboration that led to this success from Pixar sounds potentially uncomfortable: only two bathrooms for how many employees? Does anyone really want to mix and mingle with people with different specializations on their way to or from the bathroom?

While discomfort, friction, and conflict are sometimes inevitable parts of collaboration, working with others can push us to a more creative and innovative place than we can access on our own. How can we move past the buzz and hype of collaboration to meaningfully work together in team-based settings, across differences, with a commitment to putting in the work to realize these team efforts? In opposition to popular celebrations of creative collaboration that highlight serendipity and creative soul mates, this chapter emphasizes the commitment, work, and challenges of working with others in collaborative ventures. This chapter highlights shared vision, valuing differences and diversity, creating a structure or framework, creating an environment for the whole self, and committing to behind-the-scenes logistical work as building blocks of successful collaboration.

SHARED VISION

What are we working toward when we collaborate? Ideally, team-based collaborative efforts should start from a place of shared vision, a sense of mutual goals or outcomes of working together. Companies and organizations might have mission and mandate statements, but this does not mean that everyone at the company or organization will automatically support or work to actualize this mission and mandate. Rather, shared vision needs to be defined, clarified, and fostered among people working together.

In workplaces, shared vision across the organization is sometimes referred to as "buy-in." In his book *Buy In: Saving Your Good Idea from Being Shot Down*, Harvard Business School professor John Kotter writes, "Buy-in is critical to making any large organizational change happen. Unless you win support for your ideas, from people at all levels of your organization, big ideas never seem to take hold or have the impact you want. Our research has shown that 70% of all organizational change efforts fail, and one reason for this is executives simply don't get enough buy-in, from enough people, for their initiatives and ideas."[3] Though the language of "buy-in" can sometimes have an economic tone, developing good collaboration does not mean getting people to "purchase" your ideas. Furthermore, the subtitle of Kotter's book, "Saving Your Good Idea," suggests one person working alone and then presenting their idea to others to approve and support. That is a different process than collaboratively codeveloping ideas, but nonetheless, shared ownership and support for ideas is an important component of collaboration, in workplace and other settings where collaboration takes place.

This idea of shared vision within a group moves away from the hierarchical idea of one person in a leadership position making decisions and everyone else being expected to fall in line. Consider that in collaborative environments, we all have unique perspectives, views, wants, and needs, and for a collaboration to work well, we need to be moving forward together in the same direction. In *Forbes* magazine, Kristi Hedges writes, "Real buy-in involves at least some element of co-creation. It invites discussion, debate, and allows everyone to feel even more vested in the outcome."[4] Everyone feeling part of a decision or a vision means this vision is more likely to be realized and is more likely to be successful. Rather than one person deciding something and everyone else implementing it, are there ways to consult and communicate with everyone who is impacted by decisions and strategies? This is important for workplace realities, but is also important in community groups, families, and friendships.

One way to refer to a group that has a very well-formed sense of shared vision is a *community of practice*. Below, the key elements of a community of practice are outlined. It's important to recognize that this kind of culture needs to be fostered with input from all members.

What Is a Community of Practice?

The concept of the **community of practice** (CoP) was developed by anthropologist Jean Lave and educational theorist Étienne Wenger in 1991 to capture the dynamics of group learning through collaboration. As a concept, CoPs have been forwarded to capture horizontal learning-by-doing in the company of other, more seasoned practitioners. While the concept was originally articulated through examples of craft-based modes of employment, including midwifery and tailoring, it has been used to map the characteristics of a wide array of groups and locales, such as virtual and online communities, second-language learners, and more formalized workplaces.[5] The earliest outline of CoPs, developed by Lave and Wenger in their book *Situated Learning*, develops the concept of "legitimate peripheral participation," which outlines how newcomers to a community become integrated and socialized within that community through observation and initially taking on simple, low-risk tasks and gradually taking on a more central role.[6] Though this model of CoPs might suggest an apprenticeship-type model of learning, the concept emphasizes informal rather than formalized routes into the community, driven by the task at hand rather than set agendas.

In his book *Communities of Practice*, Wenger gives a definition of the CoP concept in more precise terms, suggesting that CoPs are formed through mutual engagement, joint enterprise, and shared repertoire (see table 4.1).[7] As such, CoPs are united by and driven by a clear purpose or joint enterprise that is sustained over time through the relationships and norms of mutual engagement, and this produces a common set of resources, or a shared repertoire.

These elements of a community of practice all work toward developing a shared vision, so that a community of practice can successfully collaborate. A CoP offers one outline of how to foster collaboration. The important thing about the principle of shared vision is not to take it for granted that there will be a shared vision when a team gets together. Instead, a

Table 4.1 Elements of a Community of Practice

Element	*Explanation*
Mutual Engagement	Establishing norms and building collaborative relationships, creating the ties that bind social dynamics
Joint Enterprise	A sense of shared purpose and common goals/endeavors
Shared Repertoire	Communal resources and a way of working together

Adapted from *Communities of Practice: Learning, Meaning, and Identity* by Étienne Wenger.

shared vision should be discussed, if not developed collaboratively, so that each team member feels investment in collaborative undertakings.

VALUING DIFFERENCES AND DIVERSITY

Why collaborate with others instead of working alone? The common phrases "strength in numbers" or "the more the merrier" suggest that adding numbers will increase our capacity and our pleasure in our work. Yet we can also think of the common phrase "too many cooks in the kitchen," which suggests that too many people doing the same thing in the same space creates overlap, leading to conflict and resentment.

A first step toward valuing diversity in collaborative efforts is understanding the difference between **teams** and **groups**. Psychologist Daniel Levi suggests that "a group exists for a reason or purpose and has a goal shared by the group members." In contrast, teams are "structured groups of people working on defined common goals that require coordinating interactions to accomplish certain tasks."[8] Key here is that team members work together on a project for which they share accountability, which requires complementary skills, integration, and coordination. Obviously, there is overlap between these definitions of groups and teams, but team settings are where collaboration is most required for a shared outcome. Simply put, in groups all group members could be doing independent projects or working on similar tasks, but team members need each other for interdependent team work.

Sports teams provide an easy illustration of this concept. For example, a basketball team comprises a point guard, a shooting guard, a small forward, a power forward, and a center. These positions have different skill sets and strengths but are working collaboratively toward a shared objective: winning the game. Each of these different positions is needed to do different tasks in the game toward the shared goal.

In ordinary, day-to-day situations, our differences in teams might not be as clearly defined as positions in sports teams. Still, we can strive to respect differences, and even encourage them, as a source of creativity and innovation and also as source of mutual understanding and support. Stefan Klocek of Cooper Professional Education, a design thinking consultancy company, writes, "Part of the value in difference comes from the natural tensions inherent in the differing points of view. Diversity encourages questions and healthy debate."[9]

It's important to recognize that historically, in many environments, uniformity and often conformity has been more valued than difference and diversity. In the *Harvard Business Review*, Kenji Yoshino and Christie

Smith provide an overview of the sociological phenomenon called "covering," where "people downplay their differences from the mainstream." In their research, surveying three thousand employees in more than twenty large U.S. firms, they found that "although covering was more prevalent among traditionally underrepresented groups, including gays (83%), blacks (79%), women (66%), Hispanics (63%), and Asians (61%), we found a surprising incidence among straight white men, 45% of whom told us that they downplayed characteristics such as age, physical disabilities, and mental health issues."[10] The title of Yoshino and Smith's article, "Fear of Being Different Stifles Talent," is indicative of the nature of this problem of covering. A lack of valuing of difference and diversity means people will not contribute their whole selves, to the detriment of the well-being of the individual and of the collaborative project.

In his book *Bring Your Whole Self to Work*, author Mike Robbins encourages authenticity and vulnerability in workplaces to improve performance and relationships on the job. He says this mindset and the capacity for vulnerability involves courage, because being authentic is often uncomfortable, challenging, and scary work, opening ourselves up to potential judgement, pain, and disappointment.[11] We might also consider barriers to authenticity, and how team environments do or do not encourage or permit individuals to bring their whole selves and their differences to workplace and other collaborative settings. In the "Death and Rebirth Life Skills" episode of the *Culture First* podcast, discussed in the introduction, personal coach Dara Blumenthal comments that many factors influence how we are or are not able to show up to work as our "whole selves," including intersectionality and "collective trauma."[12] For these reasons, Blumenthal suggests that the concept of bringing your whole self to work is a "beautiful aspiration," but workplaces are often not equipped to deal with this complexity of individual differences. As such, we might consider how to strive toward making this "whole selves" aspiration more available and more inclusive in a variety of collaborative settings.

Leadership and diversity expert Ritu Bhasin encourages the cultivation of environments where people can be what she terms the "Authentic Self," or "who you would be if there were no negative consequences for your actions."[13] Bhasin outlines that "being authentic is a privilege," as "not everyone has the opportunity or ability to be their Authentic Self as often as they would like."[14] In particular, people from underrepresented groups often feel pressure to conform and mask aspects of their identity and behavior, including accent, dress, diction, and emotions. These pressures can result in the "Performing Self," which Bhasin defines as "who you show up as when you feel you don't have a choice but to conform or mask who you are."[15] When individuals feel they must show up as their performing selves, this means a devaluing of diversity and difference, harming both individuals and organizational cultures, given that individuals are not able to fully contribute. In contrast to these oppositions of Authentic Self and Performing Self, Bhasin also forwards the concept of the "Adaptive Self," defined as "who you are when you willingly choose to alter your behavior from how your Authentic Self would act, to meet your needs and others' needs."[16] Key in this definition of the Adaptive Self is the element of choice. There are many situations of working collaboratively where compromise is necessary, including compromising some aspects of oneself. Valuing diversity and difference means continuing to honor and encourage aspects of others' authentic selves that are different from our own ways of thinking and doing, all the while attempting to create a common framework or structure.

In order to create organizational cultures and collaborative environments where more people feel welcomed in their authentic selves, Bhasin suggests that leaders and those in positions of power and privilege can set a tone by modeling vulnerability and choosing to bring more aspects of their authentic selves with them to collaborative environments. She encourages leaders to reveal their personal sides: "If you want to foster an authentic, inclusive culture and build trust with your team members, then they must see you as more than the representative of an organizational mandate."[17] Dara Blumenthal also points to the role of leadership, suggesting that there is "lots of unskillful leadership out there," and more inclusive and collaborative cultures needs to start with leaders who can model desired behaviors. Whether or not you are in an officially designated leadership position in the workplace, you can still showcase leadership in the ways you act and conduct yourself with those around you, in whatever context. Olympic gold medalist and FIFA Women's World Cup soccer champion Abby Wambach delivered the commencement speech to the 2018 graduating class of Barnard College and named this strategy of leading from wherever you are as "leading from the bench," underscoring individuals' capacity and agency to set the tone for how they want to work with others.[18]

To set the stage for collaboration through valuing diversity, Bhasin recommends that leaders share differences, including history, background, culture, stories, experiences, and values, so that others can also feel encouraged to do the same. Authentically sharing can be contrasted with oversharing, or revealing too much personal information that could make others uncomfortable. There is no hard line between modeling vulnerability and oversharing; Bhasin recommends listening and being responsive to others as mechanisms to calibrate this boundary.

CREATING A STRUCTURE OR FRAMEWORK

In opposition to the idea that collaboration will happen organically or serendipitously, creating a structure or framework for collaboration means being intentional about how people come together to work together. Elements of a structure or framework could include policies, procedures, or agreements, and clear roles and responsibilities. Rather then constraining action or identities, structures or frameworks can create common terms of reference so that collaboration can occur more smoothly.

The research literature on collaboration emphasizes the importance of developing structures to encourage fairness and increase participation, without resorting to a one-size-fits-all model. In their book *Collaborative Creativity*, psychology professor Dorethy Miell and educational theorist Karen Littleton explain that "underpinning many researchers' interest in exploring and conceptualising the nature of creative collaboration is the need to understand how to better support such endeavours, in order to most effectively foster opportunities for creative work." The authors suggest that there is agreement in the research community about the importance of "trying to establish supportive contexts for collaboration," but "there is also a recognition that any attempts at intervention need to reflect the requirements and preferences of particular groups and communities. There is no simple agreed formula that can be applied to promote creativity."[19] Stefan Klocek of Cooper Professional Education writes about the importance of creating a foundation for collaborative efforts: "There's many different ways people could work together, but when everyone's playing the same game (and has a shared understanding of the ground rules), things flow more easily." Like shared vision, a structure or framework shouldn't be taken for granted, but neither should a common foundation feel like a severe or imposed set of rules to follow. Klocek suggests, "It's as informal as a sketch of a calendar and a quick conversation around expectations."[20]

Clarifying expectations can set the tone for successful collaboration, including around who is doing what, when, and what the mechanisms are for reporting back or for communication. For example, do team members prefer email, phone, text, or social media messaging, or in-person communication? One famous rubric of how teams operate is from psychologist and researcher Bruce Tuckman's outline of stages of team life cycles (table 4.2).

Structure or framework might be best created in the first or second stages of team development: forming or norming. Explicitly naming common terms of engagement, rather than discovering these terms through

Table 4.2 Stages of Team Development

Stage	*Explanation*
Forming	Group formation; establishing tasks and goals
Storming	Developing a working relationship, sometimes through interpersonal conflict
Norming	Developing common group norms and clear roles and responsibilities
Performing	Executing tasks to achieve goals
Adjourning	Concluding the working relationship; debrief

Adapted from Bruce Tuckman, "Developmental Sequence in Small Groups," *Psychological Bulletin* 63, no. 6 (1965): 384–99.

disagreement and conflict, can create greater ease and enjoyment in collaborative working relationships and reduce the "storming" phase, where norms get established by working through disagreements.

Creation a structure or framework can also be more formal than a quick conversation. One way to create a structure early on through developing common terms of reference is a **group agreement**. Seeds for Change, a UK-based organization focused on workshops and training for cooperation and consensus, suggests that "group agreements are a useful tool for getting your event off to the right start and keeping it on track. They help a group to come to an agreement on how it will work together respectfully and effectively. This in turn enables people to interact more co-operatively and maintain respect for each other."[21] Creating group agreements means setting time aside to discuss how a group or team wants to work together. There could be many ways to facilitate a group agreement. Activity 4.1 provides one strategy that can be customized for different contexts or purposes.

Activity 4.1: Developing a Group Agreement

Suggested time allotment: thirty minutes.

Useful materials:

- Sticky notes
- Large sheets of paper or a white board
- Alternatively, participants can work digitally through a shared Google Document, Jamboard, or other digital collaborative means

1. Opening Prompts: A leader or facilitator asks team members to suggest important concepts for how they want to work together. Seeds for Change offers these examples of questions as opening prompts:[22]

   - What things would make this group/workshop work well for you?
   - What makes this a safe and respectful place for us to work in?
   - What would make this group a good space for learning?

   Questions for opening prompts need to be tailored to the type of team and type of task being tackled. For example, a group agreement for a postsecondary classroom may (or may not) look different than a group agreement for an industry work team or a community group. Prompts should be decided in advance by the leader or facilitator, and should be tailored to the purpose or goal of the group that will produce the group agreement.

   After asking the opening prompt, the leader or facilitator listens and organizes responses into broad key words. For example, participants might give examples of respect, communication, timeliness, fun, inclusion, and so on. The facilitator identifies and writes these key words on the material that is being used: spread out on the white board, one word per large sheet of paper, or one word on each page of a digital document.

   Depending on the size and dynamics of the team developing a group agreement, this initial stage might be done verbally, collectively, or individually, through individual written answers that are then shared with the larger group. The leader or facilitator should be mindful of team dynamics and try to create mechanisms where the greatest number of team members feel comfortable and ready to participate.
2. Concrete Examples: After a broad set of terms are established about how to work together (respect, communication, etc.), smaller subgroups can be assigned one of these terms. For example, in a team of six people, subgroups of two people can each be assigned one term. If large sheets of paper are being used, one piece of paper with one term written on it can be given to each subgroup. In this next phase of a group agreement, these subgroups are asked to develop concrete examples of what the broad term they have been assigned looks like in practice. A concrete example of respect might be "listening without interrupting." Concrete examples of communication protocols might be establishing what medium is going to be used for communication

(e.g., email, text, phone, etc.) and the expected norms for response time (four hours, two days, etc.). Assign a time limit to this phase (e.g., ten minutes), and encourage groups to develop as many concrete examples of their assigned term as possible during that time frame. Groups can be given sticky notes and be instructed to write each example on a separate sticky note. They can either add these sticky notes to their large piece of paper or to the white board.

3. Sharing and Consensus: In the final phase of a group agreement, each subgroup will share their concrete examples with the larger group. After each subgroup shares their examples, the larger group is invited to critique or add to the examples. New sticky notes can be used to add to the list that each subgroup has created. If one example is deemed not relevant by the larger group, this sticky note can be removed from the list.

At the conclusion of the group agreement, all group members agree to strive to work together within the norms established in the group agreement. If possible, it's useful for the group agreement to remain in the space where the group activity will occur as a visual reminder of the terms that have been agreed to. If large pieces of paper have been used with sticky notes added to them, these pieces of paper might be hung on a wall in the space. If a white board has been used, a photo of the terms added to the board could be shared, or a digital version of the white board could be typed up and shared.

A more formal means of developing a structure or framework for collaboration is a **team charter**. Though similar to a group agreement, the end product of a team charter more closely resembles a written contract that all team members are invited to sign. Here it is useful to recall the differences between groups and teams. While a group is a collection of people with shared interests, a team is a group of people working interdependently on a shared goal with some element of accountability. Due to this interdependence and accountability, more formalized terms of engagement can be helpful for collaborative teamwork.

Team charters can begin with team discussions about predetermined prompts, but can produce more specific outcomes than a group agreement. For example, team charter discussions might tackle team objectives, communication, team member conduct (attendance, lateness, desired behavior), roles and responsibilities, and conflict resolution strategies.

For example, a team charter discussion might begin with these prompts:

- What are the main objectives that we wish to accomplish?
- How will we make decisions?
- How will roles be divided in the team?

After the team decides its terms of engagement for its activities, a team charter is written listing the desired policies and behaviors among team members. Each of the discussed terms (objectives, communication, team member conduct) can be a header in this written document, with desired policies and behaviors listed under these headers. Each team member signs this document and receives a copy, or has access to a shared digital copy. Rather than being seen as a punitive or restrictive measure, a team charter can be viewed as a tool to clarify norms and expectations early on, to enable ease and efficiency in the collaborative working process.

Facilitation

One way to consider how best to convene people for working collaboratively together is through facilitation. A facilitator can either be an internal team member or an external, third-party consultant who is hired to facilitate visioning or decision making. Organizational policy researcher Sandor Schuman suggests that **facilitation** is a technique that emphasizes the process of collaborative work, rather than the outcome of this work. As such, "a facilitator helps a group to work collaboratively by focusing on the process of how the participants work together."[23] Key here in this definition is the emphasis on help. Working collaboratively, and creating a culture where diverse individuals feel comfortable and encouraged to contribute to generating ideas and decision making, is hard. A facilitator might bring some ease. Ease is also emphasized by adrienne maree brown in her definition of facilitation in her book *Emergent Strategy*: "At its most fundamental, facilitation is the art of making things easier for humans to work together and get things done."[24] A focus on process, or how groups or teams work together, is no easy task. Shuman recommends dividing "process" into three types, social, cognitive, and political, to conceptualize different areas that facilitation can target in groups and teams (table 4.3).

Considering these three types of process highlights the complexity of collaboration. In collaborative settings, individuals are cognitively trying to think and develop ideas together. Social dynamics will influence who is more or less comfortable participating, or whose opinion

Table 4.3 Types of Collaborative Processes That a Facilitator Can Target

Type of Process	*Explanation*
Cognitive Process	Developing ideas, thinking, analyzing
Social Process	Group dynamics, interpersonal behavior
Political Process	Equal participation, power, influence

Adapted from Schuman, "Role of Facilitation in Collaborative Groups."

and ideas take up the most space and carry the most weight. Political questions of power and privilege influence these social dynamics, including the structural factors of race, gender, social class, age, sexuality, disability, and so on.

At its best, facilitation will attempt to create a more equal forum for participation and collaboration. Schuman writes that a facilitator will allow "all perspectives to be taken into account, striving to gain the best contributions from each member." Using a facilitator to help this process of gathering perspectives and contributions can be one element of creating a structure or framework for collaboration. For groups or teams to best work together, all members need to be able to give input, and clear knowledge about what the group is trying to accomplish through collaboration can help increase participation.

Creative Problem Solving

In addition to using concrete tools such as agendas or templates as guiding structures, groups or teams might use creative methods or approaches to tackle collaboration. For example, the Creative Education Foundation (CEF) produced the *Creative Problem Solving Resource Guide* to help guide collaboration and group decision making. The Creative Education Foundation was founded by Alex Osborn in 1954 as he launched the Creative Problem Solving Institute. The creativity and idea generation technique called brainstorming, from Alex Osborn's book *How to Think Up*, is probably the best-known element of **creative problem solving** (CPS) as a method. However, this method has a broader approach with more components than only just brainstorming. The *Creative Problem Solving Resource Guide* suggests that CPS is a method "for approaching a problem or a challenge in an imaginative and innovative way. It helps people re-define the problems and opportunities they face, come up with new, innovative responses and solutions, and then take action. The tools and techniques used make the process fun, engaging, and collaborative."[25]

The CPS method is made up of four stages:

1. Clarify: This phase involves identifying, researching, and clarifying the challenge. Clarifying questions can include the following: What is the challenge that the group wants to tackle? What is the nature of this challenge?
2. Ideate: This phase involves generating many possible ideas or strategies to tackle the challenge. Ideating techniques can include brainstorming, imagining others' perspectives, or recombining existing ideas.
3. Develop: This phase involves strengthening generated ideas and formulating solutions. What is the best solution or fit among all the generated ideas?
4. Implement: This phase involves moving toward implementation through identifying resources and actions. What are the next steps? Who will do what next after the group session is finished? Who will check that this work is done? What is the timeline for next steps?

Each of these four stages of the CPS method is made up of divergent and convergent thinking. The Creative Education Foundation defines **divergent thinking** as "generating lots of ideas and options" and **convergent thinking** as "evaluating ideas and options, and making decisions."[26] Key in the CPS method is to separate and balance divergent and convergent thinking. Before jumping to decision-making or evaluating if ideas are good or not, there needs to be a free and open space for generating ideas, good or bad. As such, a key approach to the divergent thinking stage of the CPS methods is quantity over quality. For further information about particular activities for groups to participate in divergent and convergent thinking exercises, consult the *Creative Problem Solving Resource Guide*.

Design Thinking

Another term for collaborative group problem solving that is similar to the CPS method is design thinking. **Design thinking** was first coined as a concept and methodology in the second half of the twentieth century by Stanford University mechanical engineering and business administration professor John E. Arnold, particularly in his book *Creative Engineering* (1959). Though mechanical engineering might bring to mind machinery, design thinking is a process related to innovation across fields, based in rapid iteration and prototyping. This is not to say that creative thinking and design originated with Arnold in this book, as these principles have been used by people worldwide since time immemorial. Stanford University continues to emphasize design thinking methodology, and the university's d. school is known as an institute for design and "radical collaboration." The d. school defines design thinking as made up of five stages:

1. Empathize: Identifying a problem; learning more about what the problem is and how it affects the users who experience it
2. Define: Clarifying and reframing the problem by synthesizing key components of the experience of the problem
3. Ideate: Generating many possible solutions to address the problem
4. Prototype: Building simple models to see how these potential solutions do or do not work in reality
5. Test: Testing how these prototypes work by inviting user groups to interact with them[27]

As you can see, there is overlap between the CPS method and design thinking as an approach. Core tenets to retain from both of these approaches is to develop ideas quickly and collectively, in relation to a clearly identified and researched challenge. With both CPS and design thinking, it can be beneficial to have a facilitator, an external person who helps guide the idea generation and development process.

Improvisation

Creating a structure or framework should ideally not feel like imposing rules or merely re-creating an existing status quo: this will result in stifling rather than stimulating group creativity and engagement. Instead, creating a structure can enable collaborative group creativity by creating common terms for improvisation. In his TED Talk "Your Brain on Improv," brain surgeon and creativity researcher Charles Limb gives an overview of his research on the neuroscience of creativity. One of his research projects tackled the question, "What happens in the brain during something that is spontaneously generated, or improvised?" In order to investigate this research question, Limb and his team had jazz musicians improvise while playing music on a keyboard in an MRI scanner. Important to note here is that these jazz musicians already knew how to play music quite well. As such, having a set structure can act like a foundation for improvised creativity. Through MRI brain scans during this improvised music making, the research project found that parts of the brain in the frontal lobe responsible for self-monitoring shut off, resulting in people feeling "not inhibited" and "willing to make mistakes."[28] This state, of not self-monitoring, associated with improvising, results in higher levels of creativity.

When we work together, how can we foster creative cultures where people are willing to make mistakes? This is challenging in the professional and academic worlds, where our job performance and the quality of our work is evaluated. It's also challenging in our personal lives, where we sometimes don't want to risk looking foolish in front of others, or even in front of ourselves. Increasingly, workplaces recognize the importance of fostering organizational cultures where people can take risks. David Kelley, the founder of design company IDEO and creator of the Stanford d. school, and his brother and IDEO partner Tom Kelley tackle this question in their book *Creative Confidence*. They suggest that successful team environments will build what they call "karaoke confidence." What happens when someone gets up to perform karaoke in front of a crowd, even if they are not a technically gifted singer? This bravery might come from confidence, but also can come from a supportive audience that encourages the singer, even if the performance is not technically flawless. The Kelley brothers' identified elements of karaoke confidence include keeping your sense of humor, building on the energy of others, minimizing hierarchy, valuing team camaraderie and trust, and deferring judgment—at least temporarily.[29] These elements suggest that collaboration is best fostered through mutual respect, rather than top-down decision making or authority.

Further inspiration for how to maximize creativity when working with others can come from the world of improv. The Second City is a well-known professional improvisational comedy or improv company that was founded and based in Chicago. This improv company has incubated many celebrated comedians and comedy writers, including Mike Myers, Tina Fey, Jordan Peele, Dan Ackroyd, and John Candy, among many others. Two of The Second City's executives, Kelly Leonard and Tom Yorton, compiled best practices in developing this improvisational spirit in their book *Yes, And: How Improvisation Reverses "No, But" Thinking and Improves Creativity and Collaboration—Lessons from The Second City*. The premise of this book is that it is not only comedians and live performers who can benefit from improv skills. Improv can improve creativity, collaboration, and teamwork in a variety of settings. Leonard and Yorton outline seven key elements of improv in their book; these elements "set the stage" and are components of structure or framework: a foundation so that a group can collaborate (table 4.4).

Let's pause to consider the first basic rule of improv comedy, and the title of the book: "yes, and," sometimes also called the rule of agreement. When a performer starts creating a scene, others join them. For example,

Table 4.4 Elements of Improvisation

Element	*Explanation*
Yes, and	Agree with others' suggestions and building on them rather than negating them
Ensemble	Focus on the collective instead of on individual stars
Cocreation	Cede control and take risks to create new ideas together
Authenticity	Trust, support, and open communication are a basis for innovation
Failure	Accept failure as part of the creative process, using failure as an opportunity for learning
Follow the follower	Be responsive and fluid in responding, stepping up and stepping back when needed
Listening	Develop the skill of listening to understand others' intentions

Adapted from Kelly Leonard and Tom Yorton, *Yes, And: How Improvisation Reverses "No, But" Thinking and Improves Creativity and Collaboration—Lessons from The Second City* (New York: Harper, 2015).

if one performer starts miming driving a car, then the next performer can perform sitting in the passenger seat and put on their seat belt. In improv comedy, this second performer should not just decide to start another scene, for example, cooking a meal or lifting weights. This wouldn't make sense. If one person starts creating a world, others inhabit it. Outside of the space of improv comedy, this means suspending critical thought, objections, and disbelief in the early stages of collaborative work. Rather than suggesting "no" or "but" to someone else's ideas, improv suggests we answer "yes, and," which enables us to build on and extend someone else's idea rather than challenging or dismissing it from the outset.

In her memoir *Bossypants*, actress and comedian Tina Fey reflects on her experience doing improv with The Second City, and how this experience has carried over into the rest of her life. She writes,

> Now, obviously in real life you're not always going to agree with everything everyone says. But the Rule of Agreement reminds you to "respect what your partner has created" and to at least start from an open-minded place. Start with a YES and see where that takes you. As an improviser, I always find it jarring when I meet someone in real life whose first answer is no. "No we can't do that." "No, that's not in the budget." . . . What kind of way is that to live?[30]

Here Fey suggests that always agreeing with everything is not practical or even beneficial in many contexts. Nonetheless, we can retain a spirit of open-mindedness and mutual support. Daena Giardella, a senior lecturer at MIT's Leadership Center, teaches improvisational leadership and comments, "Innovation thrives in an atmosphere of safety and non-criticism. . . . Improvisation builds a muscle for trusting our own impulses and ideas, before we have to analyze how good they are, as well as helping develop an open-mindedness toward other people's ideas."[31] Key here is also the idea that improvisation is a skill to be learned or muscle to be built. Our broader culture is often competitive and judgmental, and improv asks us to pause these impulses.

Psychologist Keith Sawyer draws attention to the important role of improvisation in his research on creativity, collaboration, and learning. He suggests that improvisation happens within a structure or framework, and participants draw on "ready-mades," short motifs or clichés.[32] Using known structures might differ from common definitions of creativity, which still often rely on the idea that individual geniuses generate innovate ideas from scratch. In his book *The Myths of Creativity*, David Burkus calls this "The Eureka Myth," or the notion that creativity happens to a person and comes suddenly in a flash of insight. To counter this common myth, Burkus suggests we need to consider the work, preparation, and training that happens prior to this moment of flash or insight. For Sawyer, a definition of creativity relies on improvising on top of shared cultural knowledge. In improv comedy, these are verbal and visual cues that allow the participants to build on each other's work. For example, in the driving skit example, sitting down with hands at 10:00 and 2:00 and saying, "Buckle up," are verbal and visual cues that "driving" is happening. These "ready-mades" are shared conventions, used by performing artists to communicate with each other and their audience. As discussed above, creating shared structures, like agendas, policies, and other guidelines, enables a common frame of reference. This also means moving from an individual-driven idea of creativity toward something more collaborative. In his book, Burkus also gives an overview of what he terms "The Lone Creator Myth" about creativity, or "the belief that creativity is a solo performance and that the story of innovations can be told as the story of a single person working fervently on a new idea."[33] Instead, creativity can be recast as the improvisation teams are doing together based on common and shared tools.

Be aware that mobilizing shared conventions and known structures to cocreate is different than cultural misappropriation. As defined in chapter 3, cultural misappropriation involves a lack of consent and mobilizes the culture of marginalized and historically underrepresented communities without their involvement. To differentiate between shared conventions and cultural misappropriation, we need to consider power, access, and consent and ensure that we are not perpetuating harm and marginalization.

CREATING A SUPPORTIVE ENVIRONMENT FOR THE WHOLE SELF

In many contexts, collaboration involves a lot of thinking and developing ideas with others. Our cognitive selves—the parts of us that think and make decisions—are often most valued in our workplace and project-based environments. As discussed in chapter 1, this cognitive, thinking self has been most valued and centered in much of the history of Western culture.

But individuals are more than just thinking selves: people also have physical, emotional, spiritual, aesthetic, and other needs. For example, Indigenous worldviews have emphasized interconnectivity and connection with the natural world. One way that many Indigenous cultures depict this is through medicine wheels, which often represent Four Directions, which can include stages of life, seasons of the year, elements of nature, animals, ceremonial plants, and aspects of life. These aspects of life include the intellectual realm (the realm of the mind), the emotional realm (the realm of the heart), the physical realm (the realm of the body), and the spiritual realm (the realm of the soul).[34] In Ancient Chinese philosophy, the concept of yin and yang encapsulates the interconnectedness of dualist entities. Many traditional cultures have theories of interconnection and of the mind in relation to other elements. Recall also the concept of intersectionality, introduced in chapter 1. People have multifaceted, intersectional selves, and these complex identities and needs influence the context of how we arrive to collaborate with one another. In table 4.5, six elements of the self are identified. Are there further elements of a self that you can add to this list?

The elements of a whole self are broad and vast, and the allotted time and context of collaborative work may not allow for all aspects of a whole self to fully show up. For example, in most educational institutions, students are often expected to sit and listen to learn, which mostly engages a cognitive self. In workplace environments, cognitive selves (e.g., thinking and decision making) are also required to complete tasks in a timely fashion. However, making space for other modes of being can enable collaboration. For example, team meetings can start with a five-minute check-in, where each team member is invited to report on how their day or week is going, or how they are feeling generally. In collaborative work environments, individual team members might be invited to customize or decorate their work stations according to their own style or aesthetics.

Table 4.5 Elements of the Whole Self That Influence Collaboration

Element	*Explanation*
Cognitive Self	Thinking, decision making, problem solving
Physical Self	Embodiment, comfort, physical needs, accessibility
Emotional Self	Feelings and responses
Aesthetic Self	Appearances, pleasure, beauty
Spiritual Self	Connection, meaning, larger purpose
Social Self	Interactions, relationship building, belonging

In longer meetings, recognizing that people have physical needs to eat, stretch their legs, and go to the washroom can help everyone feel energized and ready to work together. One famous example of recognizing physical needs comes from Google corporate policy, which outlines that food must be available within 150 feet of employees at all times, so that everyone is satiated and energized.[35] Of course, small perks, like free food or beverages on site, can sometimes be an exploitative tactic to encourage employees to stay for longer hours and (unpaid) overtime. At the same time, reflecting on diverse physical and bodily needs, including dietary restrictions and access needs, can set the stage for collaboration.

Making space for the whole self in our collaborative teamwork needs to be balanced with structures of accountability, such as deadlines and set outputs or goals, so that collaboration can still be focused and effective. But making space for the whole self can help with accountability, and getting collaborators to move forward in the same direction, while allowing for individual differences and needs. Something as simple as a five-minute check-in at the beginning of a meeting can help people feel seen and heard, so that they can focus on the collaborative task at hand. It's better to acknowledge the challenges we face in our daily lives, and discuss how we can still be accountable and meet our goals, rather than pretending these challenges don't exist, should only be dealt with individually, or will not impact collaborative efforts.

COMMITTING TO BEHIND-THE-SCENES LOGISTICAL WORK

This chapter opened by questioning the outward glamor of collaboration, and in this final section we close by examining the vital component of logistics, which can make or break a collaborative effort. In her book

Creative Collaboration, Vera John-Steiner foregrounds the idea that creativity is an inherently collaborative process and identifies patterns of collaboration among artists and scientists. Discussing the concept of communities of practice, John-Steiner comments that "studies of 'communities of practice' frequently refer to the front and the backstage of situated activities. The front is visible to the outsider. It constitutes an orderly and rational sequence visible to an audience. It is in the busy backstage that the real operations, which are frequently messy or redundant, take place."[36]

Successful collaboration requires a commitment to this "busy backstage," the behind-the-scenes logistical work, which is a less glamorous process than the visible output or outcome of the collaboration. The metaphor of "front" and "backstage" suggests theater or performance, but this behind-the-scenes work is necessary for all kinds of collaboration, whether or not they have a performance element. John-Steiner describes this logistical work as "messy or redundant," highlighting that this work can often be difficult and repetitive. However, this type of logistical work is also vital for successful collaboration. Behind-the-scenes logistical work means developing clear roles and responsibilities, and ensuring that clear and effective channels of communication are in place. This final element of successful collaboration, committing to behind-the-scenes logistical work, leverages all of the previous elements of collaboration in this chapter: fostering a shared vision, valuing diversity and difference, creating a structure or framework, and supporting the whole self. This also means addressing structures of accountability. Who is doing what, on what timelines, and what are the mechanisms to check that this work has been done?

Various technologies can facilitate clarity and accountability in team logistics. These technologies could include shared calendars or shared digital workspace or messaging centers, such as Slack, GitHub, or Trello. These technologies can change over time, but it's worth spending time up front figuring out what system works best for any particular team, and ensuring the all team members have access and ease with the chosen tool or platform. These technologies are tools that can help facilitate a workflow, or, returning to the definition of a community of practice, they can be a way of developing a shared repertoire of common resources. But these technologies are not substitutes for actually executing whatever work needs to be done or communicating openly and clearly with others!

Open and clear communication, good logistics, and systems of accountability can be taken for granted as obvious elements of collaboration, but they are often the most difficult things to develop, and there are many infamous examples of these components of collaboration not being well executed, with disastrous results. For example, the Fyre Festival is a story of fraud and a music festival that never took place. The title of a 2018 Netflix documentary about this scandal, *Fyre: The Greatest Party That Never Happened*, sums it up well. Founded by entrepreneur Bill McFarland in collaboration with rapper Ja Rule, the Fyre Festival was scheduled to take place in spring 2017 on the island of Great Exuma in the Bahamas. The festival was intended to be a luxury experience, including private villas and celebrity chefs, and tickets to the festival sold for twelve thousand dollars each. This festival was well promoted and attracted a lot of investment. A successful Instagram campaign was launched, with influencers, including Kylie Jenner, promoting the supposedly forthcoming event. However, McFarland lacked skills and experience in planning and executing large-scale entertainment events. The event was underplanned, but not canceled. Festivalgoers arrived to find a hastily assembled stage and makeshift tents instead of luxury villas, and nothing being provided that they had paid for. In 2018, Bill McFarland was sentenced to six years in prison for defrauding investors and would-be concertgoers of nearly twenty-six million dollars.[37]

The Fyre Festival scandal could be read as a simple case of a fraudulent individual behaving badly, to the point of criminal negligence and fraud. Beyond fraud, the Fyre Festival is also a failure of collaboration, and a failure of various individuals working together toward a shared vision. With a planned music festival that sold tickets but did not deliver the promised event, we can see a major failure of logistical work, and of different teams being able to execute required tasks on a realistic timeline working toward a final deadline. A lack of accountability meant that the Fyre Festival went on, with nothing to show. Logistics and accountability can also mean frank discussions about when to stop, quit, apologize, or otherwise cease the collaborative effort. Though working collaboratively might be both a desired and required element of contemporary life, it's also important to realize that not every collaboration will be successful, or produce the intended outcome. Nonetheless, these challenging or failed collaborative experiences can also be learning opportunities.

MA MBA WITH GENDAI

In the profile below, we see an example of an organization, Gendai, that works to develop collaboration with an eye to fostering diversity, equity, and inclusion. While reading the profile, review what elements of successful collaboration identified in this chapter are present in Gendai's operations.

Curator Marsya Maharani and artist Petrina Ng say the seeds of their friendship and future collaborations got started just by talking, and then talking some more. As often the only person of color working at arts institutions in similar areas in Toronto, Canada, they started exchanging information about trying to navigate "very white institutions." They both found themselves feeling "very isolated and lonely."[38] These experiences, borne of the realities of systemic racism, white supremacy, precarity, and toxic workplace conditions in the arts, have long been experienced and addressed by generations of other racialized artists and cultural workers. Petrina and Marsya started ruminating about how to build on and sustain past efforts by collaborating to change this culture through connecting, listening to one another, and developing collective responses.

With Gendai collective, Marsya and Petrina's work continues and expands some of their previous projects and research, which extend past legacies of collective work that have challenged individual-centric and toxic competitive working practices. In 2020, Petrina undertook an artist residency at the Textile Museum of Canada, researching institutional colonial legacies. She extended an invitation to Souped Up (an ongoing dinner series organized by Marsya and another curator, Geneviève Wallen, for curators and cultural workers of color to share food and community) to bring together local arts collectives to discuss shared challenges and goals, while collaboratively developing curriculum to learn and discuss different working practices. Similarly, Marsya's path of learning and research developed through travel in East and Southeast Asia, motivated by a dissatisfaction with the competitive framework that characterized her education and professional training. She found inspiration for Gendai in the work and alternative pedagogies of collectives she met, including Gudskul Ecosystem, Bakudapan Food Study Group, and Dinghaiqiao Mutual Aid Society. Learning from these collectives, Marsya discovered the fun and joy of working with peers to raise one another up, rather than trying to set oneself apart and stand out.

Marsya remembers being in Shanghai when she received a text from Petrina, saying that Gendai Gallery, a Toronto-based contemporary arts organization that had supported Japanese diasporic and East Asian artists since 2000, had put out a call for new leadership, as an experiment in organizational succession planning, rather than simply retiring. Marsya and Petrina started discussing ways of working that supported a vision of cultural workers having the time and space to listen and learn from one another, "imagining what a collective future in arts work can look like, with the support and help of each other," while investing in "racialized arts practitioners as the next generation of cultural leaders, radical thinkers, and visionaries who embody new pathways towards more equitable futures."[39]

This desire to work collectively permeates the proposal that Petrina and Marsya wrote to apply to take over Gendai, which stated, "We propose to build on Gendai's history to form an intergenerational ecosystem that fosters inter-collective resource-sharing and a collaborative approach to knowledge-production."[40] In discussions with previous Gendai members and working with Gendai's existing experimental, nonhierarchical organizational structure, Marsya and Petrina proposed a stewardship, not a leadership model, working alongside and collectively with the artists that Gendai supports. Petrina says, "We don't actually have any desire to be alone at the top with lots of power, making all the decisions alone, unilaterally." Instead, what Gendai terms radical allyship involves "a way of working responsively, sustainably, and accountably" alongside peers and other BIPOC folks, as an alternative to institutional hierarchies.

For Marsya, one idea that grounds this vision of a more caring and collaborative future is found in "radical friendship." Friendship can be radical when the broader culture often pits individuals against each other. Marsya explains that radical friendship means seeing collaborators as friends, offering emotional investment and reciprocity to see friends thrive. One way that she puts this value into practice is through exclusively working in collaboration, which is unusual for curators, who still are often steeped in ideas of individual artistic vision. Her personal website invites readers into this collective mode of fun and listening to one another, asking, "Do you want to think out loud over (virtual) dinners, reading groups, co-working days, studio visits, walks, hang outs . . . ?"[41]

With Gendai, Marsya and Petrina started planning new programs to create environments to build trust and collaboration. With Gendai's "MA MBA" program, Petrina says they seek to target "professionalizing without institutionalizing," and that "professionalism" can sometimes be a code word for conformity and upholding an unequal status quo. Ideas like looking or speaking "professionally" and workplace "fit" can be used in company hiring strategies, for example, to weed out race, class, or gender difference, says Petrina. Instead, Petrina forwards a definition of professionalism that "can mean not replicating harm, a focus on relationships and your conduct with other people, not causing harm to yourself, your community, to others around you. Gendai is striving to be professional in this way, to undo harm, working in a way that's responsible and accountable to ourselves and our peers." MAs and MBAs are professionalizing graduate degrees, accredited by postsecondary institutions. Gendai's MA MBA program riffs on the title of these graduate degrees, but their version of these acronyms stands for "Mastering the

Art of Misguided Business Administration." This program is described as a "year-long think tank and workshop series for art collectives to improve capacity-building skills in a co-learning environment. Addressing sector-wide challenges of precarity and isolation, this project creates a network for collectives to resource-share, co-learn, collaborate, and improve workplace sustainability."[42] In its inaugural year in 2020, eight Toronto-based, BIPOC-led art collectives signed up for this program, to do this work alongside Gendai as a coparticipant:

- BAM—Books, Art, Music Collective: a youth- and newcomer-led collective that empowers equity-seeking young people to get involved in civics and community through art.
- BUMP TV: a 24/7 public access internet television station, supporting and commissioning artists who work in experimental and noncommercial digital and time-based mediums.
- Durable Good: a publishing studio that creates books about art, collaborating with artists, writers, and thinkers who work within feminist, equitable, and engaged frameworks.
- Glory Hole Gallery: a miniature gallery space dedicated to 2SLGBTQ+ artists.
- *MICE Magazine*: an online periodical devoted to critical writing and artist projects about and within moving image culture.
- Tea Base: a community arts space located in Toronto's Chinatown, with a focus on intergenerational programming mainly serving the GTA Asian diaspora.
- Whippersnapper Gallery: an artist-run center committed to cultivation of inclusive spaces for emerging visual and media arts, providing a flexible platform to expand parameters for professional practices.
- Younger Than Beyoncé: an arts collective for the career development of artists and cultural workers born after 1981 or who are otherwise emerging.

Gendai received funding to begin their MA MBA programming in March 2020, and because of the lockdowns of COVID-19, collaboration had to look like something different than what Marsya and Petrina had planned, which was to visit each collective's physical space and to take turns hosting one another. Instead, MA MBA began by hosting a physically distanced gathering on Marsya's porch and listening to what participants wanted, asking them, "Do you still want to do this, or do you want to postpone?" MA MBA members decided this was a good time to move forward: with many if not all arts activities postponed or canceled due to COVID-19, people had time and wanted something to work on. MA MBA is a paid program where participants are compensated for their work; Petrina says that workers in institutional contexts get paid to do professional development, and this should also be true for DIY collectives who are devoting time to collectively professionalize and build collaborative knowledge, especially in the context of the common experience of burnout due to toxic and racist work cultures and the labor of going against the grain to create change in these environments.

The inaugural MA MBA cohort began by collaboratively designing a curriculum to tackle monthly, over a ten-month period. Topics ranged from financial literacy to bylaws and governance structure for arts institutions to accessibility training. Marsya and Petrina sought out facilitators for each monthly session, inviting colleagues who have lived experience connected to the topic and who also "have desire to reimagine institutional norms to be more equitable." The monthly MA MBA sessions were held on Zoom through COVID-19, but MA MBA avoids the feeling and structure of a three-hour class or workshop, gathering to listen to an expert and ask questions. Instead, Petrina says these sessions feel like long-term relationship building, "getting to know the facilitator and getting to know each other, starting a relationship." This relationship building enables a space for racialized practitioners to rethink existing institutional practices from their perspectives, centering care rather than competition, contributing to the shift in sector values.

Marsya says there is lots to be gained from listening and learning from one another: "We're talking to people, we're hearing people's experiences. The connections made through these kinds of gatherings have been really valuable; I learn about the people I should never work with, because they have a history of taking credit for work by BIPOC women."[43] Collaborative knowledge development, bolstered by sharing and transparency, is at the heart of what Petrina and Marsya hope to do with Gendai. To counter the secrecy that can sometimes exist even between different levels of staff within an organization or institution, Marsya and Petrina make their funding applications available to the participants in their MA MBA cohort, showing their "process work" and making sure everyone is in the loop about what grants were obtained, with how much funding. Marsya jokes about a reality-TV themed meme that she's seen circulating that says, "I'm not here to make friends, I'm here to win." She wonders, though, "What if I'm here to make friends, and that is the way?" Following the wrap of the first MA MBA cohort, Marsya and Petrina put out a call to pass along MA MBA to a new collective to facilitate a second cohort, with Gendai offering mentorship and support throughout. As an effort toward making all Gendai projects open source, the inaugural cohort will collaborate on a "how-to" publication for future cohorts to learn from and build on.

For more information about Gendai, visit https://www.gendai.club/.

QUESTIONS FOR LEARNING AND REFLECTION

1. Team versus Group: Think back on past experiences working with others. According to the definition provided in this chapter, were you working in a group or in a team? Was your work with others collaborative or isolated?
2. Authentic Self Inventory: Return to Ritu Bhasin's definition of an Authentic Self that is provided in this chapter. What aspects of your Authentic Self do you habitually bring to collaborative work? Are there aspects of your Authentic Self that you feel internal or external pressure to mask or hide? Can you imagine bringing more aspects of your Authentic Self to collaborative work? How might you make more room or establish the conditions for others to bring more aspects or their Authentic Selves to collaborative work?
3. Whole Self Inventory: Take a moment to decide on your most favorite and your least favorite experience of collaborating with others. These could be experiences from your schooling, community groups, or working life. In these favorite/least favorite collaborative experiences, was there more or less space for a whole-self framework? In other words, did the recognition or lack of recognition of the self as a whole self impact your positive or negative experience of collaboration? Consider if elements of the social, physical, aesthetic, or spiritual self were encouraged in these collaborative experiences.
4. Setting the Stage for Team Success: Think back to a team experience you've had that has gone really poorly. This could be at home, at work, at school, or with friends or family. Are there elements of structure or framework that would have helped this team experience go more smoothly or be more productive? Review the building blocks of successful collaboration identified in this chapter to identify what was missing or what could have been improved.

NOTES

1. Alessandro Gandini and James Graham, "Introduction," in *Collaborative Production in the Creative Industries* (London: University of Westminster Press, 2017), 1.

2. Arianna Rebolini, "10 Habits of Highly Creative People," *Buzzfeed*, April 11, 2014, accessed May 18, 2021, https://www.buzzfeed.com/ariannarebolini/habits-of-highly-creative-people.

3. Kristi Hedges, "How to Get Real Buy-In for Your Idea," *Forbes*, March 16, 2015, accessed May 18, 2021, https://www.forbes.com/sites/work-in-progress/2015/03/16/how-to-get-real-buy-in-for-your-idea/#4ba4b75c4044.

4. Hedges, "How to Get Real Buy-In."

5. Andrew Cox, "What Are Communities of Practice? A Comparative Review of Four Seminal Works," *Journal of Information Science* 31, no. 6 (2005): 527–40; Alessia Contu, "On Boundaries and Difference: Communities of Practice and Power Relations in Creative Work," *Management Learning* 45, no. 3 (2013): 289–316.

6. Jean Lave and Étienne Wenger, *Situated Learning: Legitimate Peripheral Participation* (Cambridge: Cambridge University Press, 1991).

7. Étienne Wenger, *Communities of Practice: Learning, Meaning and Identity* (Cambridge: Cambridge University Press, 1998), 72–73.

8. Daniel Levi, "Understanding Teams," in *Group Dynamics for Teams*, 5th ed. (Los Angeles: Sage, 2017), 4, 5.

9. Stefan Klocek, "Better Together: The Practice of Successful Creative Collaboration," September 12, 2011, accessed May 25, 2021, http://www.stefanklocek.com/better-together-the-practice-of-successful-creative-collaboration/.

10. Kenji Yoshino and Christie Smith, "Fear of Being Different Stifles Talent," *Harvard Business Review*, March 14, 2014, accessed May 25, 2021, https://hbr.org/2014/03/fear-of-being-different-stifles-talent.

11. Mike Robbins, *Bring Your Whole Self to Work: How Vulnerability Unlocks Creativity, Connection, and Performance* (Carlsbad, CA: Hay House, 2018).

12. Culture Amp, "Death and Rebirth Life Skills."

13. Ritu Bhasin, *The Authenticity Principle: Resist Conformity, Embrace Differences, and Transform How You Live, Work, and Lead* (Toronto: Melanin Made Press, 2017), 30.

14. Bhasin, *Authenticity Principle*, 35.

15. Bhasin, *Authenticity Principle*, 59.

16. Bhasin, *Authenticity Principle*, 125.

17. Bhasin, *Authenticity Principle*, 163–64.

18. Wambach, "Remarks as Delivered."

19. Dorothy Miell and Karen Littleton, eds., *Collaborative Creativity: Contemporary Perspectives* (London: Free Association Books, 2004), 1–2.

20. Klocek, "Better Together."

21. Seeds for Change, "Group Agreements for Workshops and Meetings," accessed May 25, 2021, https://www.seedsforchange.org.uk/groupagree.pdf.

22. Seeds for Change, "Group Agreements."

23. Sandor P. Schuman, "The Role of Facilitation in Collaborative Groups," Executive Decision Services, 1996, accessed May 25, 2021, http://www.exedes.com/articles/Role-of-Facilitation-in-Collaboration.pdf.

24. adrienne maree brown, *Emergent Strategy: Shaping Change, Changing Worlds* (Chico, CA: AK Press, 2017), 30.

25. Creative Education Foundation, *Creative Problem Solving Resource Guide* (Scituate, MA: Creative Education Foundation, 2014), 8.

26. Creative Education Foundation, *Creative Problem Solving*, 11.

27. d. school, "Design Thinking Bootleg," Institute of Design, Stanford University, accessed May 25, 2021, https://static1.squarespace.com/static/57c6b79629687fde090a0fdd/t/5b19b2f2aa4a99e99b26b6bb/1528410876119/dschool_bootleg_deck_2018_final_sm+%282%29.pdf.

28. Charles Limb, "Your Brain on Improv," TEDxMidAtlantic, November 2010, https://www.ted.com/talks/charles_limb_your_brain_on_improv.

29. Tom Kelley and David Kelley, *Creative Confidence: Unleashing the Creative Potential within Us All* (New York City: Random House, 2013).

30. Tina Fey, *Bossypants* (New York: Little, Brown, 2011), 84.

31. Adam Bluestein, "Want to Be More Creative? Think on Your Feet," *Inc.com*, April 14, 2014, accessed May 25, 2021, https://www.inc.com/magazine/201404/adam-bluestein/companies-use-improv-to-boost-creativity.html.

32. Keith R. Sawyer, "Improvisation and the Creative Process: Dewey, Collingwood, and the Aesthetics of Spontaneity," *Journal of Aesthetics and Art Criticism* 58, no. 2 (2000): 149–61.

33. David Burkus, *The Myths of Creativity: The Truth about How Innovative Companies and People Generate Great Ideas* (San Francisco: Jossey-Bass, 2014), 105.

34. Bob Joseph, "What Is an Indigenous Medicine Wheel?," Indigenous Corporate Training Inc., May 24, 2020, accessed May 25, 2021, https://www.ictinc.ca/blog/what-is-an-aboriginal-medicine-wheel.

35. Jennifer Bain, "At Google Canada, the Meals and Snacks Are Free for 150 Employees," *Toronto Star*, June 19, 2014, accessed May 25, 2021, https://www.thestar.com/life/food_wine/2014/06/19/at_google_canada_the_meals_and_snacks_are_free_for_150_employees.html.

36. Vera John-Steiner, *Creative Collaboration* (Oxford: Oxford University Press, 2006), 92.

37. Bryan Burrough, "Fyre Festival: Anatomy of a Millennial Marketing Fiasco Waiting to Happen," *Vanity Fair*, August 2017, accessed May 25, 2021, https://www.vanityfair.com/news/2017/06/fyre-festival-billy-mcfarland-millennial-marketing-fiasco.

38. Petrina Ng, personal interview, November 27, 2020.

39. Gendai, "Gendai 2020–2022," accessed June 15, 2021, https://www.gendai.club/.

40. Akimbo, "Announcing the New Stewards of Gendai," accessed June 15, 2021, https://akimbo.ca/listings/announcing-the-new-stewards-of-gendai/.

41. Marsya Marahani, "About," accessed December 8, 2020, https://marsyamaharani.com/About.

42. Gendai, "MA MBA," accessed June 15, 2021, https://www.gendai.club/ma-mba.

43. Marsya Maharani, personal interview, November 27, 2020.

REFERENCES AND FURTHER READING

adrienne maree brown, *Emergent Strategy: Shaping Change, Changing Worlds* (Chico, CA: AK Press, 2017). Inspired by science fiction writer Octavia Butler, brown's book examines how science and science fiction can be harnessed to vision and shape social change. This book examines patterns of collaboration in the natural world found among plants and animals, and studies how these collaborative forms might teach humans how best to work together to create a more inclusive future.

Scott Doorley and Scott Witthoft, *Make Space: How to Set the Stage for Creative Collaboration* (Hoboken, NJ: John Wiley & Sons, 2012). Doorley and Witthoft compile tricks, tips, and best practices for best setting up space intentionally for collaborative work. This book ranges in topics from simple DIY hacks for creating comfortable and customizable environments to facilitating group meetings to best work with others.

Étienne Wenger, *Communities of Practice: Learning, Meaning, and Identity* (Oxford: Oxford University Press, 1998). In this book, cognitive anthropologist Etienne Wenger identifies learning as a social practice that happens through collaborative structures. Wenger explores the concept of communities of practice and how these communities support learning.

Ritu Bhasin, *The Authenticity Principle: Resist Conformity, Embrace Differences, and Transform How You Live, Work, and Lead* (Toronto: Melanin Made Press, 2017). Bhasin defines authenticity and implores readers to embrace their differences and feel confident to disrupt the status quo and common expectations to mask and conform their inner selves. Rather than delivering an individual-centric message, *The Authenticity Principle* suggests that living well means enlarged possibilities for a greater number of people to live in alignment with their core values, beliefs, and identities.

Vera John-Steiner, *Creative Collaboration* (Oxford: Oxford University Press, 2006). In this book, John-Steiner profiles how individual creativity and individual achievements are often romanticized in Western accounts of the creative process. In contrast, *Creative Collaboration* highlights the scholarly, artistic, and scientific collaborations that have produced remarkable achievements in creativity and innovation. John-Steiner profiles the relationships, support systems, joint work, and emotional bonds that are involved in creative collaborations.

Creative Education Foundation, *Creative Problem Solving Resource Guide* (Scituate, MA: Creative Education Foundation, 2014). This guide provides an overview of creative problem solving as a method, including techniques for divergent and convergent thinking.

5

Cultivate Inclusion

■ ■ ■

Taking care of other living things can be a great pleasure and also at times a great challenge. To start thinking about cultivating inclusive conditions for everyone to flourish, we can consider a very small example of this larger process of care: tending to plants. When we have a plant that doesn't flourish, it's probably easy to recognize that it wasn't given the proper conditions to thrive, namely, water and light. These components of life might sound simple, but also can be complex and complicated, and it takes skill, knowledge, and attention to provide the right blend of water and light that different plants need.

Similarly, cultivating care and the supportive conditions for people to flourish can be complex and challenging. In this chapter, we focus on cultivating inclusion, or creating supportive conditions for flourishing across differences. Let's start with the premise that living creatures need nurturance for their whole lives. We might think that young children need nurturing, but all people need encouragement and validation to foster a sense of belonging and wellbeing, throughout their entire lives. For adults, much of our sense of validation comes from employment, and *Bringing Your Whole Self to Work* author Mike Robbins suggests that inclusive workplaces need "high expectation[s] of excellence" alongside "high nurturance," which includes "being seen, being heard, being valued, being appreciated not just for what [people] do, but for who they are, being safe to be ourselves, to speak our truth, to disagree, to take risks."[1] This balance between accountability and nurturance is important for cultivating inclusion in many settings, beyond the workplace, including in school, in communities, and in relationships. Much of the research on inclusion profiled in this chapter comes from workplace settings, but the identified characteristics of inclusion are applicable in these broader settings as well.

Inclusion needs to be cultivated with intention, and there isn't a one-size-fits-all model, especially if we are considering difference and different needs. Still, a key opening idea here is *intention*, coupled with reflexivity.

Simply being "welcoming" is not always enough to be inclusive. Inclusion is ongoing work, reflecting on who can and does participate and flourish in any given context.

In her book *Radical Compassion*, psychologist Tara Brach suggests reclaiming the word *compassion*. In a podcast of the same title, Brach explains that "radical compassion means our hearts are all inclusive," with an "open, inclusive quality of heart." She suggests that "if there is ever a time in the world's history that we need [to] actively cultivate compassion and caring and stretch ourselves, widen the circles beyond where habitually we pay attention, it's now. It will be what allows us to care enough to act for our earth, that is suffering so much, for those that are most vulnerable, and live true to ourselves."[2] In this chapter, our focus is on cultivating inclusion with other people, across differences, in a variety of settings. Think of inclusion as a seed to plant, germinate, and grow with intention.

DEFINING DIVERSITY, EQUITY, AND INCLUSION

Chapter 4 outlined valuing diversity and difference as a successful component of collaboration. In this chapter, we expand this point and begin by considering the difference between diversity and inclusion. These terms are often used interchangeably, synonymously, or in tandem. For example, many organizations now have diversity and inclusion departments, often rendered as an acronym, like D&I. It's worth considering if these acronyms and the frequent pairing of these words dilutes them and minimizes the full impact of their implications.

Diversity

Here we will define **diversity** to refer to demographic difference (including race, gender, social class, sexuality, disability, age, and so on). Diversity might also mean difference in mindsets and perspectives, cognitive styles, values, assumptions, beliefs, and norms. Diversity can mean encountering difference, with people who see the world through a different lens than our own. Katherine W. Phillips, a professor of leadership and ethics at Columbia Business School, writes, "The first thing to acknowledge about diversity is that it can be difficult."[3] Some of this difficulty can be from discomfort in interactions and communication and a lessened feeling of cohesion. At the same time, Phillips provides an overview of research that shows "being around people who are different from us makes us more creative, more diligent and harder-working." Some of the strength of diversity is that it produces what Phillips terms "informational diversity," such that "when people are brought together to solve problems in groups, they bring different information, opinions and perspectives. . . . People who are different from one another in race, gender and other dimensions bring unique information and experiences to bear on the task at hand."[4]

Discussing different "paradigms" of diversity, David A. Thomas and Robin J. Ely highlight the paradigm of "integration and learning," which moves beyond mere compliance with policies and laws, and beyond the so-called business case for diversity in organizations, which is that people from underrepresented communities can make inroads into diverse markets and thereby increase revenues. The value of diversity in the "business case" is limited to market-based motivation, which "can leave some employees feeling exploited." In contrast, the integration and learning perspective on diversity suggests that people from underrepresented communities "bring different, important, and competitively relevant knowledge and perspectives about how to actually *do work*—how to design processes, reach goals, frame tasks, create effective teams, communicate ideas, and lead."[5] This framework of integration and learning highlights differences as a source of innovation and growth to develop better ways of working, whether this is in the workplace, community, or other collaborative settings.

In the past, we may have been told to be "color blind," or to not remark on or notice diversity to work toward treating everyone equally, as in treating everyone the same. Increasingly, conversations about diversity are shifting past the idea that being "color blind" is something to aspire to and toward the idea of noticing and engaging with difference. In their book *Diversity in Organizations: A Critical Examination*, Cedric Herring and Loren Henderson critique previous concepts of diversity, including (1) color-blind diversity, which embraces difference without acknowledging inequality; (2) snowflake diversity, which is rooted in individualism or celebrating "success stories" while ignoring group-based inequalities; and (3) segregated diversity, which increases diversity within a sector, though the dominant/subdominant groups remain separate, for example, in terms of people in positions of power and people in subordinate positions.[6] Herring and Henderson provide the example of the U.S. Army to illustrate the concept of segregated diversity: even if representation of women and people of color has increased in this organization, senior leadership positions remain white-male dominated.

In contrast to these flawed conceptions of diversity, Herring and Henderson forward the concept of "critical diversity" not only to celebrate demographic difference but also to register challenges of inequality. They write that critical diversity "requires an analysis of exclusion and discrimination. It therefore must challenge hegemonic notions of colorblindness and meritocracy."[7] Here Herring and Henderson reference not only including people from equity-deserving groups and moving beyond mere representation. A critical diversity framework also examines systemic social exclusion while striving for change; meaningful diversity work continually names and reflects on exclusion, and does not assume that exclusion is readily solved or no longer needs attention with increased representation alone. In her book *On Being Included*, feminist and critical race scholar Sara Ahmed analyzes the ways "diversity" is used to pay lip service to difference. "Diversity" can become a way to say "we are already diverse" rather than pointing to or addressing problems.[8] When we celebrate diversity, we may be avoiding naming or discussing inequality. Instead, we need to recognize that diversity means difference, difference can be difficult, but diversity can also create strength and innovation; meaningfully engaging with difference also means recognizing and addressing inequality.

Equity

In contrast to shallow celebrations of diversity, the concept of **equity** examines inequality and seeks to remedy or redress this problem. Independent Sector, an American umbrella organization for the charitable sector, including nonprofits, foundations, and corporations, defines equity as

> the fair treatment, access, opportunity, and advancement for all people, while at the same time striving to identify and eliminate barriers that have prevented the full participation of some groups. Improving equity involves increasing justice and fairness within the procedures and processes of institutions or systems, as well as in their distribution of resources. Tackling equity issues requires an understanding of the root causes of outcome disparities within our society.[9]

This definition underscores barriers in society that create inequality and prevent full participation of all people.

An equity framework seeks to identify and work to eliminate barriers, and sometimes generates controversy. For example, the history of affirmative action policies in the United States has been controversial. Cedric Herring and Loren Henderson outline that affirmative action, which has been most often used in employment and education contexts, "consists of government-mandated or voluntary programs and activities undertaken specifically to identify, recruit, promote and/or retain qualified members of disadvantaged minority groups in order to overcome the results of past discrimination and to deter discriminatory practices in the present."[10] Some commentators argue that equity measures, such as affirmative action, look like preferential treatment, or so-called reverse racism. Equity differs from equality, as an equity perspective considers what measures are needed to work toward equality, given historical and present-day inequality. Equity suggests equitable treatment, instead of equal treatment; in the above extract, Independent Sector defines this as fair. In some contexts, equity is increasingly recognized; for example, students with learning disabilities are recognized as needing more time to complete assignments or needing alternative arrangements or supports. Take some time to reflect on your areas of involvement in your community, schooling, personal life, and professional life and what equity measures might be needed to cultivate full participation of all members of society.

Antioppressive Practice

Fostering equity can also mean recognizing structural factors and barriers that can enable or constrain individuals to be their most fully realized selves. Originating from social work, antioppressive practice (AOP) recognizes the impact of structural factors, like race, gender, sexual orientation, ability, age, and class, on lived experience. Helen Wong and June Ying Yee define an antioppressive framework as "the lens through which one understands how race, gender, sexual orientation and identity, ability, age, class, occupation and social service usage can result in systemic inequalities for particular groups."[11] AOP foregrounds an understanding of how power dynamics and structural forces affect lived realities, and works intentionally to foster inclusion. AOP can also mean an emphasis on humanization and attempting to include the whole person.[12]

Working with an antioppressive lens, we can strive to identify barriers and work to eliminate or reduce these in order to foster inclusion. For example, imagine a single mother without child care who is also unemployed. In this situation, attending skills training or employment search workshops could be challenging, if not impossible. With this in mind, if these types of events want to include single parents, they can consider providing child care on-site. Other strategies to eliminate or reduce barriers in this example could include offering transit tokens or providing food on-site. Through this lens, we might ask what populations or demographics we are reaching, what populations are excluded, and what strategies might be put into place to include diverse populations with diverse needs.

If we consider this example of a skills training/employment workshop further through a "whole person" lens, we might also ask how this experience can be fun or enjoyable, beyond simply delivering the content. Can this event have some element of socializing or networking, which participants can opt in or out of? (Perhaps this single mother is also very tired and doesn't feel like talking to anyone.) If so, small gestures like name tags to facilitate people talking to one another, or including an ice-breaker on the agenda to allow people to get to know one another a little bit, can have a positive effect. Could there be music, enthusiasm, or positive reinforcement? An AOP framework does not mean that every event needs to be a celebration, but we can reflect on barriers, work toward removing them, and think about humanizing on an ongoing basis.

Inclusion

While diversity can refer to visible markers of difference, inclusion is a subtler concept to define, as it emerges from our feelings and experiences. **Inclusion** characterizes the nature of a climate or culture, including a feeling of belonging alongside difference being recognized and valued.[13] To clarify the difference between diversity and inclusion, diversity consultant Vernā Myers says, "Diversity is being invited to the party; inclusion is being asked to dance."[14]

Cultivating inclusion means creating environments where individuals feel valued and that they can belong for being themselves and for their unique contributions. Melanie Dunn, CEO of marketing agency Cossette, addresses this topic in her provocatively titled article "Stop Telling Women They Must Change Themselves to Become Leaders."[15] In this article, Dunn raises the point of changing organizational culture to become inclusive instead of changing people so they fit into the organizational culture. This concept of building inclusive cultures differs from the advice from Sheryl Sandberg, the chief operating officer of Facebook. Her famously titled book *Lean In* encourages women to feel empowered to "lean in" at work in order to be heard, project confidence, and push to reach top roles. This phrase "lean in" widely caught on, leading to the formation of "lean in" support and empowerment groups for women. But this term has also been critiqued for not adequately recognizing systemic gender bias, discrimination, and barriers to advancement. At its worst, a "lean in" model suggests adopting a false confidence or bravado to fit in and get ahead. In an equally provocatively titled article called "Why Do So Many Incompetent Men Become Leaders," business psychology professor Tomas Chamorro-Premuzic suggests that certain personality qualities, like hubris, charm, and charisma, are often seen as having leadership potential. Other, more destructive qualities, like narcissism, psychopathy, and being risk prone, are also oversampled in leaders. Chamorro-Premuzic writes, "It struck me as a little odd that so much of the recent debate over getting women to 'lean in' has focused on getting them to adopt more of these dysfunctional leadership traits."[16] Other leadership traits, important for fostering inclusion, include listening, being responsive and attentive, and facilitating consensus, but these subtler traits are sometimes less visible and less celebrated.

One way to conceptualize building an inclusive culture is the shift from the idea of "culture fit" toward the idea of "culture add." In workplaces, emphasis on an applicant's "fit" with the organizational culture when hiring is now thought to minimize difference and diversity and encourage individuals to conform and mask. In the *New York Times*, Lauren Rivera gives an overview of the history of this "culture fit" idea, originating in the 1980s: "the original idea [behind culture fit] was that if companies hired individuals whose personalities and values—and not just their skills—meshed with an organization's strategy, workers would feel more attached to their jobs, work harder and stay longer."[17] Rivera characterizes this idea of culture fit as "potentially dangerous," as it too narrowly relies on personal characteristics rather than qualifications. A focus on fit can produce biased assumptions about what type of person is best, reduce diversity, and create too much similarity. In contrast, the idea of culture add asks what skill sets or qualifications add to the existing pool of resources and experience in an organization. Culture add allows for a wider range of characteristics to been seen as valuable to an organization.

We can see this dynamic dramatized in the Pixar short film *Purl*, written and directed by Kristen Lester. In this short film, the titular character is a ball of yarn named Purl. When Purl gets hired into an all-male corporate environment called B.R.O. Capital, she learns to adopt a masculine bravado, swagger, and appearance, after initially being ignored and overlooked. When a second ball of yarn, Lacy, gets hired, Purl chooses to drop this persona and revert back to her more authentic self, to include and reach out to Lacy. The conclusion of this short film shows a more balanced, comfortable, and inclusive work environment that benefits everyone.[18]

One indicator of a sense of inclusion and the comfort of being oneself is **psychological safety**. Amy Edmondson, professor at Harvard Business School, profiles the importance of this quality in her book *The Fearless Organization: Creating Psychological Safety in the Workplace for Learning, Innovation, and Growth*. Edmondson's research on psychological safety in the workplace, the quality of a "climate where people feel safe enough to take interpersonal risk by speaking up and sharing concerns, questions, or ideas," identifies that this quality of a workplace helps to facilitate a "continuous loop of learning."[19] Edmondson's research on this concept began with studies of work teams in hospitals in the 1990s.

Her research investigated whether or not more cohesive teams in hospitals would make fewer mistakes. She found that the more cohesive a team was, the more willing they were to report mistakes. Edmondson's research suggests that a sense of psychological safety allows teams and organizations to perform better through a willingness to admit, reflect on, and learn from mistakes.

As introduced above, being inclusive doesn't simply mean being "welcoming." Similarly, Edmondson clarifies that creating the conditions for psychological safety doesn't mean just being nice. She says the term psychological safety "implies to people a sense of coziness. . . . You know, that we're all going to be nice to each other and that's not what it's really about. What it's about is candor; what it's about is being direct, taking risks, being willing to say, 'I screwed that up.' Being willing to ask for help when you're in over your head."[20] In this way, a sense of psychological safety relates to a sense of empowerment to speak up rather than needing to be "nice." Edmondson notes that "hiring for diversity is not enough," as inclusion and belonging also need to be targeted.[21] Important to note in these discussions of the differences between diversity and inclusion is that inclusion is an active process that needs to be fostered through reflexivity on working practices—a focus on diversity alone cannot ensure equitable or inclusive experiences in the workplace. Psychological safety is important in and beyond the workplace and can also impact education and learning environments, community and volunteer groups, and other group and team environments.

One concrete example of a workplace culture that invites workers to report mistakes is the famous *andon* or "stop the line" system in Toyota car manufacturing plants in Japan. At Toyota, *andon* could be a button or cord for workers to stop a production line if they notice an error in car assembly, so that the error could be corrected. This system, developed by Taiichi Ohno, differed from common manufacturing principles at the time, which emphasized continuous output through production quotas with targets or benchmarks to reach. Profiling "the Toyota Way," engineering professor Jeffrey Liker describes this system as "building a culture of stopping to fix problems, to get quality right the first time."[22] In the context of inclusion, we want to consider how to build this culture so diverse members feel empowered to speak up and contribute their ideas, including pointing out mistakes or problems.

Inclusive Leadership

Outside of a manufacturing context, inclusive culture can take on more complexity than being allowed to push a button or pull a cord. Research on diversity and inclusion identifies the key role that leaders play in setting the tone to develop inclusive cultures.[23] In her book *How to Be an Inclusive Leader*, Jennifer Brown suggests that individuals in leadership positions have a responsibility and an opportunity to "build a different future, a better future" that is more inclusive.[24] Brown maps four stages of inclusive leadership: unaware, aware, active, and advocate (see figure 5.1). Brown's continuum suggests that there is ongoing work to be done to foster inclusion, and that a leader may be an advocate in one particular area of diversity work but be unaware in other areas. This continuum suggests the importance of learning and continual self-reflection alongside committed action.

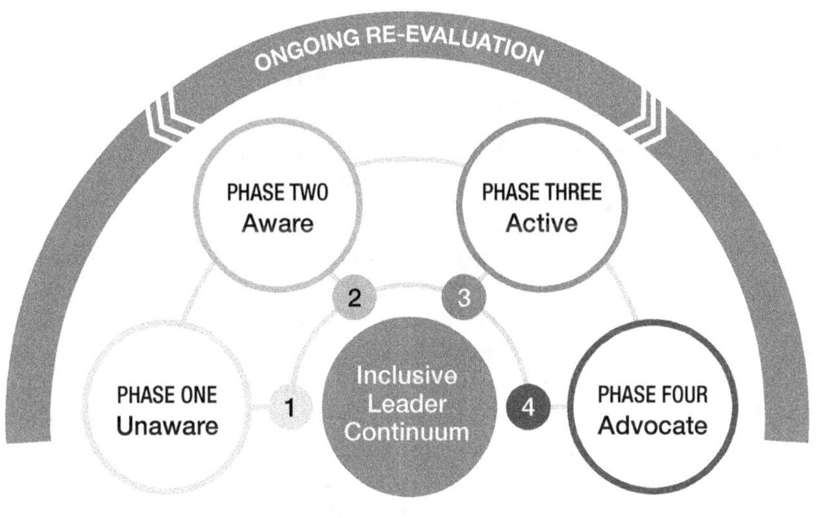

UNAWARE
You think diversity is compliance-related and simply tolerate it. It's someone else's job–not yours.

AWARE
You are aware that you have a role to play and are educating yourself about how best to move forward.

ACTIVE
You have shifted your priorities and are finding your voice as you begin to take meaningful action in support of others.

ADVOCATE
You are proactively and consistently using your privilege to the avantage of others. You consider their issues your issues and stand in solidarity with them.

Private // Low Risk // Individual Perspective ⟫ Public // High Risk // Organizational Perspective

Figure 5.1 The Inclusive Leader Continuum

Reprinted with permission from *How to Be an Inclusive Leader* by Jennifer Brown

Table 5.1 Components of Inclusive Leadership

Visible Commitment	Articulating authentic commitment to diversity; challenging the status quo; holding others accountable; making diversity and inclusion a personal priority
Humility	Being modest about capabilities; admitting mistakes; creating the space for others to contribute
Awareness of Bias	Showing awareness of personal blind spots as well as flaws in the system; working hard to ensure meritocracy
Curiosity about Others	Demonstrating an open mindset and deep curiosity about others; listening without judgment; seeking with empathy to understand those around them
Cultural Intelligence	Being attentive to others' cultures and adapting as required
Effective Collaboration	Empowering others; paying attention to diversity of thinking and psychological safety; focusing on team cohesion

Adapted from Bourke and Titus, "Key to Inclusive Leadership."

Similarly, Juliet Bourke and Andrea Titus, from the Human Capital division of insurance company Deloitte, conducted a research project about inclusion, surveying 4,100 employees, interviewing identified inclusive leaders, and conducting academic literature reviews on leadership. In the *Harvard Business Review*, they share their research findings that highlight six traits or behaviors of inclusive leaders (table 5.1).[25] Across these six identified characteristics, we can note elements of responsiveness rather than top-down authority. Fostering inclusion can be thought of as setting the stage for success and enabling an environment that allows psychological safety and engagement so that individuals can be their more fully realized selves.

In her TEDx talk, "3 Steps to Turn Everyday Get-Togethers into Transformative Gatherings," author of *The Art of Gathering: How We Meet and Why it Matters* Priya Parker outlines strategies to create what she terms "transformative gatherings." One of her strategies is creating a structure or framework for social events, allowing for "temporary alternative worlds through the use of pop-up rules." Although rules sometimes have a restrictive and even punitive connotation (follow the rules or you will get punished), Parker suggests that rules don't have to be boring or controlling. Is it possible to think of rules as liberating, creating a structure for meetings so we know how to behave or act? Parker comments, "In this multicultural, intersectional society . . . unspoken norms are trouble, whereas pop-up rules allow us to connect meaningfully. They are one-time-only constitutions for a specific purpose. Rules are powerful because they allow us to temporarily change or harmonize our behavior. In diverse societies, pop-up rules carry special force. They allow us to gather across difference, to connect, to make meaning together, without having to be the same."[26]

Parker's discussion of inclusive social gatherings that enable differences, not conformity or masking, emphasizes temporary structures, guidelines, or foundations. When we consider inclusive leadership, we can also consider being leaders in our-day-to-day lives, while reflecting on what barriers might impact individuals' capacities to meaningfully engage with one another, and what strategies are within our means to foster more inclusion.

INCLUSION IN DESIGN: FROM DESIGN THINKING TO DESIGN JUSTICE

Recall the principles of design thinking, introduced as a tool for collaboration in chapter 4. Design thinking involves starting from a place of empathy or research, but it can sometimes result in attempting to solve a problem on behalf of or for others, and this can minimize impacted individuals' capacity and agency to meaningfully contribute to change making. **Design justice** shifts this strategy, working toward "designing with" instead of "designing for" individuals and communities, and is a more meaningfully inclusive design strategy.

The Design Justice Network emerged from the Allied Media Conference in Detroit in 2015. This conference is an annual social justice gathering organized by Allied Media Projects (AMP), an organization working toward personal and societal transformation through all ways people communicate with one another. AMP's vision includes attempting to "model a world in which we, collectively care for ourselves, each other, other species, and the planet; dismantle supremacist systems as they operate upon us and within us; assume responsibility for creating new liberatory ways of being, and; cultivate life affirming joy."[27] The Design Justice Network follows from these principles, seeing design not just as something that professional designers use to make things aesthetically pleasing but as the way that we define and solve problems. The network's mission statement says, "The Design Justice Network challenges the ways that design and designers can harm those who are marginalized by systems of power. We use design to imagine and build the worlds we need to live in—worlds that are safer, more just, and more sustainable. We advance practices that center those who are normally excluded from and adversely impacted by design decisions in design processes." Design Justice Network principles include sharing knowledge and tools with communities, believing that lived experience brings innovation to design, and looking for what is already working at the community level before seeking new design solutions.[28] The Design Justice Network holds workshops and events to engage with communities and has local nodes in cities worldwide.

In her book *Design Justice: Community Led Practices to Build the Worlds We Need*, Sasha Costanza-Chock discusses the framework of design justice, raising social justice concerns of equity and inclusion. Costanza-Chock outlines that design can be a tool of discrimination, highlighting Ruha Benjamin's definition of **discriminatory design** as "the normalization of racial hierarchies within the underlying design of sociotechnical systems." Acknowledging that "most designers do not intend to systematically exclude marginalized groups of people," Costanza-Chock identifies that the impact of design can be exclusionary and discriminatory, whether or not this consequence is intentional.[29] Costanza-Chock illustrates the concept of discriminatory design with Robert Moses' urban planning of overhead passes in the mid-twentieth century that blocked public buses from reaching the Rockaway Beaches in Queens, New York City, showing how the built environment can structure racism and embody power. But discriminatory design is not a thing of the past and is encoded in many contemporary designs. Costanza-Chock gives the example of facial detection softwares that fail to detect dark-skinned faces, highlighting research from Joy Buolamwini and Timnit Gebru that shows that these softwares were developed on "pale males" and perform "best on images of white men and worst on images of Black women."[30]

In contrast to discriminatory design, Costanza-Chock outlines that a design justice perspective of centering people who are normally marginalized by design is "ethical" and can lead to better outcomes: "the tacit and experiential knowledge of those marginalized within the matrix of domination is sure to produce ideas, approaches, and innovations that a nonmember of the community would be very unlikely to come up with."[31] This framework for inclusion does not attempt to integrate marginalized peoples into dominant and unchanged norms, but instead values difference and differing perspectives as a source of innovation. Design justice moves away from a top-down approach of inclusion into the mainstream, and works toward community-led and community-controlled outcomes to build a better world.

ACCESS

Considering equity and fostering inclusion can also mean considering the physical space and environment, including who is and is not able to access a space and the different physical needs of diverse individuals. Scott Doorley and Scott Witthoft are codirectors of Environments Collaborative at Stanford University's d. school, an institute for design and "radical collaboration." Their book *Make Space: How to Set the Stage for Creative Collaboration* provides instructions for building tools to customize physical spaces to better collaborate, including objects like foam cubes for seating for quickly convening informal meetings and creating dry-erase boards with affordable materials, like shower board or tile board. Beyond these DIY hacks, *Make Space* contains profiles about "situations," or different kinds of configurations of space for different kinds of collaborative purposes, and "insights," with small tips for best practices about how to work together, like "Get There a Little Early, Leave a Little Late" and "Don't Blow the Whole Budget."

Beyond these small hacks for customizable space, considering the space of collaboration through the lens of access means considering different needs and abilities. "Radical collaboration" might truly mean creating spaces that all people can access and participate in. Much of the built world has been structured around dominant norms of able-bodied individuals and can be inaccessible to individuals with physical, sensory, and intellectual disabilities. The *Accessibility Toolkit* is a practical guide for making art spaces accessible, produced by Tangled Art + Disability, a charitable organization dedicated to enhancing opportunities for artists with disabilities. This toolkit opens by contrasting the medical model and the social model for disability. The medical model of disability "frames individuals as disabled by their impairments or differences" and seeks to "fix" the perceived impairment in the affected individual. In contrast, the social model of disability "says that disability is caused by the way society is designed and organized, rather than by a person's impairment or difference. This model looks at ways of removing barriers that restrict life choices and access for disabled people."[32] For example, the *Accessibility Toolkit* provides the example of a wheelchair user who is unable to access a building due to steps. In the social model of disability, the steps are a barrier, rather than the wheelchair being the source of the problem.

Universal Design

One type of design that moves away from dominant able-bodied norms is called universal design. This form of design requires a shift in thinking about norms and the "normal" user. Who is this "norm," and does this "norm" include everyone? Historically, the physical environment has been built for one standard norm, which was able-bodied, and then adaptations were created for those who fell outside of dominant norms, such as people with physical disabilities. The Centre for Excellence in Universal Design defines **universal design** as follows:

> Universal Design is the design and composition of an environment so that it can be accessed, understood and used to the greatest extent possible by all people regardless of their age, size, ability or disability. An environment (or any building, product, or service in that environment) should be designed to meet the needs of all people who wish to use it. This is not a special requirement, for the benefit of only a minority of the population. It is a fundamental condition of good design.[33]

In a TEDx talk titled "When We Design for Disability, We All Benefit," disability rights lawyer Elise Roy gives an overview of design thinking and how design can be used to create more inclusion. She talks about her own experience of woodworking as a Deaf person. Drawing on Warren Berger, who says, "Design thinking teaches us to look sideways," Roy gives an overview of products and services that were designed for disability users but now have mainstream use and popularity, like text messaging and ergonomic vegetable peelers. She says, "What if we started designing for disability first—not the norm? As you see, when we design for disability first, we often stumble upon solutions that are not only inclusive, but also are often better than when we design for the norm."[34]

Universal design can shift a perspective away from accommodating disability and being tolerant toward difference (like in the medical model of disability) and shift toward questioning that there is one stable norm that everyone needs to adapt or conform to (like in the social model of disability). A simple example of this problem of one dominant norm is common air-conditioning settings in North America. Have you ever been inside an air-conditioned building in the summer months and found yourself too cold, or maybe even brought a sweater to work or to a movie theater? Research shows that "most office buildings set temperatures based on a decades-old formula that uses the metabolic rates of men."[35] These formulas, developed in the 1960s, reflected a workforce that was predominantly male. Furthermore, common office attire in the 1960s was often more formal that today's workplace requirements: many contemporary office cultures don't suggest that men wear heavy suits to work, especially in the summer. The takeaway point here is that these temperatures were set for one body type, which in this example was male and heavily dressed, and this norm does not reflect the diversity of people who make up contemporary working environments and use public space. Universal design aims to disrupt and shift these norms to be more inclusive for more people.

One example of shifting the dominant norm to be more inclusive is "relaxed performances," which emerged in performing arts and theater with a recognition that there were barriers for people with autism, Tourette's, or intellectual disabilities to attend live performance. These events often expect that the audience sit still or be quiet for the duration of the performance. However, a person with Tourette's might have outbursts that prevent them from being quiet for long stretches. In a relaxed performance, the audience is permitted or even encouraged to make noise. This means that people with disabilities can attend, but also children or other people who might want to circulate or make noise for any number of reasons. Have you ever tried to stifle a cough or very quietly tried to unwrap a candy at a live performance where there was an expectation of silence in the room? A relaxed performance creates an environment that can still be respectful of an artist or performer and their craft, while also being more inclusive, and possibly being more fun for everyone.

When we reflect on cultivating inclusion, we can also reflect on where, when, and how our contemporary norms and expectations got formed. This reflection process might need research and gathering of more historical information, but the thought process can nonetheless open up our thinking from one set way of being to multiple different and valid ways of being. In the example of a relaxed performance, we can note that the idea of a theater audience being quiet throughout a performance is not necessarily the way that live theater has always been done. In "Elizabethan Theater Etiquette and Audience Expectations Today," Austin Tichenor reflects on audience composition and behavior in Shakespeare's day, noting that audience members came from every social class: "Elizabethan audiences clapped and booed whenever they felt like it. Sometimes they threw fruit."[36] This is not to say that disrespectful or aggressive behavior should be encouraged from contemporary audiences; in fact, historical progress sometimes means more inclusion and respect for diverse groups of people. However, we can still question where we got our ideas that there is one "correct" or "normal" way of doing things, and consider if these ideas are necessarily helpful or if they maintain power and privilege in exclusionary ways. We can ask, who benefits from dominant norms, and who is excluded?

In their book *Building Access: University Design and the Politics of Disability*, Aimi Hamraie brings a critical lens to the history and mainstreaming of universal design, asking how it can remain "attentive to issues of power and privilege," rather than taking for granted that designing for everyone is common sense and that "accessible design [is] easy to achieve and simple to practice."[37] Universal design can sometimes now just appear like good common sense that produces good products and services. Hamraie brings attention to continued inclusion and exclusion in society, even if universal design has become popular: "the built world is inseparable from social attitudes, discriminatory systems, and knowledge about which users designers must keep in mind. Put another way, how we structure knowledge, interact with material things, and tell stories about the users of built environments matter for belonging and justice."[38]

Hamraie identifies that universal design shifts the emphasis away from disability and toward "everyone," but this emphasis is "confusing" as we still live in a world "that devalues particular bodies."[39] Instead of designing for "everyone," Hamraie recommends continued attention to disability and people who are marginalized by dominant norms, because dominant exclusionary norms still exist in society. Hamraie draws attention to "The Principles of Universal Design" from the Center of Universal Design at North Carolina State University, which does discuss specific users, including disabled people.

What does design look like if we acknowledge that it is not possible to design a product that is truly accessible by all potential users and aim to be "inclusive" rather than "universal"? One variation of universal design is *user-sensitive inclusive design*. Rather than aiming for a one-size-fits-all universal model, user-sensitive inclusive design acknowledges the challenges of marginalized groups of people, including disabled people and the elderly, and aims to develop a close relationship with the user and cultivate empathy. User-sensitive inclusive design considers the whole person, not just the functionality of products they will use.[40] This means also considering aesthetic needs and the desire for products to be attractive and enjoyable to use. Why do major brands and fashion labels produce eyeglasses but not walking sticks? Mobility aids and devices are often still largely functional, but other types of assistive technology, like eyeglasses, have become more normalized. Only recently has maternity clothing been designed to be stylish. In the past, pregnancy has been treated like something to conceal or hide. More recently, women have expressed a continued desire to feel glamorous and even sexy through pregnancy. What could design look like if difference was not stigmatized or seen as inferior but was centered and celebrated?

Crip Theory

The limitations of universal design to be truly inclusive in a universal way in a society that is still unequal suggests the need for models and frameworks that center disability while working toward inclusion. Following from the social model of disability, **crip theory** is a framework that centers disability and celebrates differing ways of being. In *Building Access*, Aimi Hamraie traces the term *crip* to the 1970s independent living movement for people with disabilities and the reclamation of the term *cripple*. Unlike the universal design movement, crip theory does not seek to normalize and neutralize disability. Instead, crip theory sees disability as a "a valuable cultural identity, a source of knowledge, and a basis for relationality," opening up ways of being, knowing, and relating.[41] Hamraie outlines that crip theory expands the focus on physical environment and environmental design found in universal design and investigates the broader system of cultural norms, power, and economics that treat disability as a "disqualification."

In her TED Talk, Elise Roy asserts the value in her disability as a Deaf person, suggesting her lived experience gives her a different perspective about problem solving, involving ingenuity and creativity. She provides the example of woodworking and inventing a pair of safety googles that visually alert users to danger before a pitch-shift safety sound is audible to the ear. She asks, "Why hadn't tool designers thought of this before? Two reasons: one, I was a beginner. I wasn't weighed down by expertise or conventional wisdom. The second is: I was Deaf. My unique experience of the world helped inform my solution."

The idea that unique experience and wisdom comes from disability and provides value and innovation is at the heart of crip theory. In *Care Work: Dreaming Disability Justice*, Leah Lakshmi Piepzna-Samarasinha writes, "In the deficiency model of disability, there's nothing good about disability, no skills or brilliance. We are just a fault to be cured. The only good crip is a cured crip, one who has ceased to exist. Cure is healing is elimination." Piepzna-Samarasinha suggests that flipping this script, moving beyond the medical or deficit model for disability, "is a giant paradigm shift. Our crip bodies aren't seen as liabilities, something that limits us and brings pity, or something to nobly transcend, 'cause I'm just like you. Our crip bodies are gifts, brilliant, fierce, skilled, valuable. Assets that teach us things that are relevant and vital to ourselves, our communities, our movements, the whole goddamn planet."[42] Building a more caring and more just society means celebrating the strengths, innovation, and contributions of all individuals. When society still adheres to dominant norms that are exclusionary, these diverse contributions are lost. Cultivating inclusion benefits everyone, enabling a broader range of people to live well and contribute to society as their whole selves. In this closing profile of Roots to Harvest, we learn about cultivating inclusion through collectively growing food.

CULTIVATING INCLUSION BY GROWING FOOD TOGETHER: ROOTS TO HARVEST

Roots to Harvest has existed in Thunder Bay, Canada, since 2007, and was inspired by the Food Project, based in Boston, which envisions "a world where youth are active leaders, diverse communities feel connected to the land and each other, and everyone has access to fresh, local, healthy, affordable food," while treating youth as "powerful agents of change" by placing them in responsible roles, doing meaningful work.[43] Roots to Harvest now operates at three sites across the city of Thunder Bay, and the centerpiece of the project is a summer garden, and the Youth Garden program that employs ten youth between the ages of fifteen and eighteen for six weeks in the summer to work and harvest the garden and bring and sell produce at markets while earning high school co-op credits. Roots to Harvest also runs the Seasonal Horticultural Outdoor Worker (S.H.O.W.) program, an employment program for older youth aged eighteen to thirty, "aimed at breaking down barriers to employment and instilling broader based employment skills and agricultural training."[44] The organization also runs educational programs in local schools, such as Forest Meets Farm, teaching about wild and cultivated food in the local area.

Speaking about the Youth Garden program, Roots to Harvest Executive Director Erin Beagle says the program serves youth for whom the formal education system can be a tough fit and who can be pushed out of school, or youth who might be struggling with their sense of self and place in the world and are trying to find positive places to fit and belong. Erin says the institutional setting and expectations of school are hard to get past, even if there are supportive teachers working in that space. Roots to Harvest offers an alternative for youth learning, and gardening outdoors can offer a "good authentic setting" for open and supportive conversations. Youth who come to the Youth Garden Program can "face some serious barriers to employment, whether that's the programs they're involved in, or their life situation, or their different learning needs, or whatever it is. A lot of them are really undervalued for what they are really good at, because at school, they're not really good at what's going on there, reading and writing, and sitting still, and listening, and attendance. But talking to the public, or hands on, or creative ideas, or lots of energy, and hard worker—totally."[45]

This search for support and belonging that marginalized youth can experience is also true for participants in the S.H.O.W. program, and Erin says that the "sympathy of the world drops off for people when they hit eighteen," and in some contexts, homelessness can become a reality, or mental health or addiction struggles can become all the more challenging for individuals in this phase of their lives. Employment at S.H.O.W. often happens through a referral process and partnerships with other socially engaged organizations, for example, adult education centers or cooking programs that Roots to Harvest runs with Indigenous partner organizations. Erin says more doors into Roots to Harvest allows for more entry levels and groups of people; Roots to Harvest has built community trust with LGBTQ+ communities, as the organization has become known as a safe place to undertake a gender transition while at work, and has become known as a place that provides good and respected work, where people are treated well, among Indigenous and refugee communities.

With these contexts in mind, Roots to Harvest endeavors to provide supportive employment programming that allows for different chances to succeed. Erin says, "Success looks different for everybody" and is not a recipe. At Roots to Harvest, expectations are still high; it's not a program or treatment—it's employment. But the organization aims to provide a different kind of employment, and Roots to Harvest hires people for their skills to be with people, not because they are good farmers. She says inclusive skill development and learning happen not always through explanation and instruction at Roots to Harvest but is "lived in every moment" with ongoing conversations. At Roots to Harvest, youth "feel valued and know that they have something to offer." Skill development follows individual pathways and desires to learn, whether it's learning to interact with the public when selling produce at the market, or listening to how people are feeling or doing, or learning to be vulnerable. Erin says the work of Roots to Harvest is relational, in that the organization wants to have relationships with people it is employing, getting to know people for who they are and also for who they think they want to be, while offering support for these pathways of becoming and development. The context of Roots to Harvest lends itself well to creating belonging, with people coming from different backgrounds where they might not typically encounter each other, and also working outdoors side by side, day in, day out, which allows time for connection and conversation alongside garden work. At Roots to Harvest, program staff and youth employees do all the garden jobs together, and program staff don't ask youth employees to do tasks they wouldn't do themselves.

In this light, Roots to Harvest often targets relationships, not learning about food in itself, but the experience of growing food is nonetheless a particular and often empowering process. Growing food offers good work that is productive, valuable, and meaningful. Learning to grow food also means learning to work through challenges, whether those challenges are hot weather, being soaking wet, or dealing with bugs, and then seeing the fruits of your labor and celebrating by having meals and eating together, which allows youth to feel pride: the pride of, "I grew this." The responsibility of growing food also means a concrete and tangible reason to come to work: youth employees have to be there to take care of things and help things grow. At work, there is a role for everybody; everybody is needed and necessary with the many tasks involved in planting and maintaining a community garden, whether it is harvesting carrots, staking tomatoes, tending to the compost, or building sheds or greenhouses.

Though everyone has a common purpose at the garden, everyone also has different roles and tasks. When everyone is needed and valuable, this also helps foster belonging, when people can feel part of a bigger whole, in a specific way. This atmosphere can also help form important and lasting friendships, where people support each other and look out for each other. Erin underscores the importance of trust and finding a place of belonging, where "someone is excited to see them, remembers great things about them, has seen them at their most vulnerable, and at their most powerful." Cultivating inclusion can mean cultivating relationships, nurturing people's development, and finding purpose and pride in the fruits of our collective labors.

Activity 5.1: Inclusive Design Challenge

This activity was originally developed by Daniel Drak, cofounder of Drakberry, a social enterprise that seeks to leverage design thinking to advance social change.

To complete this exercise, you will need to cut some paper to create some blank cards, just big enough to write a word or two on each one. Additionally, the cards you created in the intersectionality activity (chapter 1, activity 1.2) will be helpful here.

1. Services/Platforms You Use Regularly: On one side of your cards, write down services/platforms that you use regularly (regularly could mean daily, monthly, or yearly). Write down things you actually use so that you are reflecting on things that you have a working knowledge of. For example, services and platforms might include Twitter, Instagram, Airbnb, Amazon Echo, Spotify, and local transit apps. Write one word or one service/platform per card.
2. Physical Spaces You Frequent/Use Regularly: On the other side of your cards, write down physical spaces you frequent or use

regularly. For example, you might consider where you do your grocery shopping, where you exercise, where you go to school or work, community spaces, entertainment spaces, and shopping spaces. Aim to list a variety of spaces you use for different reasons (i.e., functional spaces vs. relaxing spaces vs. inspiring places).

3. Selection and Research: Choose one card to work with that has one service/platform on one side and one physical space on the back side. Here we are narrowing down to do further research and inclusive planning, but the purpose of listing many services/platforms and spaces is to reflect on the broad number of ways we interact with our physical and digital environments. Do some research to place these services/spaces in context. Where/when were they invented/founded? What was their original purpose, and has this original purpose expanded or been modified?
4. Intersectional Selves: Look through the cards you created for the intersectionality activity from chapter 1 (activity 1.2) and consider if there are aspects of your intersectional self that impact how you use the service/platform that you have selected. Place these intersectional cards next to your service/platform cards. For example, you might reflect on gender, race, sexuality, disability, socioeconomic class, age, or religion, or other aspects of your intersectional self. You can also reflect or research if there have been news stories or controversies about members from diverse groups experiencing barriers or being prevented from accessing the service/platform you are reflecting on.
5. Access and Inclusion Plan: Research whether or not there are government plans, policies, or existing guidelines to increase or improve accessibility in your area. If you can locate a plan, identify how improved accessibility will be targeted. Consider accessibility from a broad perspective. Often when we think about accessibility, we think about physical mobility, but we can think about ability and disability broadly, both visible and invisible. Additionally, we can consider accessibility more broadly than ability and disability when we also consider intersectionality, and barriers to use or access that diverse groups of people might experience. Consider, for example, racialized groups, the LGTBQ+ community, parents, the working poor, and so on. Develop a plan for the service/space you have selected. How can it be made more accessible? More inclusive? One strategy for creative exploration is design thinking, introduced in chapter 4. Review those guidelines and consider what the various stages or steps of design thinking would involve for an accessibility

improvement process. Further consider how a design justice model would impact the development of an accessibility plan. If you have found an accessibility plan or policy for your area, you can see if funding has been allocated toward improving accessibility. In addition to major policy or structural changes, consider also if there are any possible low- or no-cost strategies that could be readily implemented to improve inclusion and accessibility to the service/platform you have selected.

6. Reflection and Debrief: Return to look at the other services and spaces you wrote down in step 1 of this exercise. It's not necessary to go through this exercise again with all of those services and spaces, but take a moment to reflect on the relative ease or difficulty you experience in accessing these services and platforms, and reflect on what barriers to access might exist for users from diverse groups. Reflect also on what was missing in this exercise, for example, testing, seeking input, or codesigning with user groups who represent a diversity of abilities/body sizes/identities. How can we include diverse perspectives into design processes so that designs are inclusive from the outset?

QUESTIONS FOR LEARNING AND REFLECTION

1. "Same-Same" versus Difference Inventory: Take a personal inventory of your workplace environment, personal relationships, community spaces, and other gatherings or groups that you frequent. Do you mostly encounter people who are similar to you? Consider similarity not only demographically but also in terms of ways of thinking and values. If you self-identify as someone who is part of dominant norms, what opportunities exist for you to encounter difference on a more regular basis if you don't do so already? If you self-identify as someone who experiences marginalization, what opportunities are there for you to strengthen and bolster your community?
2. Psychological Safety: Consider a situation where you did not fully contribute to a group or team. Were there any aspects of yourself that you did not feel comfortable to fully reveal or present? From this experience, consider what a more inclusive environment could look like for you. Conversely, if you often feel comfortable in groups or teams, consider why these environments feel safe or inclusive for you. Can you imagine other elements of an environment that might enable more diverse expressions and contributions in your group or

team environments? Who is showing up, who isn't, and who is forwarding their ideas?

3. Leadership: Think of a leader you admire or who has created an environment where you felt included and thrived. Reflect on the qualities of this leader and how they created this environment. Do you think this inclusive culture worked just for you or also worked for all members of the group? Learning from this leader, how might you create inclusive conditions for others, regardless of whether or not you are in an official leadership position?

NOTES

1. Mike Robbins, "Bring Your Whole Self to Work," TEDxBerkeley, March 26, 2015, https://www.youtube.com/watch?v=bd2WKQWG_Dg.

2. Tara Brach, "Radical Compassion Part 2: Loving Ourselves and Our World into Healing," *Tara Brach* podcast, December 13, 2019.

3. Katherine Phillips, "How Diversity Makes Us Smarter," *Scientific American*, October 1, 2014, accessed May 10, 2021, https://www.scientificamerican.com/article/how-diversity-makes-us-smarter/.

4. Phillips, "How Diversity Makes Us Smarter."

5. David A. Thomas and Robin J. Ely, "Making Differences Matter: A New Paradigm for Managing Diversity," *Harvard Business Review*, September-October 1996, accessed March 17, 2021, https://hbr.org/1996/09/making-differences-matter-a-new-paradigm-for-managing-diversity.

6. Cedric Herring and Loren Henderson, *Diversity in Organizations: A Critical Examination* (New York: Routledge, 2015), 15–17.

7. Herring and Henderson, *Diversity in Organizations*, 24.

8. Sara Ahmed, *On Being Included: Racism and Diversity in Institutional Life* (Durham, NC: Duke University Press, 2012).

9. Monisha Kapila, Ericka Hines, and Martha Searby, "Why Diversity, Equity, and Inclusion Matter," Independent Sector, October 6, 2016, accessed May 10, 2021, https://independentsector.org/resource/why-diversity-equity-and-inclusion-matter/.

10. Herring and Henderson, *Diversity in Organizations*, 13.

11. Helen Wong and June Ying Yee, *An Anti-Oppression Framework for Child Welfare in Ontario* (Toronto: Ontario Association of Children's Aid Societies, 2010), 6.

12. Jeff Karabanow and Ted Naylor, "Using Art to Tell Stories and Build Safe Spaces: Transforming Academic Research into Action," *Canadian Journal of Community Mental Health* 34, no. 3 (2015): 67–85.

13. Lynn Shore et al., "Inclusion and Diversity in Work Groups: A Review and Model for Future Research," *Journal of Management* 37, no. 4 (2010): 1262–89; Lynn Shore, Jeanette N. Cleveland, and Diana Sanchez, "Inclusive

Workplaces: A Review and Model," *Human Resource Management Review* 28, no. 2 (2018): 176–89.

14. Vernā Myers, "Diversity and Inclusion Training," VernaMyers.com, accessed June 7, 2021, https://www.vernamyers.com/.

15. Melanie Dunn, "Stop Telling Women They Must Change Themselves to Become Leaders," *Globe and Mail*, March 2, 2019, accessed May 10, 2021, https://www.theglobeandmail.com/business/careers/leadership/article-stop-telling-women-they-must-change-themselves-to-become-leaders/.

16. Tomas Chamorro-Premuzic, "Why Do So Many Incompetent Men Become Leaders," *Harvard Business Review*, August 22, 2013, accessed May 14, 2021, https://hbr.org/2013/08/why-do-so-many-incompetent-men.

17. Sophia Lee, "Culture Fit: What You Need to Know," *Culture Amp*, accessed May 10, 2021, https://www.cultureamp.com/blog/culture-fit-what-you-need-to-know/.

18. Kristen Lester, dir., *Purl* (PixarSparkShorts, 2018).

19. Amy Edmondson, *The Fearless Organization: Creating Psychological Safety in the Workplace for Learning, Innovation, and Growth* (Hoboken, NJ: John Wiley & Sons, 2018), 22, 69.

20. *HBR Idea Cast*, "Creating Psychological Safety in the Workplace," episode 666, February 12, 2019, https://hbr.org/podcast/2019/01/creating-psychological-safety-in-the-workplace.

21. Edmondson, *Fearless Organization,* 201–2.

22. Jeffrey Liker, *The Toyota Way: 14 Management Principles from the World's Greatest Manufacturer* (New York: McGraw-Hill, 2005).

23. Kathleen Buse, Ruth Sessler Bernstein, and Dina Bilimoria, "The Influence of Board Diversity, Board Diversity Policies and Practices, and Board Inclusion Behaviors on Nonprofit Governance Practices," *Journal of Business Ethics* 133, no. 1 (2016): 179–91; Will Hammonds and Lakhbir Bhandal, "Where to Next for Diversity? An Assessment of Arts Council England's Race Equality and Cultural Diversity Policies and Emerging Trends," *Journal of Policy Research in Tourism, Leisure and Event*s 3, no. 2 (2011): 187–200; Quinetta Roberson, "Disentangling the Meanings of Diversity and Inclusion in Organizations," *Group & Organization Management* 31, no. 2 (2006): 212–36.

24. Jennifer Brown, *How to Be an Inclusive Leader: Your Role in Creating Cultures of Belonging Where Everyone Can Thrive* (San Francisco: Berrett-Koehler, 2019), 7.

25. Juliet Bourke and Andrea Titus, "The Key to Inclusive Leadership," *Harvard Business Review*, March 6, 2020, accessed May 10, 2021, https://hbr.org/2020/03/the-key-to-inclusive-leadership.

26. Priya Parker, "3 Steps to Turn Everyday Get-Togethers into Transformative Gatherings," TED2019, April 2019, https://www.ted.com/talks/priya_parker_3_steps_to_turn_everyday_get_togethers_into_transformative_gatherings?language=en.

27. Allied Media Projects, "Vision," accessed May 14, 2021, https://alliedmedia.org/about.

28. Design Justice Network, "Design Justice Network Principles," Summer 2018, accessed June 8, 2020, https://designjustice.org/read-the-principles.

29. Sasha Costanza-Chock, *Design Justice: Community Led Practices to Build the Worlds We Need* (Cambridge, MA: MIT Press, 2020), 42, 40.

30. Costanza-Chock, *Design Justice*, 19.

31. Costanza-Chock, *Design Justice*, 26.

32. Anne Zbitnew, with Kim Fullerton, Lenore McMillan, and Fran Odette, *Accessibility Toolkit: Guide to Making Art Spaces Accessible*, https://tangledarts.org/wp-content/uploads/2018/10/Accessibility_Toolkit-1.pdf.

33. Center for Excellence in Universal Design, "What Is Universal Design," accessed May 14, 2021, http://universaldesign.ie/What-is-Universal-Design/.

34. Elise Roy, "When We Design for Disability, We All Benefit," TEDxMidAdlantic, September 2015, https://www.ted.com/talks/elise_roy_when_we_design_for_disability_we_all_benefit?language=en.

35. Pam Belluck, "Chilly at Work? Office Formula Was Devised for Men," *New York Times*, August 3, 2015, https://www.nytimes.com/2015/08/04/science/chilly-at-work-a-decades-old-formula-may-be-to-blame.html.

36. Austin Tichenor, "Elizabethan Theater Etiquette and Audience Expectations Today," Folger Shakespeare Library, September 25, 2018, accessed May 14, 2021, https://shakespeareandbeyond.folger.edu/2018/09/25/elizabethan-theater-etiquette-audience-expectations/.

37. Aimi Hamraie, *Building Access: Universal Design and the Politics of Disability* (Minneapolis: University of Minnesota Press, 2017), 5, 7.

38. Hamraie, *Building Access*, 3.

39. Hamraie, *Building Access*, 11.

40. Alan F. Newell, et al., "User-Sensitive Inclusive Design," *Universal Access in the Information Society* 10, no. 3 (2011): 235–43.

41. Newell, et al., "User-Sensitive Inclusive Design," 12.

42. Piepzna-Samarasinha, *Care Work*, 232, 75.

43. Food Project, "What We Do" and "Our Vision," accessed June 7, 2021, https://thefoodproject.org/who-we-are/.

44. Roots to Harvest, "S.H.O.W. Program," accessed June 7, 2021, http://www.rootstoharvest.org/show-program.html.

45. Erin Beagle, personal interview, June 2021.

REFERENCES AND FURTHER READING

Sara Ahmed, *On Being Included: Racism and Diversity in Institutional Life* (Durham, NC: Duke University Press, 2012). Diversity has become a buzzword, often used by organizations in celebratory ways. Ahmed traces the ways that inequality still exists and how the celebration of diversity is often used to mask this inequality. Through interviews with diversity practitioners in higher education, Ahmed investigates the possibilities and challenges of doing meaningful diversity work within organizations.

Jennifer Brown, *How to Be an Inclusive Leader* (San Francisco: Berrett-Koehler, 2019). Focusing on workplace environments, Brown suggests how leaders can engage diversity through the Inclusive Leader Continuum. Brown suggests that the qualities associated with inclusive leadership can be utilized by everyone, not only those in management positions.

Eli Clare, *Brilliant Imperfection: Grappling with Cure* (Durham, NC: Duke University Press, 2017). Disability has historically been conceived of as a deficit or a problem to be cured. Eli Clare investigates the complexity of the relationship between the body and the mind, moving past either an anti-cure politics or a pro-cure worldview in investigating diverse stories, spanning from disability stereotypes to weight loss surgery, gender transition to skin lightening creams.

Sasha Costanza-Chock, *Design Justice: Community-Led Practices to Build the Worlds We Need* (Cambridge, MA: MIT Press, 2020). Exploring the relationships between design, power, and social justice, Sasha Costanza-Chock explores the concept of design justice, which challenges structural inequality through cocreation with marginalized communities in order to build a better world.

Aimi Hamraie, *Building Access: Universal Design and the Politics of Disability* (Minneapolis: University of Minnesota Press, 2017). Hamraie's book offers a critical account and history of universal design. This book "investigates twentieth-century strategies for designing the world with disability in mind," rather than assuming that universal design is common sense or the same as good design for everyone.

Anne Zbitnew, with Kim Fullerton, Lenore McMillan, and Fran Odette, *Accessibility Toolkit: Guide to Making Art Spaces Accessible*, https://tangledarts.org/wp-content/uploads/2018/10/Accessibility_Toolkit-1.pdf. This toolkit provides definitions and concepts of disability, including the medical model and the social model. Focusing on the art world, the *Accessibility Toolkit* provides practical considerations for making art exhibits accessible, including exhibition content, label design and text, lighting, image description, audio description, transcription and captioning, language usage, and access symbols.

6
Love

■ ■ ■

"If you can't love yourself, how in the hell are you going to love anyone else?" This phrase concludes every episode of the television show *RuPaul's Drag Race*, where host and drag queen RuPaul implores contestants and by extension the audience to commit to self-love. RuPaul raises an important provocation: can we love others if we don't love ourselves first?

In the *New York Times*, cultural critic and journalist Jenna Wortham discusses the positive impact she sees *Drag Race* having on society, "challenging norms and making space for people to be themselves, whatever that means to them." *Drag Race* has raised the visibility of drag as an art and performance form in the LGBTQ+ community, and has also raised the visibility and acceptance of LGBTQ+ issues more broadly. One way *Drag Race* has been able to do this is through the positive celebration of being who you are. Wortham discusses the impact of the TV show on her, personally, as it "has taught me a lot about how to form community, to take myself less seriously and lose some ego."[1]

These qualities that Wortham names here—humility and connecting with others—correspond well with the major components of care outlined in this book. At the same time, as we close this book here with a final chapter on love, we also want to find a balance between caring for others and centering ourselves and loving ourselves, and between humility and retaining our core selves.

SELF-CARE AND CENTERING THE SELF

We started our exploration of care in chapter 1 with an examination of the self in relation to others. Much of contemporary capitalistic culture stresses individualism, independence, and self-reliance. In this light, thinking about care as a relational quality, prioritizing relationships, and investing in care as an action are antidotes to an overly individualistic and competitive culture. At the same time, we don't want to lose our sense of self or see ourselves exclusively in relation to others. Here we need to find a sense of balance: the self in response and in relation to others, yet still an intact and whole sense of self. Only thinking of others can result in self-sacrifice, leading to burnout and resentment. In chapter 1, we examined the ways that care has been historically gendered, divided, and devalued. As such, women and people from historically marginalized communities, for example, people of color, the LGBTQ+ community, and people with disabilities have been allocated care work and have had to care for themselves, even if this work has not also been seen as "work." We need to counter the expectation that some groups of people should self-sacrifice and put others first and themselves last. Instead, we need to work toward a culture where care is celebrated as the foundational engine that allows everyone to survive and thrive—a culture that acknowledges that everyone needs care, receives care, and provides care.

One easy way to picture this concept is the airplane oxygen mask: on an airplane, you are instructed that, in case of emergency, you need to put your own oxygen mask on before you are able to assist others with theirs. How are you going to help anyone if you can't take care of yourself or survive? In everyday life, we need to make sure that we are taking care of ourselves alongside investing and committing to causes and other people. These two ideas don't need to be mutually exclusive, but each person needs to find a balance between attending to the self and attending to others. At times, it's important to say no to requests from others, set boundaries, and reflect on one's own capacity, wants, needs, and desires.

In her talk "Decolonizing Our Creativity," holistic health, antiharm, wellness, and consent educator Chloe Kirlew, who works as the "The ReiQueer," discusses how Western capitalistic and colonial views reduce the value and worth of individuals to their productivity and output. In opposition to these views, Kirlew highlights the value of rest as a radical act of resistance, and that daydreaming and visualization can be self-care tools. In opposition to a narrow and isolated view of the self, Kirlew places the self and self-care in dialogue with community and community care.[2] Looking to Indigenous worldviews and knowledge, Kirlew suggests that the health and wellbeing of the individual is connected to the health and wellbeing of the community. As such, we need to find ways to prioritize self and wellbeing, outside of productivity and output, so that we can both care for ourselves and care for our communities (see figure 6.1). Kirlew explains that the Care Continuum describes a practice of community care that is not a hard line with a start and end point, but a continued circle that involves self-care and community care as two parts of the same process. She explains, "Community care practices have been intentionally disrupted and attempted to be severed by white supremacy,

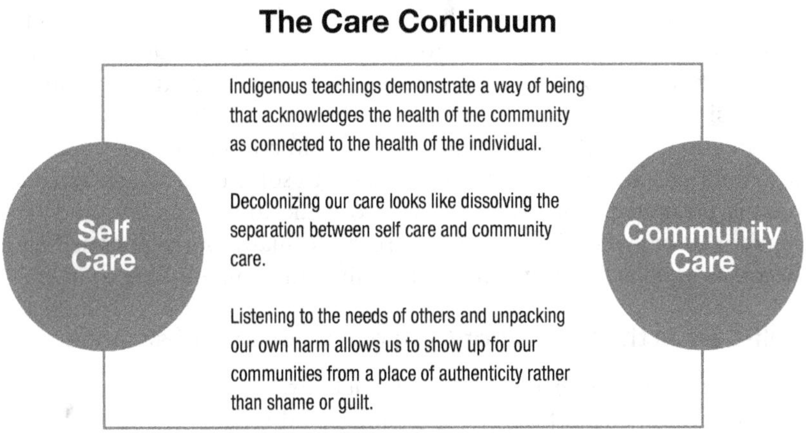

The Care Continuum

Self Care

Indigenous teachings demonstrate a way of being that acknowledges the health of the community as connected to the health of the individual.

Decolonizing our care looks like dissolving the separation between self care and community care.

Listening to the needs of others and unpacking our own harm allows us to show up for our communities from a place of authenticity rather than shame or guilt.

Community Care

Figure 6.1 The Care Continuum

Courtesy of Chloe Kirlew-Geddes "The ReiQueer," @thereiqueer, www.thereiqueer.com

[which] impacted people's ability to feel worthy of an abundance of support and care—thus also interrupting the natural ability for people to extend these gifts of love to community members and loved ones."

In recent years, we've heard a lot about the idea of self-care. In an article for the *Baffler*, journalist Laurie Penny critiques the rise of self-care, as much of this idea has been directed toward individualism at the expense of social and collective action. Self-care is just that—a focus on the self—and has become a "modern mania for clean eating, healthy living, personal productivity, and 'radical self-love'—the insistence that, in spite of all evidence to the contrary, we can achieve a meaningful existence by maintaining a positive outlook, following our bliss, and doing a few hamstring stretches as the planet burns."[3] In this version of "self-care," if something is wrong, it's up to you to fix your life, and by extension, if something is wrong, there is no one to blame other than yourself. While personal responsibility and accountability are important, persistent messages of self-care can ignore inequality and structural barriers and suggest that challenges are only individual problems, ignoring broader social issues.

Discussing how self-care can sometimes be very self-centered and self-focused in a negative way, Penny writes, "Anxious millennials now seem to have a choice between desperate narcissism and crushing misery." There are many reasons why the world might make individuals feel anxious these days, including environmental, economic, social, and political conflicts. An emphasis on self and self-care might not provide adequate tools for meaningfully intervening in these sources of anxiety, or actually feeling well or whole. We can ask the questions: What kinds of emotional labor are needed for a positive attitude? Does this emotional labor mask and sublimate problems instead of acknowledging or addressing root causes?

In addition to this individualistic outlook, critiques of self-care have also noticed some of the costs associated with some of the ways that self-care is promoted. For example, yoga, organic foods, candles, and face masks can be expensive and out of reach to many. Sometimes self-care becomes another form of consumerism instead of an antidote to it.

Self-Care in the Context of Marginalization and Resistance

At the same time, in her article, Penny acknowledges the important role that a popular form of self-care, yoga, has had in her own life. Self-care practices can and should feel good. Often, Penny writes, the work of "self-care and mutual care that keeps hope alive and health possible" is devalued as women's work or inferior to other kinds of social organizing or collective action. In contrast to this devaluation, in her book *Pleasure Activism: The Politics of Feeling Good*, adrienne maree brown defines pleasure as a "feeling of happy satisfaction and enjoyment." In this vein, "pleasure activism is the work we do to reclaim our whole, happy, and satisfiable selves from the impacts, delusions, and limitations of oppression and/or supremacy. Pleasure activism asserts that we all need and deserve pleasure and that our social structures must reflect this. In this moment, we must prioritize the pleasure of those more impacted by oppression."[4] According to brown, feeling good is a worthy goal to pursue, and we must also recognize pleasure is not equally available to all: experiences of oppression make self-care and pleasure all the more vital.

Though self-care has become a popular contemporary phrase, it's also important to look at some previous, deeper discussions of caring for the self. In 1988, Black feminist and poet Audre Lorde published a collection of essays called *A Burst of Light*. The titular essay, "A Burst of Light: Living with Cancer," is Lorde's journal reflection on her process of being diagnosed and living with liver cancer. In this context, self-care is about physical survival, both in the context of health challenges and in the context of experiencing marginalization and oppression as a Black queer woman. Lorde's now famous proclamation from this essay is that "caring for myself is not self-indulgence, it is self-preservation, and that is an act of political warfare."[5]

In her reflective essay, Lorde makes explicit links between these two contexts of health and of marginalization, declaring, "Racism. Cancer. In both cases, to win the aggressor must conquer, but the resisters need only survive. How do I define that survival and on whose terms?"[6] Through her essay, Lorde articulates survival on her own terms, choosing resistance and also joy. Part of Lorde's resistance is self-education and never resorting to fatalism that the status quo is unchangeable:

> But attending my own health, gaining enough information to help me understand and participate in the decisions made about my body by people who know more medicine than I do, are all crucial strategies in my battle for living. They also provide me with important prototypes for doing battle in all other arenas of my life. Battling racism and battling heterosexism and battling apartheid share the same urgency inside me as battling cancer. None of these struggles are ever easy, and even the smallest victory is never to be taken for granted. Each victory must be applauded, because it is so easy not to battle at all, to just accept and call that acceptance inevitable.[7]

For Lorde, resistance, survival, and caring for the self are also commitments to creativity, to working, to teaching and mentoring others. Through her journals, Lorde chronicles her activities of developing a small press to publish women's writing, traveling to give speeches and foster international solidarity among Black women, and leading a meaningful life, on her own terms. She concludes "A Burst of Life" by remarking, "I work, I love, I rest, I see and learn. And I report," showcasing commitment to relate to others, to take care of the self, and to do good work.[8]

In her book *Living a Feminist Life*, Sara Ahmed chronicles the often difficult work of speaking up to point out problems related to inequality, which can result in being labelled a "killjoy." Ahmed reclaims this label and the importance of speaking up, and writes a "killjoy survival kit" to bring self-care to these challenges. Items in Ahmed's survival kit include books, favorite objects, taking time, enjoying life, laughing, and finding community. Here, Ahmed traces Lorde's influence through her lived example, in particular in *A Burst of Light*. Ahmed draws attention to a documentary film about Lorde's time teaching and living abroad called *The Berlin Years*, which closes with images of Lorde dancing, enjoying life, "sequences that seem to capture so well the generosity of her black feminist spirit."[9]

Ahmed chronicles that in queer, feminist, and antiracist work, "self-care is about the creation of community," highlighting the relational qualities of self-care and looking out for one another, as the impact of protesting can be difficult. In this vein, Ahmed's survival toolkit includes celebrating and staying with the beauty of life, including the natural world, friends, and pleasure: "being a killjoy is too occupying, if it takes you away from the worlds you are in; the rise and fall of the sun, the way the trees are angled like that, the smile of a friend when you share a joke, the cold fresh water; the feel of the sea as an immersion; the familiar smells of spices cooking."[10] Ahmed also comments on the joy of animals in her life, including riding a horse in her youth, and her beloved dog, Poppy. This joy in life and prioritizing self-care counters the unflattering, external "killjoy" label, which often perpetuates a strident, unfun, unloving stereotype of feminists. Ahmed's reclaimed killjoy figure speaks up because she loves life and wants equality, not because she hates fun.

With these contexts in mind, we can reformulate an enlarged and socially engaged definition of self-care. *Caring for Yourself Is a Radical Act* is a self-care guide oriented to youth workers, but it has broad applicability outside of this particular employment pathway. At the same time, this guide describes the particular context of this job, which is "often underpaid and undervalued with high amounts of stress and trauma."[11] This experience of stress and trauma is also applicable in the context of the ongoing realities of structural inequality and marginalization, and in this context, anchoring the self through self-care for survival and resistance is important. In *Caring for Yourself Is a Radical Act*, self-care is defined as

> creating and maintaining practices that help you sustain your energy and spirit in whatever life path you choose. It also makes you a better friend, community member, lover, partner, and caregiver. When you give to others but neglect yourself, feelings of resentment can arise because you sacrifice your own needs. Taking care of yourself allows you to enjoy time with others while also sustaining yourself. Self-care is not selfish. Self-care is being intentional with your day to reflect, nurture your body, remember your heart, grieve your sorrows and attend to your daily needs.[12]

At the end of this chapter, you will be invited to reflect on what practices you can create and maintain to sustaining yourself, so you can enjoy your time with others while also nurturing yourself and your communities.

SELF-CARE AND LESS IS MORE

Let's return to Penny's proposition that young people today are faced with the options of narcissism (too much of a focus on the self, often enabled by social media) or misery (being paralyzed by despair that the world is a bad place and there is nothing to do to make it better). How can self-care expand these options and enable us to engage in the types of activities that fulfill us and contribute to society? The goal is to think about taking care of the self so that we can show up and engage with the world, not retreat from the world. An expanded definition of care, discussed in this book, can offer an alternative option beyond either narcissism or misery.

It's important to note that self-care might not always immediately feel "good." Examples of self-care might include going to bed at a decent time instead of staying up scrolling through social media; eating nourishing foods; staying in and resting; exercise that focuses on enjoying movement; talking with friends and loved ones. In the first example, it might be more immediately pleasurable to look at your phone than to go to sleep, but we know that prioritizing sleep is a better practice in the larger scheme of things. Our always-busy, always-on culture does not necessarily encourage rest and relaxation as a daily, ordinary practice. Instead, we go hard when we go out, sometimes travel across the world to take a vacation, expect each other to immediately respond to email and texts, fill up spare time with more work, and otherwise operate at a frenetic, overdrive pace. In this context, self-care can feel like going against the grain, perhaps doing less rather than doing more.

You can also see in the above list that one example of self-care is talking with friends and loved ones. Being with others is also a way to take care of ourselves. Self-care doesn't mean we have to isolate or exist apart from our relationships. At the same time, we can question whether or not our relationships with others are mutually supportive and relational. It can be difficult to do, but it is sometimes needed to set boundaries, say no, or take time for yourself.

RADICAL SELF-LOVE

What would the world look like if every person was able to love their bodies and every body was celebrated as beautiful and worthy, just the way it is? What products would or would not be for sale on drugstore shelves? Who would we see on TV and in movies and in the media? What would you eat? Who would you love? How would you spend your time? You can see from this broad list of questions that the seemingly simple concept of loving your body opens up a world of possibilities of ways of living—ways that might be more grounded and whole than what is currently dominant in our society.

In her book *The Body Is Not an Apology*, activist and poet Sonya Renee Taylor hones in on the concept of body shame and how so many people have been taught to feel shame about their bodies. She discusses that bodies have been the targets and objects of oppression, whether through racism, sexism, homophobia, transphobia, religious persecution, or ableism. These forms of hate are experienced and internalized in people's bodies. We also live in a world where media and culture deliver repeated images that thin, white, cisgender able-bodied bodies are a norm and ideal. To counter this toxic and harmful environment of internalized body shame, Taylor suggests we first work on our relationships with our own bodies. Rather than just "accepting" ourselves, Taylor suggests striving toward radical self-love. She writes, "A radical self-love world is a world that works for every body. Creating such a world is an inside-out job. How we value and honor our own bodies impacts how we value and honor the bodies of others."[13] Radical self-love is an ongoing journey and process of learning love and unlearning toxicity. Taylor suggests that this journey be guided by what she terms the "three peaces":

1. Make peace with not understanding: accepting there are things and people that we don't know about, rather than fearing the unknown.
2. Make peace with difference: striving to cultivate a "difference-celebrating" culture, recognizing the joy of different ways of being.
3. Make peace with your body: unlearning internalized body shame.

On the surface, these three concepts or types of peace might seem straightforward or easy to accept, but Taylor acknowledges that these three guiding principles can be difficult and need ongoing work. In this process, Taylor suggests compassion for the self, as the broader culture does not suggest we "make peace" in the ways she outlines: for example, the diet and beauty industries thrive and profit from ongoing messages that we fix or change or bodies, rather than love ourselves the way we are at the present moment. To this end, Taylor accompanies her three peaces with four pillars of practice to take practical steps toward realizing these objectives (table 6.1).

Table 6.1 Four Pillars of Practice for Radical Self-Love

Element	*Explanation*
Taking out the Toxic	Avoiding negative media messages and interrupting negative self-talk
Mind Matters	Developing new thought patterns and self-affirmations
Unapologetic Action	Moving, being physical, and loving your body
Collective Compassion	Being with others who support you and being kind and patient with yourself on your journey

Adapted from Taylor, *The Body Is Not an Apology*.

These four pillars of practice suggest intentionality alongside kindness toward the self. Even the first pillar, avoiding negative media messages, could require a big shift in which films, television shows, magazines, or games we consume. Change can to be difficult, but the end goal here is liberation: to love oneself and to be able to more truly love others. In the profile below, we learn about a short documentary film called *#LoveYourz*, which profiles one group of teens' efforts to develop healthy self-love.

#LOVEYOURZ, DIRECTED BY NICK BENTGEN

#LoveYourz started as a small Facebook group, a place for teens to support each other and encourage self-love and creativity. Directed by Nick Bentgen, the *#LoveYourz* short documentary film profiles Black youth from New York who have spearheaded a positivity and affirmation movement among themselves. Collectively, these youth speak to contemporary coming-of-age struggles and realities: family conflict, living in New York, fear of failure, killing and the Black Lives Matter movement, coming out as gay, finding authentic gender expressions, low-self esteem, among other pressing and complex issues.

The initial Facebook group and #LoveYourz movement was sparked by a simple post, asking: "who thinks they're ugly?"[14] Feelings of discomfort and body shame are broad experiences but can be particularly acute for people and communities that face oppression and marginalization. In this context, the affirmation of the #LoveYourz movement is particularly powerful. The *#LoveYourz* film profiles teens doing average teen stuff, like hanging out, talking, skateboarding, and rapping, while being interviewed about their experiences and perspectives on their lived realities. The creativity of these teens shines through. Commenting about the group, one teen in the film says, "Everybody's so expressive, everybody's so artistic, they're writing it down, or painting it, or rapping or singing it." Creative projects and goals include skateboarding, modelling, poetry, photography, art, recording music, drawing, painting, and designing clothing lines. The #LoveYourz group helps support these ambitions. In the words of the teens in the film, #LoveYourz is "good energy," a space where "people can feel love and just be," where "you cannot make anyone feel alienated or isolated."

What is particularly notable is the kindness and affirmation that the teens in the film show one another—notable in particular because youth can sometimes be portrayed as a time of friendship conflict, pettiness, and meanness. Instead, in the film when one teen receives a breakup text and says they want to go home and cry, one friend encourages the group,

"Guys, group hug," supporting the friend who is hurting. In another scene, a group of teens are hanging out in a park, rapping. When one youth stumbles and loses his flow, his friends chime in to set him back on track, reassuring him that it's okay and that he should keep going. Often broader societal messages do not offer this kind of affirmation, in particular to Black youth, and these teens show that they have developed the awareness of the importance of nonjudgement in friendship. Hanging out might seem like a simple or ordinary thing, but affirming spaces and friends can be an essential component of loving ourselves, being creative, and persevering in the face of challenges. As one teen in the film says, "People assume teenagers running around just get into a bunch of mischief. Honestly, we didn't know where we would go, and because of each other now we all have a common journey."

FEELINGS

When we work toward investing ourselves in caring more, feelings will arise. Alongside feelings like joy and fulfillment we might experience feelings like resentment, anger, frustration, sadness, confusion, cynicism, despair—or whatever else comes up for you. It's important to note that these emotions might not be positive ones: caring might make you feel bad. Still, making space for feelings is part of moving toward a more relational concept of self. As discussed in chapter 4, in many contexts, our rational, cognitive, thinking selves are most valorized. A whole self is made up of many components, including an emotional self, and making space for others to bring their whole selves can begin internally, making space for our whole selves, and our feelings, including hard or bad feelings.

At the same time, though the world is often full of turmoil and strife, it's okay to feel okay, even through times of societal grief or despair. In an interview at the beginning of the COVID-19 pandemic in 2020, adrienne maree brown, author of *Pleasure Activism*, speaks to finding joy even in difficult times. brown says that joy is found through connecting with others and making space for grief and fear, rather than avoiding these feelings, and that joy and sorrow can sometimes be parallel emotional states. She gives the example of coming together with family members through COVID-19 to have needed but difficult conversations, about how death would be handled and who would take care of the children in the family. brown stresses intentionality and being on purpose and facing these fears, and feeling good after these intense conversations. Joy can come from a sense of being alive, based on finding a sense of agency.[15]

In her blog post "If You're Good, Say You're Good," brown acknowledges the difficulty of wellbeing during times of crisis, like the COVID-19 pandemic, and acknowledges the hard work in takes to feel good: "Whatever you have done to get to a good place right now took labor—spiritual, mental, emotional . . . and probably physical."[16] Feeling good doesn't need to be based in willful ignorance of the world. Instead, feeling good "doesn't negate reality, it weaves your reality into the fabric of this complex time." Rather than avoiding speaking about feeling well, brown suggests that speaking about wellness creates more possibility for support and mutual aid, and enables others to ask us for help. brown also advocates for sharing the practices that enable wellness, offering her own examples, including music playlists, meditation, reducing her belongings, drinking more water, and redirecting time to reading rather than social media. She characterizes all of these practices as "learned behaviors," given that dominant norms often do not direct us to take care of ourselves in meaningful ways.

Love and Ethics of Care

When we discuss love and self-care here in the context of an ethics of care, we are positioning love as an active process, taking care of and centering the self alongside being responsive and in relationships with others. Indeed, in her discussion of love in *All About Love*, bell hooks suggests that "the word 'love' is most often defined as a noun, yet . . . we would all love better if we used it as a verb," suggesting love as an action. "To begin by always thinking of love as an action rather than a feeling is one way in which anyone using the word in this manner automatically assumes accountability and responsibility," she writes.[17]

While love can be a powerful, active force, we also need to make space for feelings as we discuss love and an ethics of care that is grounded in a whole self. In many contexts, feelings are often denigrated or unwelcome. hooks acknowledges, "We are often taught we have no control over our 'feelings,'" highlighting the societal message that feelings can be irrational and disruptive.[18] Feelings can be denigrated because they are associated with feminine qualities and are hence devalued. In *Living a Feminist Life*, Sara Ahmed repositions feelings to be a source of strength rather than a problem to constrict, bury, or numb. She writes, "Our emotions can be a resource; we draw on them. To be a killjoy is often to be assigned as being emotional, too emotional; letting your feelings get in the way of your judgement." In this context, "your feelings can be a site of rebellion," as feelings can also galvanize action, speaking up, and striving for equality.[19]

Discussing philosophic traditions, philosophy professor Anthony Weston notes that "the formal tradition in ethics . . . does not speak much of love."[20] Love can be expressed in many ways, but it is also a feeling, and the philosophy of ethics, or theories of how moral principles guide behavior and action, has highlighted judgement and rationality, not feeling or intuition. An ethics of care has a different orientation to feelings than other philosophic traditions. This difference is also based in the relational understanding of identity or being (also known as ontology), as discussed in chapter 1. In her book *Caring: A Relational Approach to Ethics and Moral Education*, Nel Noddings provides an overview of these differences, stating, "Taking relation as ontologically basic simply means that we recognize human encounter and affective response as a basic fact of human existence."[21] With the reference to "affective response," Noddings foregrounds affect or emotion as an essential fact of humans as they relate to one another. This relational, affective concept of self differs from an individual, isolated concept of self; Noddings suggests that the basic human affect of a relational self is joy, whereas the affect of the individual, isolated self can be anguish and emptiness. An ethic of care starts from this place of relational joy, and the experience of this relational joy can further strengthen the commitment to care: "it is the recognition of and longing for relatedness that form the foundation of our ethic, and the joy that accompanies fulfilment of our caring enhances our commitment to the ethical ideal that sustains us."[22]

As suggested from the subtitle of her book, Noddings applies this understanding of ethics of care to the educational space, suggesting that care and support nurture lifelong learning. While most education is oriented around learners absorbing content, Noddings suggests forming supportive and relational bonds between teacher and learner is the most important component of education, and that the content that needs to be learned can flow from this established relationality. As such, Noddings brings love and care into a space that has become dominated by mastery of content.

This framework of ethics of care for education is similar to **critical pedagogy**, which is a framework that suggests teaching and learning are important components of striving toward a more just society. Paulo Freire is often named as a key thinker in what we term critical pedagogy, and in his foundational text *Pedagogy of the Oppressed*, he infuses education with love. His vision of critical pedagogy is defined as a process of humanization, or striving to become a more fully realized and free self, which has particular salience for marginalized and historically oppressed people and communities. For Freire, critical pedagogy and humanization is based in a problem-posing methodology through dialogue, in which learners investigate critical questions that impact their lived realities, rather than what he terms the banking model of education, in which an expert teacher "deposits" knowledge into a learner, which can be a vehicle for domination and disempowerment. Though historical, political, and social conditions have created oppression, Freire centers this process of learning and unlearning in love: "because love is an act of courage, not of fear, love is a commitment to others. No matter where the oppressed are found, the act of love is commitment to their cause—the cause of liberation. . . . If I do not love the world—if I do not love life—if I do not love people—I cannot enter into dialogue."[23] Here love is a way of being in the world, being in dialogue, and committing to other people.

Critical pedagogy views education as a lifelong process that happens in many contexts, not solely in classrooms with children and youth. That said, classroom learning remains a key site of education. In the Freirian tradition, bell hooks reflects on herself as a classroom educator and on bringing love into this space. Love and feelings are sometimes not wanted in education, and to be clear, in the unfortunate but real context of abuse of power and sexual violence, love in education can sometimes have unwelcome overtones. hooks positions love in the context of care and loving students by caring for their learning. With a foundation of love, true learning can take place (rather than just absorption of content), as learning can involve vulnerability and growth that needs support:

> Teachers who extended care and respect that is a component of love make it possible for students to address their fears openly and to receive affirmation and support. Contrary to the notion that love in the classroom makes teachers less objective, when we teach with love we are better able to respond to the unique concerns of individual students while simultaneously integrating those of the classroom community. When teachers work to affirm the emotional wellbeing of students we are doing the work of love.[24]

Teachers may be in a particular position to affirm the emotional wellbeing of others, but we can further consider how we can do the work of love in our own contexts, regardless of our roles or profession. We need to understand that this kind of affirmation of the self and others is work, but this can be joyful and necessary work. This work starts with acknowledging that emotional wellbeing is a necessary and needed foundation for everyone, including ourselves, and requires attention and commitment to foster. While reading the following profile of an organization called H.O.L.L.A! (How Our Lives All Link Together), reflect on how prioritizing love and healing, for ourselves and for others, is a potent pathway to personal and societal transformation.

H.O.L.L.A!—HOW OUR LIVES LINK ALTOGETHER: "HEALING JUSTICE IS OUR STRATEGY / RESPONDING TO HISTORICAL TRAGEDY"

In his "Healing Justice Is Our Strategy" spoken word piece, H.O.L.L.A! cofounder Cory Greene opens by asking "we came to heal, what you came to do / We came to build, what you came to do?"[25] These pressing questions of healing and building suggest that the internal work of restoring one's self is a first step to building a better, more just, and more inclusive world.

H.O.L.L.A! is a nonprofit organization focused on empowering youth of color to understand themselves as embedded in systems of oppression that affect their everyday realities. H.O.L.L.A! engages youth in learning about tools for healing, which is deeply rooted in ancestry and grassroots movements that have fought back against oppression, using these teachings to help in the fight for freedom. This internal, healing work happens in a historical context, with an understanding of the legacy and ongoing realities of white supremacy, structural violence, mass incarceration, and police brutality.

H.O.L.L.A! as an organization was created by six Black men coming together to share their experiences and responses while incarcerated in Otisville, a New York State Correctional Facility—Marlon Peterson, Gregory "Butta Lab/Worldwide" Barnes, Thomas "Arocks" Porter, Craig "Shaq" Colston, Clifton "Bill" Hall, and Andrew "Cory" Greene—with Terrell Tate joining as the seventh cofounder outside of prison. These young men crossed paths in their individual healing journeys, including in places like parenting and anger management classes. Over time, these men developed bonds of trust and forged a collective vision to share their learnings and journeys with other young people. The healing work that this group pursued was not only individual and interpersonal, but also involved learning and studying prison organizing work, such as the Bedford Hills Sisters, the Green Haven Think Tank, the Resurrection Study Group, and the Attica Revolt. These prison movements of the 1960s, 1970s, and 1980s saw political prisoners engaging in nontraditional approaches of organizing for better living conditions and political rights. H.O.L.L.A!'s analysis of cultural and political history examines how white supremacy facilitates by mass incarceration, disproportionately affecting seven neighborhoods in New York City, the communities of Brownsville, East New York, Crown Heights, Southside/South Jamaica, Central Harlem, the Lower East Side, and the South Bronx, which disproportionately feed the New York State Prison System. While in Otisville, the cofounders of H.O.L.L.A! petitioned prison administration to be able to share their stories, experiences, and learning with youth, but it wasn't until these young men were released from prison that they were able to start the work of healing, community organizing, building their families, mentorship, and supporting young people, starting with volunteer work in local high schools in the seven neighborhoods.

For H.O.L.L.A!, healing is social and political change, and starts within and with other people, focusing on their relationships, reimagining self-love, and journeying with others through "deepening our (H.O.L.L.A!) commitments to each other, working together, throwing ourselves into resisting systems of oppression, organizing and taking care of each other."[26] This work also consists of studying history, having circles for deep reflection as well as hard conversations, and decolonizing from Eurocentric ideology. The organization says, "To sustain collective participation in social change, we need to be able to grow and build together."[27] H.O.L.L.A! works to break the cycle of intergenerational violence by first understanding root causes in historical and present-day oppression and injustice that inflict harm on individuals and perpetuate the cycle.

To do this work, H.O.L.L.A! has developed workshops, facilitates healing justice circles, and has developed its own nontraditional approach to healing-centered curriculum, called the "Youth Leadership, Transformation, and Healing Process." Named after Nat Turner, an enslaved Black preacher who led a rebellion of Black enslaved people, the first phase of this curriculum is called the "Nat Turner Revolutionary Leadership Training" and targets internal growth, learning, and healing. This six-month program is for youth thirteen to twenty-eight years old and emphasizes individuals who have been pushed out of or are unengaged by mainstream institutions. The program works with youth to build their capacity for critical social analysis through political education and socio-emotional spiritual development. The next phase of H.O.L.L.A!'s "Youth Leadership, Transformation, and Healing Process" is the "Ella Baker Sustainability, Transformation, and Organizing Portal." In this program, youth participants develop leadership skills and become "Healing Justice Organizers," learning how to facilitate healing justice circles and create spaces for others to begin their journeys of healing and learning. Youth leaders/organizers participating in the training are provided with a financial stipend for their engagement in the eighteen-month process.

H.O.L.L.A!'s nontraditional approach to healing justice circles creates a space for vulnerability and sharing through developing community agreements as well as through storytelling and creative expression, including poetry, spoken word, rapping, and singing. In the H.O.L.L.A! documentary *We Came to Heal*, one H.O.L.L.A! healing justice organizer says, "I heal through hearing other people's stories. We don't do this enough, these circles, and talking about what we've been through, and really listening." One youth participant says, "A lot of people have been through similar things as you, or [have] some sort of trauma that you connect to. Every time that you heal, every time that you open up and share your story, every time that you build with somebody, every time that you connect with your community, it leads to someone getting justice."[28] H.O.L.L.A!'s understanding of justice involves centering the individual through healing and creating positive spaces and bonds of trust. This is part of the process of resisting larger forces and structures.

On the Healing Justice Movement mixtape album called *The Report Back*, made by the Youth Organizing Committee, the track "Nat Turner" opens with the lines, "We was born into a system designed to keep us behind / But knowledge is power, keep that in mind / Pay attention to the road and the signs / You gonna shine, you gonna know when it's time."[29] This sums up H.O.L.L.A!'s work well, developing and deepening individual and collective knowledge about systems of oppression so that individuals can shine—linking our lives altogether.

For more information about H.O.L.L.A!, visit https://healwithholla.com/.

SUSTAINABLE PROSPERITY AND WELLBEING

What does it mean to live well? Often in our capitalistic society, prosperity is tied to economic prosperity and wealth, oriented around individual advancement, benchmarks, and possessions. This economic definition of prosperity can come with a cost: to the self, to the community, and to the planet. The individual cost can be burnout and exhaustion. When we are always striving for more, how do we know that we have enough? Does working assume the primary or even sole role for personal identity and activities? What other parts of the self get neglected or fall away completely? When individuals strive for individual goals of economic wealth, community and societal goals can get put on the back burner or completely fall away. And continually purchasing products brings short-term pleasure and short-term economic impact, but longer term there are environmental costs and personal costs, including lack of true fulfillment.

Discussions of **sustainable prosperity** suggest redefining living well and fully within ecological limits. In his book *Prosperity without Growth: Economics for a Finite Planet*, ecological economist Tim Jackson differentiates wellbeing from economic growth, defining prosperity to differ from economic wealth. Mobilizing political philosopher Martha Nussbaum's "capabilities approach," Jackson recuperates wellbeing at the level of human capabilities. Wellbeing can mean feeling like we have capacity and feel capable, including with life and bodily health; bodily integrity; practical reason; affiliation; play and control over one's environment.[30] These components of wellbeing exceed a simple economic definition. We need economic means to be able to take care of ourselves, but truly flourishing goes beyond economic prosperity in the capabilities approach.

This capabilities approach is also evident in the Centre for the Understanding of Sustainable Prosperity's mission statement, where Jackson is the director, which states, "People everywhere have the capability to flourish as human beings—within the ecological and resource constraints of a finite planet. A prosperous society is concerned not only with income and financial wealth, but also with the health and wellbeing of its citizens, with their access to good quality education, and with their prospects for decent and rewarding work."[31] Developing a good society can involve developing mechanisms for more people to feel more capable, rather than suggesting individuals rise and fall all on their own. The environmental component is also important to recognize, as the destruction of our natural habitat is not sustainable, and negative environmental impacts also affect individuals' capacities to flourish.

There are many different examples of what sustainable prosperity can look like in practice. Kate Oakley and Jon Ward emphasize being creative and engaging in community life in their definition of prosperity: "human flourishing is not linked to high levels of material consumption but rather the capabilities to engage with cultural and creative practices and communities."[32] Another famous example comes from the country of Bhutan, which has shifted away from economic wealth as the main definition of societal success. While a country's impact is usually measured economically through its gross domestic product or GDP, this measure has also been critiqued, as GDP includes things that have negative economic impacts and environmental costs: it is an overly broad brush that includes anything that's been paid for, including environmental cleanup after disasters and pollution, which doesn't necessarily correlate with success or advancement.

In 2008, Bhutan developed an alternative to GDP with a measure called gross national happiness, or GNH. "Happiness" might feel subjective and be difficult to measure, and Bhutan's GNH is guided by four pillars: (1) sustainable and equitable socioeconomic development, (2) environmental conservation, (3) preservation and promotion of culture, and (4) good governance. These four pillars are accompanied by nine domains of GNH: psychological wellbeing, health, time use, education, cultural diversity and resilience, good governance, community vitality, ecological diversity and resilience, and living standards.[33]

Another way of measuring and quantifying wellbeing has been developed in the Canadian context. Drawing from data from Statistics Canada, the Canadian Index of Wellbeing (CIW) uses 64 indicators in eight domains to map quality of life including community vitality, democratic engagement, education, environment, healthy populations, leisure and culture, living standards, and time use. Though "living standards" includes economic elements such as cost of living, these eight domains offer an expansive definition of wellbeing and provide a concrete example of how to discuss wellbeing that includes but goes beyond an economic framework. The 2016 CIW report, *How Are Canadians Really Doing?*, highlights a "wellbeing gap," noting a distinction and divide between growth in GDP and in CIW.[34] In short, increasing GDP does not automatically mean increasing wellbeing or quality of life; in fact, this report showcases the opposite, that increased GDP can have negative impacts on wellbeing and quality of life. These examples offer a few possible alternatives to an overreliance on economic indicators to measure success and prosperity. In the questions below, you will be encouraged to develop your own definitions of self-care, prosperity, and love.

Activity 6.1: Personal Self-Care Guide

As discussed in this chapter, self-care is an increasingly popular talking point in our society, and you may already have a well-developed self-care routine. In this final activity in this book, we will take some time to reflect on your self in the context of the past, present, and future.

Use a piece of paper of sketch some drawings in response to the following prompts, or simply reflect with journal-style writing if you prefer.

1. Goals and Values: On the top right side of the paper, identify your goals and values in the context of care. What do you care about? What actions do you want to take toward these goals and values?
2. Self: In the center of your page, draw yourself, who you are, and what makes you, you. What can you do to nurture these core parts of yourself? Is this similar or different than how you currently practice (or do not practice) self-care?
3. Collaborators: Who do you have to support you on your journey? Are there friends, family, or community members who share your identified goals and values? If so, draw them in. Are there spaces, places, or organizations you can identify that

would help support you in nurturing your core self and in realizing your goals and values? Is striving toward these places and spaces similar or different than how you currently practice (or do not practice) self-care?

QUESTIONS FOR LEARNING AND REFLECTION

1. Less Is More: In this chapter, we reviewed popular definitions of self-care that sometimes overemphasize individualism and consumerism, and then reviewed that self-care can instead mean doing less, not more. Are there parts of your life that you are able to constrict or reduce in order to practice better self-care? What barriers or opportunities exist to do less, rather than more, to practice self-care? After reviewing the discussion and definitions of self-care in this chapter, identify your own personal definition of self-care.
2. Take Space, Make Space: In this chapter, we reviewed the importance of centering the self, especially in the contexts of marginalization and devaluation of care work. Reflect on your social location in the context of intersectionality (discussed in chapter 1). Are there areas of your life where decentering your self and making space for others' voices and lived experiences could be a useful part of social change? Are there areas of your life where centering yourself more and taking up space would be a useful part of social change? Can tensions between taking space and making space in different contexts be part of a definition of love?
3. Prosperity: In this chapter, we reviewed a definition of prosperity that includes but transcends economic wealth, which often assumes primary importance in capitalist definitions of prosperity. Reflect on your personal definition of sustainable prosperity. What does being prosperous in a sustainable way mean to you, and what are the components of your definition that are not economic? Can you include nurturing these components of sustainable prosperity in your definition of self-care?
4. Love: This chapter gave an overview of how emotions and feelings can sometimes be unwelcome and have not had a lot of discussion in major philosophic discussion of ethics. What challenges and opportunities are there with bringing love into areas where love is not part of the mainstream discussion? This chapter discussed love in education—are there other fields or professions that could benefit from love?

NOTES

1. Jenna Wortham, "It's RuPaul's Moment (Can I Get an Amen?)," *New York Times*, January 26, 2018, accessed May 17, 2021, https://www.nytimes.com/2018/01/26/insider/rupaul-drag-race-cultural-influence.html.

2. Chloe Kirlew, "Decolonizing Our Creativity: Daydreaming and Visualization as Resistance," YouTube, February 23, 2021, https://www.youtube.com/watch?v=EH4dLXeRQ88&t=13s.

3. Laurie Penny, "Life-Hacks of the Poor and Aimless," *Baffler*, July 8, 2016, accessed May 5, 2021, https://thebaffler.com/war-of-nerves/laurie-penny-self-care.

4. adrienne maree brown, *Pleasure Activism: The Politics of Feeling Good* (Chico, CA: AK Press, 2019), 13.

5. Lorde, "Burst of Light," 131.

6. Lorde, "Burst of Light," 109.

7. Lorde, "Burst of Light," 114–15.

8. Lorde, "Burst of Light," 133.

9. Sara Ahmed, *Living a Feminist Life* (Durham, NC: Duke University Press, 2017), 247.

10. Ahmed, *Living a Feminist Life*, 242, 243.

11. Farrah Khan for ArtReach, *Caring for Yourself Is a Radical Act: Self-Care Guide for Youth Working in Community* (Toronto: ArtReach, n.d.), 4.

12. Khan, *Caring for Yourself*, 3.

13. Sonya Renee Taylor, *The Body Is Not an Apology* (San Francisco: Berrett-Koehler, 2018), 4–5.

14. Olwen Lynch, "The NY Teen Collective Providing IRL & URL Love," *Dazed*, September 7 2017, accessed May 20, 2021, https://www.dazeddigital.com/film-tv/article/37296/1/the-ny-teen-loveyourz-collective-providing-irl-url-love.

15. Megna Chakrabarti and Wes Martin, "adrienne maree brown on Finding Joy during the Coronavirus Crisis," WBUR.org, April 6, 2020, accessed June 8, 2021, https://www.wbur.org/onpoint/2020/04/06/finding-joy-during-coronavirus.

16. adrienne maree brown, "If You're Good, Say You're Good," adriennemareebrown.net, February 8, 2021, accessed May 21, 2021, https://adriennemareebrown.net/2021/02/08/if-youre-good-say-youre-good/.

17. hooks, *All About Love*, 13.

18. hooks, *All About Love*, 13.

19. Ahmed, *Living a Feminist Life*, 246.

20. Weston, *21st Century Ethical Toolbox*, 198.

21. Noddings, *Caring*, 4.

22. Noddings, *Caring*, 6.

23. Paulo Freire, *Pedagogy of the Oppressed*, 50th anniversary ed., trans. Myra Bergman Ramos (New York: Bloomsbury Academic, 2018), 89–90.

24. bell hooks, *Teaching Community: A Pedagogy of Hope* (New York: Routledge, 2003), 133.

25. Faolan Jones and H.O.L.L.A!, *We Came to Heal Documentary*, YouTube, June 29, 2020, https://www.youtube.com/watch?v=o1lTejZrw6Y.

26. H.O.L.L.A!, "Our History," accessed October 28, 2020, https://healwithholla.com/about-the-movement.

27. H.O.L.L.A!, "We've Build a Curriculum Tailored to Our Youth," accessed October 28, 2020, https://holla-inc.com/.

28. Jones and H.O.L.L.A!, *We Came to Heal*.

29. Y.O.C. the Youth Organizing Collective, "Nat Turner," *The Report Back* (HOLLA Music Group, 2019).

30. Tim Jackson, *Prosperity without Growth: Economics for a Finite Planet*, 2nd ed. (New York: Routledge, 2017), 46.

31. Centre for Sustainable Prosperity, "About: Vision," accessed May 19, 2021, https://www.cusp.ac.uk/about/.

32. Kate Oakley and Jon Ward, "The Art of the Good Life: Culture and Sustainable Prosperity," *Cultural Trends* 27, no. 1 (2018): 4.

33. Michael Givel, "Mahayana Buddhism and Gross National Happiness in Bhutan," *International Journal of Wellbeing* 5 (2015): 14–27.

34. Canadian Index of Wellbeing, *How Are Canadians Really Doing? The 2016 CIW National Report* (Waterloo, ON: Canadian Index of Wellbeing and University of Waterloo, 2016).

REFERENCES AND FURTHER READING

Tara Brach, *Radical Compassion: Learning to Love Yourself and Your World with the Practice of RAIN* (New York: Viking, 2019). Brach suggests that the journey toward a more inclusive society starts with looking inwardly, and with accepting and loving ourselves. Her RAIN methodology includes the steps of recognizing, accepting, investigating, and nurturing one's feelings.

bell hooks, *All About Love: New Visions* (New York: Harper Perennial, 2018). "The word 'love' is most often defined as a noun, yet . . . we would all love better if we used it as a verb," writes bell hooks. We most often define love as (heterosexual) romantic love, and overemphasize this definition of love in our society for women in particular, resulting in undue focus on being loved and romantic love in individual self-worth. In this book, hooks underlines the extreme importance of love, but repositions this word, suggesting in some ways we don't value love enough in our society. hooks suggests that love is how we care for ourselves and for our communities.

Paulo Freire, *Pedagogy of the Oppressed*, 50th anniversary ed., trans. Myra Bergman Ramos (New York: Bloomsbury Academic, 2018). Originally published in Portuguese, this book outlines a view of education that empowers individuals and communities to make sense of their experiences and the experience of marginalization and oppression, in the goal of humanization, liberation, and social change. These goals might involve struggle, but Freire suggests this process of critically learning about and unlearning dominant systems in society is an act of love.

Farrah Khan for ArtReach, *Caring for Yourself Is a Radical Act: Self-Care Guide for Youth Working in Community* (Toronto: ArtReach, n.d.). This practical toolkit offers journaling exercises and self-care practices, specifically in the context of the stress and trauma of the youth worker profession. This context of stress and trauma is important, but the strategies and information provided in this guide also have broader applicability beyond this profession.

Fariha Róisín, *Being in Your Body: A Journal for Self-Love and Body Positivity* (New York: Abrams Noterie, 2019). This illustrated journal offers prompts and space for written reflections on approaching your body with compassion, given the context of body shame and socially entrenched beauty norms, which are intensified by social media. This journal encourages cultivating confidence alongside broader definitions for beauty.

Audre Lorde, *A Burst of Light and Other Essays* (Ithaca, NY: Firebrand Books, 1988). This collection offers Lorde's insightful reflections on a range of topics, including building intersectional, international alliances, lesbian parenting, and living with cancer. The essay "A Burst of Light," Lorde's journal over a two-year period, offers incisive and critical engagement with the intertwined struggles of racism and cancer and includes the now famous proclamation, "Caring for myself is not self-indulgence, it is self-preservation, and that is an act of political warfare."

Sonya Renee Taylor, *The Body Is Not an Apology: The Power of Radical Self-Love* (San Francisco: Berrett-Koehler, 2018). In this book, Taylor argues that our contemporary culture encourages shame about our bodies through "body terrorism." Taylor provides a practical toolkit with strategies to transform this body shame into radical self-love.

Conclusion

Remaining Resilient

■ ■ ■

On September 27, 2019, I attended a Climate Strike event as part of the Global Week for Future. In Toronto, where I live, more than twenty thousand people attended a rally, march, and final concert. After my toddler got up from her nap, I biked downtown with her on my bike seat, met a friend, sat on the grass in front of our local legislation building, and listened to some musical performance in support of action on climate change, while feeding my kid some snacks. The atmosphere was calm and festive, but the stakes were high, as demonstrators sought to draw attention to the increasing urgency of the climate crisis.

The Global Week for Future took place in 4,500 locations in 150 countries, drawing six million participants worldwide, the largest climate protest ever. But these widespread climate demonstrations started with a small action. On August 20, 2018, then fifteen-year-old Greta Thunberg did a solo protest outside of the Swedish parliament building in Stockholm. That summer in 2018 was the hottest on record at the time, coupled by mass wildfires, and Thunberg decided to take action, leaving school to sit outside of the Swedish parliament for three weeks leading up to the Swedish election, demanding that politicians take a stand. Thunberg's impact has spread far beyond her local context. Her individual strike led to the #FridaysforFuture movement, with youth striking from school on Fridays to demand politicians take action on climate change.

One youth marching in the 2019 Climate Strike events, seventeen-year-old Pascal Morimanno, commented that Thunberg "has revolutionized how we look at activism. She is one person but there are millions of youth out here now because of her. She is the face of new activism."[1] Grace King, a student and organizer with Climate Justice Toronto, commented, "Youth are rising."[2] Though Thunberg has become one of the faces of climate change activism, it's also important to recognize that this activism has been long ongoing in many communities, though it may not have received the same media attention.

On March 22, 2018, thirteen-year-old Anishnaabe Indigenous activist Autumn Peltier addressed the United Nations General Assembly about access to clean water and water conservation for the International Decade for Action on Water for Sustainable Development. Peltier is the chief water protector for the Anishinabek Nation and asked UN delegates to "warrior up," to do more to protect water. In this context, being a warrior does not suggest aggression or violent action, but instead suggests bold commitment and taking a stand. Peltier has spoken nationally and internationally at more than two hundred events and explains that she has been inspired by her aunt Josephine Mandamin, a longtime activist for clean water. In turn, Greta Thunberg cites that she was inspired by the activism from teens in Parkland, Florida, and the March for Our Lives movement for gun control after the shooting at Marjory Stoneman Douglas High School that killed seventeen people in 2018. Sources and examples of youth activism are everywhere and suggest the importance and impact of collective action and inspiration.

Though Thunberg may have galvanized a resurgence of climate awareness among youth, this hasn't always been an easy or straightforward path for her. She's been mocked in the media and by politicians, some critics even suggesting it was her parents, not her, who planned her actions and her activism. Thunberg has persevered in the face of this criticism and was seemingly not deterred by starting and continuing alone with her personal commitment to seek change and protest alone. Here in this conclusion to this book, we end with the note of remaining resilient with commitments to care more. As outlined in the introduction, care is an ongoing process that commits to action. Caring can be enriching and revitalizing, a way of anchoring ourselves in our communities and working toward social change. But caring can also be challenging, and it can sometimes be difficult to see how small or personal actions and growth connect with bigger change, and social problems can sometimes seem vast or unsurmountable.

In the first step of Bernice Fisher and Joan Tronto's outline of the process of care, discussed in chapter 1, care involves paying attention. Often with individual, competitively driven mindsets, our attention is directed to ourselves, but a relational mindset invites us to consider how we relate to others and pay attention to matters beyond ourselves. Paying attention, as a step of care, involves making choices. Fisher and Tronto write, "There are often more things to care about than we can comprehend, and we often care about more than that to which we can respond." Discussing this discrepancy between the many things that can pull our attention and the number of things we can reasonably respond to, the authors note that the Old Saxon etymological root of the word *care* means "sorrow."[3]

Knowing that caring is not always easy, and in fact can sometimes also be an experience of sorrow, alongside joy, we need to fortify ourselves for the journey. One important reminder is that personal and social change is not linear or straightforward and can take time. In this context, it's important to learn the characteristics of resilience to be perseverant and remain resilient, which includes taking care of ourselves.

CHARACTERISTICS OF RESILIENCE

Life is full of challenges that require us to respond. The American Psychological Association (APA) defines resilience as "the process of adapting well in the face of adversity, trauma, tragedy, threats, or significant sources of stress."[4] Being resilient doesn't mean that we don't experience discomfort or distress, but instead that we can navigate difficult experiences, keep going, and keep ourselves intact. The APA emphasizes that resilience is not innate, but instead is a set of skills that can be learned and practiced. In particular, the APA outlines that resilience is made up of finding connection with others, fostering wellness, healthy thinking, and finding purpose. These skills are important to practice as we commit to caring more as an ongoing and active process. To close, we reflect on these skills, while learning some examples of these resilient characteristics from activists and collectives working toward social change. Continue expanding your learning about these collectives and groups, and reflect on what further inspiring examples of activism and community building you are aware of in your communities.

Build Connections

Although our society often celebrates individual initiatives and individual achievements, developing resilience involves support from others, rather than tackling problems or challenges alone. The APA encourages developing relationships and "genuinely connecting with people who care about you" through times of struggle. Furthermore, remaining resilient while committing to care can mean collective rather than individual action. For example, in 2013, the Nishiyuu journey saw Cree youth walking 1,600 kilometers from a Cree village in Northern Quebec to the seat of Canadian government in Ottawa, in support of the Idle No More movement that protests for Indigenous people's rights. Idle No More is an Indigenous-led social movement based in Canada that protests the Canadian government's dismantling of environmental protection and has built an expansive movement for Indigenous rights and the protection of land, water, and sky.[5]

Idle No More continues to mount and sustain numerous campaigns to protect and defend Indigenous rights and the planet, from supporting

Indigenous treaty fishing rights to addressing housing, supporting protestors who are blocking pipeline developments to protect land and water, and more, connecting these broad areas of activism to the overarching goal of "peaceful Indigenous revolution . . . rising around the planet."[6]

Idle No More also builds connections through a focus on public education and nonviolent direct action. For example, the Idle No More website offers a variety of public education resources so that readers can educate themselves on the ongoing impacts of colonial institutions, such as schools and the mass media, which often "normalize the inequities and injustices Indigenous people continue to face."[7] Suggested resources from Idle No More, created by Indigenous land protectors, academics, and community members, include podcasts, magazines, and reports, providing a connected web of expertise and resources.

Indigenous youth continue to protest and call for change, to protect their ways of life, worldviews, and sovereignty in many shapes, forms, and movements. For example, the Indigenous Youth Movement is a collective of land defenders and water protectors committed to protest of the injustices faced by Indigenous peoples. One member, Ezra Green, a young Mi'kmaw activist, commenting on protest actions, stated, "We're trying to create a space where we can engage with community and have conversations but also try to make and encourage active change to the justice system and the child welfare system."[8] Engaging with community, having conversations, and encouraging change can all be part of a process of caring more, and resilience in this process can be practiced through finding support and solidarity with others and building those connections.

Foster Wellness

As discussed in chapter 6, self-care has become a trendy buzzword, but meaningful wellness takes time and effort, including taking care of your body, practicing mindfulness, and avoiding negative outlets. These wellness practices are part of developing resilience and persevering while experiencing challenges. Something as seemingly simple as trying to be more caring toward others can go against the grain, and spearheading personal and social change can sometimes take time.

Bearing witness to traumatic historical moments and injustice can also take its toll. In the context of the global uprisings of the summer of 2020 after the murder of George Floyd, Yasmine Cheyenne, a self-healing teacher and author, advocated for "making time for rest. I like being on social media and it's where I reach a lot of my audience, but sometimes, it's important to just log off. The things that we're ingesting are traumatic. There is no other way around it. We're watching people be attacked, abused, killed. These are traumatic things that we're witnessing, whether we're white or Black." Balancing self-care and activism can be challenging, and Cheyenne suggests finding balance between remaining informed and finding joy: "we all need to be keeping up with the news, but every now and then, we should be taking a moment to do something to bring us joy. Especially for Black people, finding time for joy is important. We don't always have to be in the fight. We can take time to rest and to take care of ourselves, too."[9]

Cheyenne says that striving for long-term change is a marathon not a sprint, and needs a balance of commitment and rest alongside "finding ways of showing up that make the most sense for *us*." Take a moment here to further reflect on what rest looks like for you, and in what ways you want to show up, be present, and be engaged in personal and social change. Finding this personal balance is a personal pathway to resilience that honors wellness.

Embrace Healthy Thoughts

While social change can be slow, we are surrounded by change on a day-to-day basis that sometimes can feel destabilizing and dehabilitating. The APA suggests resilience is based in accepting change and keeping things in perspective, and this is the basis of healthy thought patterns. For example, Nobel Peace Prize Laureate Malala Yousafzai became internationally known because of the attack that nearly killed her, and she continues to advocate for universal education. A long-term advocate for girls' access to schooling, Malala was shot by the Taliban at the age of fifteen in 2012. Malala both survived this attack and continued on with her resolve to fight for educational rights. Her organization, the Malala Fund, is striving to create a world where all girls have access to attending school through a nontraditional approach. Rather than trying to build more schools, the Malala Fund develops a network of activists, like Malala, investing in "education advocates and activists who are challenging the policies and practices that prevent girls from going to school in their communities."[10] In 2015, at aged seventeen, Malala received the Nobel Peace Prize for her educational activism work, the youngest ever recipient at the time. She continued on with her own educational journey, completing high school in England, all the while recovering and rehabilitating from her injuries from her attack. Malala completed her bachelor's degree in philosophy, politics, and economics at Oxford University in 2020.

Her continued work toward her activism goals, after her attack, demonstrates Malala's resilience, but Malala also demonstrates the characteristic of embracing healthy thoughts. In a 2018 interview with David Letterman on his show *My Next Guest Needs No Introduction*, Malala said about her attackers, "I forgive them because that's the best revenge I can have."[11] In addition to forgiveness, Malala has continued on with the same activist work that she was pushing for prior to her attack—and caused her to be attacked. Her focus, energy, and efforts seem to have remained on the same goals rather on those that caused her harm, and this offers an inspiring example of what embracing healthy thoughts can look like. As adrienne maree brown writes in her book *Emergent Strategy*, "What we pay attention to grows." This perspective also offers inspiration for the idea of being intentional, directing our thoughts to our goals and desires, while keeping a balanced perspective about challenges and the need for rest.

Find Purpose

Resilience is based in connecting with a broader path and finding meaning outside of ourselves. While we might individually experience challenges, successes, or failures, we can build resilience by pursuing goals and helping others. For example, the popular Netflix documentary *Knock Down the House* follows four grassroots candidates trying to get elected for the first time in the U.S. congressional primaries, all going up against long-term, well-funded incumbents. Though politics can often be a space of corporate donors, these profiled candidates find purpose with community organizing, focusing on getting young people and people of color to vote, and choose not to accept corporate donations to not be swayed by the influence of corporations on politics.

In the film, grassroots organizing and campaigning is showcased through knocking on doors to meet prospective voters, town hall events and rallies, mobilizing social media, learning about how electoral systems work from more experienced organizers, and connecting with and offering support to other candidates who are also spearheading their own grassroots campaigns. One of these candidates, Alexandria Ocasio-Cortez, decides to run against a heavily funded, veteran, ten-term incumbent. In one scene of *Knock Down the House*, she is shown handing out campaign flyers to prospective voters on the street, accompanied by her niece. She tells her young niece, "For every ten rejections, you get one acceptance, and that's how you win everything."[12] In 2018, Ocasio-Cortez won her primary election to become the Democratic candidate, and in 2019 she was elected to the U.S. Congress, the youngest person elected to Congress in U.S. history. Though Ocasio-Cortez's story is one of overcoming great odds to reach a goal, we can also see the sense of purpose and drive that guides this goal, finding purpose in small-scale action and small-scale results that grow into larger impact.

As a component of resilience, finding purpose doesn't mean doggedly persevering until you are successful or win. Instead, resilience is based in finding meaning and purpose in small-scale actions and results themselves, regardless of the outcome. Through committing to care, we can find larger-scale results or impacts, but chasing results as a benchmark of success can sometimes be a fool's errand. Caring more instead means we ground ourselves, take care of ourselves, and take care of those around us in the ways that we can, connecting with larger causes and actions along the way. While our broader society often directs us to individual goals and success, caring finds joy and purpose in connections and relationality. From this relational place, we can take action, and from this relational place, we can remain resilient in the face of adversity.

NOTES

1. Mia Rabson, "Canadian Youth Gather across Canada to Demand Drastic Climate Action," CTV News, September 27, 2019, accessed June 3, 2021, https://www.ctvnews.ca/canada/canadian-youth-gather-across-canada-to-demand-drastic-climate-action-1.4612987.
2. CBC News, "'Youth Are Rising': Thousands Hit Queen's Park as Part of Global Climate Strikes," September 27, 2019, accessed June 28, 2021, https://www.cbc.ca/news/canada/toronto/climate-strike-toronto-1.5299504.
3. Fisher and Tronto, "Toward a Feminist Theory of Caring," 42.
4. American Psychological Association, "Building Resilience," 2012, accessed June 2, 2021, https://www.apa.org/topics/resilience.
5. Idle No More, "An Indigenous-Led Social Movement," accessed June 4, 2021, https://idlenomore.ca/about-the-movement/.
6. Idle No More, "Campaigns and Actions," accessed June 28, 2021, https://idlenomore.ca/campaigns-actions/.
7. Idle No More, "Resources and Education," accessed June 28, 2021, https://idlenomore.ca/resources-education/.
8. Rhiannon Johnson, "Indigenous Youth Set Up Protest Outside Toronto's Old City Hall," CBC News, March 6, 2018, accessed June 4, 2021, https://warriorpublications.wordpress.com/2018/03/07/indigenous-youth-set-up-protest-camp-outside-torontos-old-city-hall/.
9. Eliza Dumais, "How to Balance Activism and Self-Care, According to a Wellness Coach," *Refinery29*, July 14, 2020, accessed June 2, 2021, https://www.refinery29.com/en-us/activism-burnout-self-care.
10. Malala Fund, "How We Work," accessed June 6, 2021, https://malala.org/about?sc=header.
11. David Letterman, "You Know, She Has a Nobel Peace Prize," *My Next Guest Needs No Introduction with David Letterman*, dir. Michael Bonfiglio (Netflix, 2018).
12. Rachel Lears, dir., *Knock Down the House* (Jubilee Films, Atlas Films, and Artemis Rising, 2019).

Bibliography

■ ■ ■

11th Principle: Consent! "Rape Culture Pyramid." https://www.11thprinciple consent.org/consent-propaganda/rape-culture-pyramid/.

Ahmed, Sara. *Living a Feminist Life*. Durham, NC: Duke University Press, 2017.

——. *On Being Included: Racism and Diversity in Institutional Life.* Durham, NC: Duke University Press, 2012.

Akimbo. "Announcing the New Stewards of Gendai." Accessed June 15, 2021. https://akimbo.ca/listings/announcing-the-new-stewards-of-gendai/.

Alcid, Sara. "Navigating Consent: Debunking the 'Gray Area' Myth." *Everyday Feminism*, January 4, 2013. Accessed November 26, 2020. https://everydayfeminism.com/2013/01/navigating-consent-debunking -the-grey-area-myth/.

Alexander, Liz. "What Millennials Learned about Bias from This Harvard Test." *Psychology Today*, May 8, 2017. Accessed October 21, 2020. https://www.psychologytoday.com/us/blog/preparing-the-unpredict able/201705/what-millennials-learned-about-bias-harvard-test.

Allied Media Projects. "Vision." Accessed May 14, 2021. https://alliedmedia .org/about.

American Psychological Association. "Building Resilience." 2012. Accessed June 2, 2021. https://www.apa.org/topics/resilience.

Anderson, Bruce M. "The Most In-Demand Hard and Soft Skills of 2020." *LinkedIn Talent Blog*, January 9, 2020. Accessed May 28, 2021. https://business.linkedin.com/talent-solutions/blog/trends-and-re search/2020/most-in-demand-hard-and-soft-skills.

Anti-Oppression Network. "Allyship." Accessed November 13, 2020. https:// theantioppressionnetwork.com/allyship/.

Arendt, Hannah. *On Violence.* Boston: Houghton Mifflin Harcourt, 1970.

Bain, Jennifer. "At Google Canada, the Meals and Snacks Are Free for 150 Employees." *Toronto Star*, June 19, 2014. Accessed May 25, 2021. https:// www.thestar.com/life/food_wine/2014/06/19/at_google_canada_the _meals_and_snacks_are_free_for_150_employees.html.

Baldwin, James, and Margaret Mead. *A Rap on Race.* Philadelphia: J. B. Lippincott & Co., 1971.

Bassel, Leah. *The Politics of Listening: Politics and Challenges for Democratic Life.* London: Palgrave Pivot, 2017.

Beagle, Erin. Personal interview, June 2021.

Belluck, Pam. "Chilly at Work? Office Formula Was Devised for Men." *New York Times*, August 3, 2015. https://www.nytimes.com/2015/08/04/science/chilly-at-work-a-decades-old-formula-may-be-to-blame.html.

Bhasin, Ritu. *The Authenticity Principle: Resist Conformity, Embrace Differences, and Transform How You Live, Work, and Lead.* Toronto: Melanin Made Press, 2017.

Bluestein, Adam. "Want to Be More Creative? Think on Your Feet." *Inc.com*, April 14, 2014. Accessed May 25, 2021. https://www.inc.com/magazine/201404/adam-bluestein/companies-use-improv-to-boost-creativity.html.

Bourke, Juliet, and Andrea Titus. "The Key to Inclusive Leadership." *Harvard Business Review*, March 6, 2020. Accessed May 10, 2021. https://hbr.org/2020/03/the-key-to-inclusive-leadership.

Brach, Tara. *Radical Compassion: Learning to Love Yourself and Your World with the Practice of RAIN*. New York: Viking, 2019.

——. "Radical Compassion Part 2: Loving Ourselves and Our World into Healing." *Tara Brach* podcast, December 13, 2019.

brown, adrienne maree. *Emergent Strategy: Shaping Change, Changing Worlds.* Chico, CA: AK Press, 2017.

——. "If You're Good, Say You're Good." adriennemareebrown.net, February 8, 2021. Accessed May 21, 2021. https://adriennemareebrown.net/2021/02/08/if-youre-good-say-youre-good/.

——. *Pleasure Activism: The Politics of Feeling Good.* Chico, CA: AK Press, 2019.

——. *We Will Not Cancel Us: And Other Dreams of Transformative Justice.* Chico, CA: AK Press, 2020.

Brown, Jennifer. *How to Be an Inclusive Leader: Your Role in Creating Cultures of Belonging Where Everyone Can Thrive.* San Francisco: Berrett-Koehler, 2019.

Brucculieri, Julia. "The Difference between Cultural Appropriation and Appreciation Is Tricky. Here's a Primer." *Huffington Post*, July 2, 2018. Accessed December 15, 2020. https://www.huffingtonpost.ca/entry/cultural-appropriation-vs-appreciation_n_5a78d13ee4b0164659c72fb3.

Buchwald, Emilie, Pamela Fletcher, and Martha Roth, eds. *Transforming a Rape Culture.* Minneapolis: Milkweed Editions, 1994.

Burkus, David. *The Myths of Creativity: The Truth about How Innovative Companies and People Generate Great Ideas.* San Francisco: Jossey-Bass, 2014.

Burrough, Bryan. "Fyre Festival: Anatomy of a Millennial Marketing Fiasco Waiting to Happen." *Vanity Fair*, August 2017. Accessed May 25, 2021. https://www.vanityfair.com/news/2017/06/fyre-festival-billy-mcfarland-millennial-marketing-fiasco.

Buse, Kathleen, Ruth Sessler Bernstein, and Dina Bilimoria. "The Influence of Board Diversity, Board Diversity Policies and Practices, and Board Inclusion Behaviors on Nonprofit Governance Practices." *Journal of Business Ethics* 133, no. 1 (2016): 179–91.

Butt, David, and Chi Nguyen. "AfterMeToo Report." #AfterMeToo, March 6, 2018. Accessed November 26, 2020. https://a085d11e-6d13-4974-83f0-d75131b04e1c.filesusr.com/ugd/1766c7_398ee90fdbb047af951203f20a5f3db3.pdf.

Call Your Girlfriend. "About Us." Accessed June 22, 2021. https://www.callyourgirlfriend.com/about.

Canadian Federation of Students. "Gender-Based Violence." Accessed November 26, 2020. https://cfsontario.ca/campaigns/gender-based-violence/.

Canadian Index of Wellbeing. *How Are Canadians Really Doing? The 2016 CIW National Report.* Waterloo, ON: Canadian Index of Wellbeing and University of Waterloo, 2016.

Canadian Press. "AfterMeToo Group Creating Digital Centre for Survivors of Workplace Violence." CBC News, October 14, 2018. https://www.cbc.ca/news/entertainment/aftermetoo-digital-centre-survivors-1.4862446.

Care More. "Our Vision." Accessed October 21, 2020. https://www.letscaremore.com/.

CBC News. "'Youth Are Rising': Thousands Hit Queen's Park as Part of Global Climate Strikes." September 27, 2019. Accessed June 28, 2021. https://www.cbc.ca/news/canada/toronto/climate-strike-toronto-1.5299504

Center for Excellence in Universal Design. "What Is Universal Design." Accessed May 14, 2021. http://universaldesign.ie/What-is-Universal-Design/.

Centre for Sustainable Prosperity. "About: Vision." Accessed May 19, 2021. https://www.cusp.ac.uk/about/.

Chakrabarti, Megna, and Wes Martin. "adrienne maree brown on Finding Joy during the Coronavirus Crisis." WBUR.org, April 6, 2020. Accessed June 8, 2021. https://www.wbur.org/onpoint/2020/04/06/finding-joy-during-coronavirus.

Chamorro-Premuzic, Tomas. "Why Do So Many Incompetent Men Become Leaders." *Harvard Business Review*, August 22, 2013. Accessed May 14, 2021. https://hbr.org/2013/08/why-do-so-many-incompetent-men.

Chira, Susan. "The Universal Phenomenon of Men Interrupting Women." *New York Times*, June 14, 2017. Accessed November 11, 2020. https://www.nytimes.com/2017/06/14/business/women-sexism-work-huffington-kamala-harris.html.

Ciciolla, Lucia, and Suniya S. Luthar. "Invisible Household Labor and Ramifications for Adjustment: Mothers as Captains of Households." *Sex Roles* 81 (2019): 467–86.

Clare, Eli. *Brilliant Imperfection: Grappling with Cure.* Durham, NC: Duke University Press, 2017.

Collins, Patricia Hill, and Sirma Bilge. *Intersectionality.* Cambridge: Polity Press, 2016.

Costanza-Chock, Sasha. *Design Justice: Community Led Practices to Build the Worlds We Need.* Cambridge, MA: MIT Press, 2020.

Contu, Alessia. "On Boundaries and Difference: Communities of Practice and Power Relations in Creative Work." *Management Learning* 45, no. 3 (2013): 289–316.

Cox, Andrew. "What Are Communities of Practice? A Comparative Review of Four Seminal Works." *Journal of Information Science* 31, no. 6 (2005): 527–40.

Creative Education Foundation. *Creative Problem Solving Resource Guide.* Scituate, MA: Creative Education Foundation, 2014.

Crenshaw, Kimberlé. "Demarginalizing the Intersection of Race and Sex: A Black Feminist Critique of Antidiscrimination Doctrine, Feminist Theory and Antiracist Politics." *University of Chicago Legal Forum* 1 (1989): 139–67.

Culture Amp. "Death and Rebirth Life Skills." *Culture First* podcast, season 1, episode 5, February 5, 2020.

Design Justice Network. "Design Justice Network Principles." Summer 2018. Accessed June 8, 2020. https://designjustice.org/read-the-principles.

Dobson, Andrew. *Listening for Democracy.* Oxford: Oxford University Press, 2014.

Doolittle, Robyn. *Had It Coming: What's Fair in the Age of #MeToo?* Toronto: Penguin Random House, 2019.

Doorley, Scott, and Scott Witthoft. *Make Space: How to Set the Stage for Creative Collaboration.* Hoboken, NJ: John Wiley & Sons, 2012.

d. school. "Design Thinking Bootleg." Institute of Design, Stanford University. Accessed May 25, 2021. https://static1.squarespace.com/static/57c6b79629687fde090a0fdd/t/5b19b2f2aa4a99e99b26b6bb/1528410876119/dschool_bootleg_deck_2018_final_sm+%282%29.pdf.

Du Bois, W. E. B. *Black Reconstruction in America, 1860–1880.* 1935. New York: Free Press, 1998.

Dumais, Eliza. "How to Balance Activism and Self-Care, According to a Wellness Coach." *Refinery29*, July 14, 2020. Accessed June 2, 2021. https://www.refinery29.com/en-us/activism-burnout-self-care.

Dunn, Melanie. "Stop Telling Women They Must Change Themselves to Become Leaders." *Globe and Mail*, March 2, 2019. Accessed May 10, 2021. https://www.theglobeandmail.com/business/careers/leadership/article-stop-telling-women-they-must-change-themselves-to-become-leaders/.

Edmondson, Amy. *The Fearless Organization: Creating Psychological Safety in the Workplace for Learning, Innovation, and Growth.* Hoboken, NJ: John Wiley & Sons, 2018.

Elan, Priya. "Blackfishing: 'Black Is Cool, Unless You're Actually Black.'" *Guardian*, April 14, 2020. Accessed March 15, 2021. https://www.theguardian.com/fashion/2020/apr/14/blackfishing-black-is-cool-unless-youre-actually-black.

Estrada, Mica, et al. "The Influence of Microaffirmations on Undergraduate Persistence in Science Career Pathways." *CBE Life Sciences Education* 18 (2019): ar40.

Ethics of Care. "Carol Gilligan." July 16, 2011. Accessed October 19, 2020. https://ethicsofcare.org/carol-gilligan/.

Fey, Tina. *Bossypants.* New York: Little, Brown, 2011.

Field Museum. "Field Museum to Renovate Native North America Hall, to Open 2021." October 29, 2018. Accessed June 24, 2021. https://www.fieldmuseum.org/about/press/field-museum-renovate-native-north-america-hall-open-2021.

Fink, Marty. *Forget Burial: HIV Kinship, Disability, and Queer/Trans Narratives of Care*. New Brunswick, NJ: Rutgers University Press, 2021.

Fisher, Bernice, and Joan Tronto. "Toward a Feminist Theory of Caring." In *Circles of Care*, edited by Emily Abel and Margaret Nelson, 36–54. Albany, NY: SUNY Press, 1990.

Food Project. "What We Do" and "Our Vision." Accessed June 7, 2021. https://thefoodproject.org/who-we-are/.

Foucault, Michel. *Discipline and Punish: The Birth of the Prison*. Translated by Robert Sheridan. New York: Pantheon Books, 1977.

———. *The History of Sexuality: An Introduction*. Vol. 1, Translated by Robert Hurley. New York: Pantheon Books, 1978.

Freire, Paulo. *Pedagogy of the Oppressed*. 50th anniversary ed. Translated by Myra Bergman Ramos. New York: Bloomsbury Academic, 2018.

Friedman, Jaclyn. "'Yes Means Yes' and Enthusiastic Consent." Our Bodies Ourselves, October 15, 2011. Accessed November 26, 2020. https://www.ourbodiesourselves.org/book-excerpts/health-article/yes-means-yes-enthusiastic-consent/.

Gagnon, John H., and William Simon. *Sexual Conduct: The Social Sources of Human Sexuality.* Chicago: Aldine Books, 1973.

Gandini, Alessandro, and James Graham. "Introduction." In *Collaborative Production in the Creative Industries*, 1–14. London: University of Westminster Press, 2017.

Gendai, "Gendai 2020–2022." Accessed June 15, 2021. https://www.gendai.club/.

———. "MA MBA." Accessed June 15, 2021. https://www.gendai.club/ma-mba.

Giblin, John, Imma Ramos, and Nikki Grout. "Dismantling the Master's House: Thoughts on Representing Empire and Decolonising Museums and Public Space in Practice; An Introduction." *Third Text* 33, nos. 4–5 (2019): 471–86.

Givel, Michael. "Mahayana Buddhism and Gross National Happiness in Bhutan." *International Journal of Wellbeing* 5 (2015): 14–27.

Hagi, Sarah. "Cancel Culture Is Not Real—at Least Not in the Way People Think." *Time*, November 21, 2019. Accessed November 13, 2020. https://time.com/5735403/cancel-culture-is-not-real/.

Hammonds, Will, and Lakhbir Bhandal. "Where to Next for Diversity? An Assessment of Arts Council England's Race Equality and Cultural

Diversity Policies and Emerging Trends." *Journal of Policy Research in Tourism, Leisure and Events* 3, no. 2 (2011): 187–200.

Hamraie, Aimi. *Building Access: Universal Design and the Politics of Disability.* Minneapolis: University of Minnesota Press, 2017.

Hatzipanagos, Rachel. "The 'Decolonization' of the American Museum." *Washington Post*, October 11, 2018. Accessed December 16, 2020. https://www.washingtonpost.com/nation/2018/10/12/decolonization-american-museum/.

HBR Idea Cast. "Creating Psychological Safety in the Workplace." Episode 666, February 12, 2019. https://hbr.org/podcast/2019/01/creating-psychological-safety-in-the-workplace.

Hedges, Kristi. "How to Get Real Buy-In for Your Idea." *Forbes*, March 16, 2015. Accessed May 18, 2021. https://www.forbes.com/sites/work-in-progress/2015/03/16/how-to-get-real-buy-in-for-your-idea/#4ba4b75c4044.

Herring, Cedric, and Loren Henderson. *Diversity in Organizations: A Critical Examination.* New York: Routledge, 2015.

H.O.L.L.A! "Our History." Accessed October 28, 2020. https://healwithholla.com/about-the-movement.

——. "We've Build a Curriculum Tailored to Our Youth." Accessed October 28, 2020. https://holla-inc.com/.

hooks, bell. *All About Love: New Visions.* New York: Harper Perennial, 2000.

——. *Feminist Theory: From Margin to Center.* 3rd ed. New York: Routledge, 2014.

——. *Teaching Community: A Pedagogy of Hope.* New York: Routledge, 2003.

Idle No More. "Campaigns and Actions." Accessed June 28, 2021. https://idlenomore.ca/campaigns-actions/.

——. "An Indigenous-Led Social Movement." Accessed June 4, 2021. https://idlenomore.ca/about-the-movement/.

——. "Resources and Education." Accessed June 28, 2021. https://idlenomore.ca/resources-education/.

Indigenous Corporate Training Inc. *Indigenous Peoples: A Guide to Terminology.* https://www.ictinc.ca/indigenous-peoples-a-guide-to-terminology.

Intellectual Property Issues in Cultural Heritage Project. "Think Before You Appropriate: Things to Know and Questions to Ask in Order to Avoid Misappropriating Indigenous Cultural Heritage." Simon Fraser University, 2015.

Jackson, Tim. *Prosperity without Growth: Economics for a Finite Planet.* 2nd ed. New York: Routledge, 2017.

Jana, Tiffany, and Matthew Freeman. *Overcoming Bias: Building Authentic Relationships across Difference.* Oakland, CA: Berrett-Koehler, 2016.

Johnson, Rhiannon. "Indigenous Youth Set Up Protest Outside Toronto's Old City Hall." CBC News, March 6, 2018. Accessed June 4, 2021. https://warriorpublications.wordpress.com/2018/03/07/indigenous-youth-set-up-protest-camp-outside-torontos-old-city-hall/.

John-Steiner, Vera. *Creative Collaboration.* Oxford: Oxford University Press, 2006.

Jones, Faolan, and H.O.L.L.A! *We Came to Heal Documentary.* YouTube, June 29, 2020. https://www.youtube.com/watch?v=o1lTejZrw6Y.

Jones, Feminista. "Black Women Have Been Calling Out R. Kelly for Years. Nobody Listened." *Vox*, January 9, 2019. Accessed June 9, 2021. https://www.vox.com/first-person/2017/7/21/16008230/r-kelly-surviving-sex-cult-abuse-john-legend-chance-the-rapper.

Joseph, Bob. "Indigenous or Aboriginal: Which Is Correct?" CBC News, September 21, 2016. Accessed December 16, 2020. https://www.cbc.ca/news/indigenous/indigenous-aboriginal-which-is-correct-1.3771433.

——. "What Is an Indigenous Medicine Wheel?" Indigenous Corporate Training Inc., May 24, 2020. Accessed May 25, 2021. https://www.ictinc.ca/blog/what-is-an-aboriginal-medicine-wheel.

Just Be Inc. "About Us." Accessed November 24, 2020. https://justbeinc.wixsite.com/justbeinc/purpose-mission-and-vision.

Kapila, Monisha, Ericka Hines, and Martha Searby. "Why Diversity, Equity, and Inclusion Matter." Independent Sector, October 6, 2016. Accessed May 10, 2021. https://independentsector.org/resource/why-diversity-equity-and-inclusion-matter/.

Karabanow, Jeff, and Ted Naylor. "Using Art to Tell Stories and Build Safe Spaces: Transforming Academic Research into Action." *Canadian Journal of Community Mental Health* 34, no. 3 (2015): 67–85.

Kasmani, Shaheen. "How Can You Decolonise Museums?" *Museum Next*, June 2, 2020. https://www.museumnext.com/article/decolonising-museums/.

Keene, Adrienne. "But Why Can't I Wear a Hipster Headdress." *Native Appropriations*, April 17, 2010. Accessed December 16, 2020. http://nativeappropriations.com/2010/04/but-why-cant-i-wear-a-hipster-headdress.html.

Kelley, Tom, and David Kelley. *Creative Confidence: Unleashing the Creative Potential within Us All.* New York City: Random House, 2013.

Khan, Farrah, for ArtReach. *Caring for Yourself Is a Radical Act: Self-Care Guide for Youth Working in Community.* Toronto: ArtReach, n.d.

Kimmerer, Robin Wall. "Returning the Gift." *Minding Nature* 7, no. 2 (2014): 18–24.

Kirlew, Chloe. "Decolonizing Our Creativity: Daydreaming and Visualization as Resistance." YouTube, February 23, 2021. https://www.youtube.com/watch?v=EH4dLXeRQ88&t=13s.

Klocek, Stefan. "Better Together: The Practice of Successful Creative Collaboration." September 12, 2011. Accessed May 25, 2021. http://www.stefanklocek.com/better-together-the-practice-of-successful-creative-collaboration/.

Landsbaum, Claire. "Obama's Female Staffers Came up with a Genius Strategy to Make Sure Their Voices Were Heard." *The Cut*, September

13, 2016. https://www.thecut.com/2016/09/heres-how-obamas-female-staffers-made-their-voices-heard.html.

Lave, Jean, and Étienne Wenger. *Situated Learning: Legitimate Peripheral Participation.* Cambridge: Cambridge University Press, 1991.

Lears, Rachel, dir. *Knock Down the House.* Jubilee Films, Atlas Films, and Artemis Rising, 2019.

Lee, Sophia. "Culture Fit: What You Need to Know." *Culture Amp*. Accessed May 10, 2021. https://www.cultureamp.com/blog/culture-fit-what-you-need-to-know/.

Leonard, Kelly, and Tom Yorton. *Yes, And: How Improvisation Reverses "No, But" Thinking and Improves Creativity and Collaboration—Lessons from The Second City.* New York: Harper, 2015.

Lester, Kristen, dir. *Purl.* PixarSparkShorts, 2018.

Letterman, David. "You Know, She Has a Nobel Peace Prize." *My Next Guest Needs No Introduction with David Letterman*. Directed by Michael Bonfiglio. Netflix, 2018.

Levi, Daniel. "Understanding Teams." In *Group Dynamics for Teams*, 5th ed., 1–18. Los Angeles: Sage, 2017.

Liker, Jeffrey. *The Toyota Way: 14 Management Principles from the World's Greatest Manufacturer.* New York: McGraw-Hill, 2005.

Limb, Charles. "Your Brain on Improv." TEDxMidAtlantic, November 2010. https://www.ted.com/talks/charles_limb_your_brain_on_improv.

Locker, Melissa. "Call Your Girlfriend: Podcast Dishes on Everything from Benghazi to Bieber." *Guardian*, March 5, 2016. Accessed June 11, 2021. https://www.theguardian.com/culture/2016/mar/05/call-your-girlfriend-podcast-politics-pop-culture.

Lorde, Audre. "A Burst of Light: Living with Cancer." In *A Burst of Light and Other Essays*, 40–133. Ithaca, NY: Firebrand Books, 1988.

——. "Learnings from the 60s (1982)." Black Past, August 12, 2012. Accessed October 20, 2021. https://www.blackpast.org/african-american-history/1982-audre-lorde-learning-60s/.

Lynch, Olwen. "The NY Teen Collective Providing IRL & URL Love." *Dazed*, September 7 2017. Accessed May 20, 2021. https://www.dazeddigital.com/film-tv/article/37296/1/the-ny-teen-loveyourz-collective-providing-irl-url-love.

Lynskey, Dorian. "This Means War: Why the Fashion Headdress Must Be Stopped." *Guardian*, July 30, 2014. Accessed December 15, 2020. https://www.theguardian.com/fashion/2014/jul/30/why-the-fashion-headdress-must-be-stopped.

Malala Fund. "How We Work." Accessed June 6, 2021. https://malala.org/about?sc=header.

Marcantonio, Tiffany L., and Kristen N. Jozkowski. "Assessing How Gender, Relationship Status, and Item Wording Influence Cues Used by College Students to Decline Different Sexual Behaviors." *Journal of Sex Research* 57, no. 2 (2020): 260–72.

Marahani, Marsya. "About." Accessed December 8, 2020. https://marsyamaharani.com/About.

——. Personal interview. November 27, 2020.

Marsh, Calum. "Osheaga's Headress Ban Shows Festival's Zero Tolerance for Cultural Appropriation." *Guardian*, July 17, 2015. Accessed December 15, 2020. https://www.theguardian.com/culture/2015/jul/17/osheaga-music-festival-headdress-cultural-appropriation

McIntosh, Peggy. "White Privilege: Unpacking the Invisible Knapsack." National Seed Project. Originally published 1989. Accessed October 21, 2020. https://nationalseedproject.org/Key-SEED-Texts/white-privilege-unpacking-the-invisible-knapsack.

McKenzie, Mia, ed. *The Solidarity Struggle: How People of Color Succeed and Fail at Showing Up for Each Other in the Fight for Freedom*. Oakland, CA: BDG Press, 2016.

Me Too. "Tarana Burke, Founder." Accessed October 26, 2020. https://metoomvmt.org/get-to-know-us/tarana-burke-founder/.

Miell, Dorothy, and Karen Littleton, eds. *Collaborative Creativity: Contemporary Perspectives.* London: Free Association Books, 2004.

Mingus, Mia. "Pods and Pod Mapping Worksheet." Bay Area Transformative Justice Collective, June 2016. Accessed June 29, 2021. https://batjc.wordpress.com/resources/pods-and-pod-mapping-worksheet/.

Moniuszko, Sara, and Cara Kelly. "Harvey Weinstein Scandal: A Complete List of the 87 Accusers." *USAToday.com*, June 1, 2018. Accessed October 26, 2020. https://www.usatoday.com/story/life/people/2017/10/27/weinstein-scandal-complete-list-accusers/804663001/.

Montreal Urban Aboriginal Community Strategy Network. "Indigenous Ally Toolkit." March 2019. https://reseaumtlnetwork.com/wp-content/uploads/2019/04/Ally_March.pdf.

Moore, Joseph. Personal interview, November 15, 2019.

Mussell, Bill. "Cultural Pathways for Decolonization." *Visions Journal* 5 (2008): 4–5. https://www.heretohelp.bc.ca/visions/aboriginal-people-vol5/cultural-pathways-for-decolonization.

Myers, Vernā. "Diversity and Inclusion Training." VernaMyers.com. Accessed June 7, 2021. https://www.vernamyers.com/.

Newell, Alan F., et al. "User-Sensitive Inclusive Design." *Universal Access in the Information Society* 10, no. 3 (2011): 235–43.

Nichols, Ralph G., and Leonard A. Stevens. "Listening to People." *Harvard Business Review*, September 1957. https://hbr.org/1957/09/listening-to-people.

Ng, Petrina. Personal interview, November 27, 2020.

Noddings, Nel. *Caring: A Relational Approach to Ethics and Moral Education.* 2nd ed. Berkeley: University of California Press, 2013.

Oakley, Kate, and Jon Ward. "The Art of the Good Life: Culture and Sustainable Prosperity." *Cultural Trends* 27, no. 1 (2018): 4–17.

Parker, Priya. "3 Steps to Turn Everyday Get-Togethers into Transformative Gatherings." TED2019, April 2019. https://www.ted.com/talks

/priya_parker_3_steps_to_turn_everyday_get_togethers_into_transformative_gatherings?language=en.

PDX Non-Binary Community Effort. “Collective Cares,” n.d. Accessed March 16, 2021. https://docs.google.com/document/d/1XBDKJjQsSQOCT64ADuuCaPognKHUTZD7syc_RliGg3o/edit.

Penny, Laurie. “Life-Hacks of the Poor and Aimless.” *Baffler*, July 8, 2016. Accessed May 5, 2021. https://thebaffler.com/war-of-nerves/laurie-penny-self-care.

Phillips, Katherine. “How Diversity Makes Us Smarter.” *Scientific American*, October 1, 2014. Accessed May 10, 2021. https://www.scientificamerican.com/article/how-diversity-makes-us-smarter/.

Piepzna-Samarasinha, Leah Lakshmi. *Care Work: Dreaming Disability Justice.* Vancouver: Arsenal Pulp Press, 2018.

——. “Half Assed Disabled Prepper Tips for Preparing for a Coronavirus Quarantine.” March 10, 2020. Accessed March 16, 2021. https://docs.google.com/document/d/1rIdpKgXeBHbmM3KpB5NfjEBue8YN1MbXhQ7zTOLmSyo/edit.

Popova, Milena. *Sexual Consent.* Cambridge, MA: MIT Press, 2019.

Rabson, Mia. “Canadian Youth Gather across Canada to Demand Drastic Climate Action.” CTV News, September 27, 2019. Accessed June 3, 2021. https://www.ctvnews.ca/canada/canadian-youth-gather-across-canada-to-demand-drastic-climate-action-1.4612987.

RAINN. “Key Terms and Phrases.” Accessed November 26, 2020. https://www.rainn.org/articles/key-terms-and-phrases.

Rebolini, Arianna. “10 Habits of Highly Creative People.” *BuzzFeed*, April 11, 2014. Accessed May 18, 2021. https://www.buzzfeed.com/ariannarebolini/habits-of-highly-creative-people.

Robbins, Mike. *Bring Your Whole Self to Work: How Vulnerability Unlocks Creativity, Connection, and Performance.* Carlsbad, CA: Hay House, 2018.

——. “Bring Your Whole Self to Work.” TEDxBerkeley, March 26, 2015. https://www.youtube.com/watch?v=bd2WKQWG_Dg.

Roberson, Quinetta. “Disentangling the Meanings of Diversity and Inclusion in Organizations.” *Group & Organization Management* 31, no. 2 (2006): 212–36.

Róisín, Fariha. *Being in Your Body: A Journal for Self-Love and Body Positivity.* New York: Abrams Noterie, 2019.

Roots to Harvest. “S.H.O.W. Program.” Accessed June 7, 2021. http://www.rootstoharvest.org/show-program.html.

Rosa, Hartmut. *Resonance: A Sociology of Our Relationship to the World.* Translated by James C. Wagner. Cambridge: Polity Press, 2019.

Rosman, Katherine. “The Reinvention of Consent.” *New York Times*, February 24, 2018. Accessed November 26, 2020. https://www.nytimes.com/2018/02/24/style/antioch-college-sexual-offense-prevention-policy.html.

Rothman, Joshua. “The Origins of Privilege.” *New Yorker*, May 14, 2014. Accessed October 21, 2020. https://www.newyorker.com/books/page-turner/the-origins-of-privilege.

Roy, Elise. "When We Design for Disability, We All Benefit." TEDxMidAdlantic, September 2015. https://www.ted.com/talks/elise_roy_when_we_design_for_disability_we_all_benefit?language=en.

Saad, Layla F. *Me and White Supremacy: Combat Racism, Change the World, and Become a Better Ancestor.* Naperville, IL: Sourcebooks, 2020.

Sauers, Jenna. "Urban Outfitters and the Navajo Nation: What Does the Law Say?" *Jezebel*, October 13, 2011. Accessed June 24, 2021. https://jezebel.com/urban-outfitters-and-the-navajo-nation-what-does-the-l-5849637.

Sawyer, Keith R. "Improvisation and the Creative Process: Dewey, Collingwood, and the Aesthetics of Spontaneity." *Journal of Aesthetics and Art Criticism* 58, no. 2 (2000): 149–61.

Schuman, Sandor P. "The Role of Facilitation in Collaborative Groups." Executive Decision Services, 1996. Accessed May 25, 2021. http://www.exedes.com/articles/Role-of-Facilitation-in-Collaboration.pdf.

Schumer, Amy. "Information about My 'Formation.'" *Medium*, October 27, 2016. Accessed December 15, 2020. https://medium.com/@amyschumer/information-about-my-formation-b416d2adfc71#.ot3a3gptr.

Seeds for Change. "Group Agreements for Workshops and Meetings." Accessed May 25, 2021. https://www.seedsforchange.org.uk/groupagree.pdf.

SexInfo Online. "Bodily Autonomy." November 1, 2018. Accessed November 26, 2020. https://sexinfoonline.com/bodily-autonomy/.

Shore, Lynn, Jeanette N. Cleveland, and Diana Sanchez. "Inclusive Workplaces: A Review and Model." *Human Resource Management Review* 28, no. 2 (2018): 176–89.

Shore, Lynn, et al. "Inclusion and Diversity in Work Groups: A Review and Model for Future Research." *Journal of Management* 37, no. 4 (2010): 1262–89.

Simmons, Tamra, Dream Hampton, Jesse Daniels, Joel Karsberg, Jessica Everleth, and Maria Pepin, executive producers. *Surviving R. Kelly.* Lifetime, 2019.

Simpson, Leanne Betasamosake. *As We Have Always Done: Indigenous Resurgence through Radical Resistance.* Minneapolis: University of Minnesota Press, 2017.

Smith, Mercedes. "The Artful Gift of Care." TEDx Lincoln University. YouTube.com, February 3, 2020. https://www.youtube.com/watch?v=wIDJyVYHQ1w.

Sow, Aminatou, and Ann Friedman. *Big Friendship: How We Keep Each Other Close*. New York: Simon & Schuster, 2020.

Sue, Derald Wing. *Microaggressions in Everyday Life: Race, Gender, and Sexual Orientation*. Hoboken, NJ: Wiley, 2010.

Taylor, Sonya Renee. *The Body Is Not an Apology.* San Francisco: Berrett-Koehler, 2018.

Thomas, David A., and Robin J. Ely. "Making Differences Matter: A New Paradigm for Managing Diversity." *Harvard Business Review*, September–October 1996. Accessed March 17, 2021. https://hbr.org/1996/09/making-differences-matter-a-new-paradigm-for-managing-diversity.

Tichenor, Austin. "Elizabethan Theater Etiquette and Audience Expectations Today." Folger Shakespeare Library, September 25, 2018. Accessed May 14, 2021. https://shakespeareandbeyond.folger.edu/2018/09/25/elizabethan-theater-etiquette-audience-expectations/.

Torino, Gina. "How Racism and Microaggressions Lead to Worse Health." Center for Health Journalism, USC Annenberg, November 10, 2017. Accessed November 12, 2020. https://centerforhealthjournalism.org/2017/11/08/how-racism-and-microaggressions-lead-worse-health.

Trần, Ngọc Loan. "Calling In: A Less Disposable Way of Holding Each Other Accountable." In *The Solidarity Struggle: How People of Color Succeed and Fail at Showing Up for Each Other in the Fight for Freedom*, edited by Mia McKenzie, 59–63. Oakland: BDG Press, 2016.

Tronto, Joan. *Caring Democracy: Markets, Equality and Justice*. New York: New York University Press, 2013.

Tuckman, Bruce. "Developmental Sequence in Small Groups." *Psychological Bulletin* 63, no. 6 (1965): 384–99.

United Nations, Office of the Human Rights for High Commissioner. "Declaration on the Elimination of Violence against Women." General Assembly resolution 48/104, December 20, 1993. Accessed November 26, 2020. https://www.ohchr.org/EN/ProfessionalInterest/Pages/ViolenceAgainstWomen.aspx.

University of Iowa, Office of Sexual Misconduct Response Coordinator. "Sexual Misconduct." Accessed November 26, 2020. https://osmrc.uiowa.edu/policy/sexual-misconduct.

Vikram, Anuradha. *Decolonizing Culture: Essays on the Intersection of Art and Politics*. San Francisco: Art Practical Books and Sming Sming Books, 2017.

Viso, Olga. "Decolonizing the Art Museum: The Next Wave." *New York Times*, May 1, 2018. Accessed June 24, 2021. https://www.nytimes.com/2018/05/01/opinion/decolonizing-art-museums.html.

Wallace-Wells, David. *The Uninhabitable Earth: Life after Warming*. New York: Tim Duggan Books, 2019.

Wambach, Abby. "Remarks as Delivered: Commencement 2018." Barnard College. Accessed November 11, 2020. https://barnard.edu/commencement/archives/2018/abby-wambach-remarks.

Way, Katie. "'I Went on a Date with Aziz Ansari. It Turned into the Worst Night of My Life." *Babe*, January 13, 2018. Accessed November 24, 2020. https://babe.net/2018/01/13/aziz-ansari-28355.

Wenger, Étienne. *Communities of Practice: Learning, Meaning and Identity*. Cambridge: Cambridge University Press, 1998.

Weston, Anthony. *A 21st Century Ethical Toolbox*. 2nd ed. New York: Oxford University Press, 2008.

Wikipedia. "*RiP!: A Remix Manifesto*." Accessed December 15, 2020. https://en.wikipedia.org/wiki/RiP!:_A_Remix_Manifesto.

Wong, Helen, and June Ying Yee. *An Anti-Oppression Framework for Child Welfare in Ontario.* Toronto: Ontario Association of Children's Aid Societies, 2010.

Woolf, Nicky. "Urban Outfitters Settles with Navajo Nation after Illegally Using Tribe's Name." *Guardian*, November 19, 2016.

Wortham, Jenna. "It's RuPaul's Moment (Can I Get an Amen?)." *New York Times*, January 26, 2018. Accessed May 17, 2021. https://www.nytimes.com/2018/01/26/insider/rupaul-drag-race-cultural-influence.html.

Y.O.C. the Youth Organizing Collective. "Nat Turner." *The Report Back.* HOLLA Music Group, 2019.

Yoshino, Kenji, and Christie Smith. "Fear of Being Different Stifles Talent." *Harvard Business Review*, March 14, 2014. Accessed May 25, 2021. https://hbr.org/2014/03/fear-of-being-different-stifles-talent.

Zacharek, Stephanie, Eliana Dockterman, and Haley Sweetland Edwards. "The Silence Breakers." *Time.com*, December 8, 2017. Accessed October 26, 2020. http://time.com/time-person-of-the-year-2017-silence-breakers/.

Zbitnew, Anne, with Kim Fullerton, Lenore McMillan, and Fran Odette. *Accessibility Toolkit: Guide to Making Art Spaces Accessible*. https://tangledarts.org/wp-content/uploads/2018/10/Accessibility_Toolkit-1.pdf.

Index

About the Author

■ ■ ■

Dr. **Miranda Campbell** is associate professor in the School of Creative Industries at Ryerson University in Toronto, Canada, where she teaches courses in creative collaboration, diversity, equity, and inclusion, and care ethics. Her research focuses on creative employment, youth culture, and small-scale and emerging forms of cultural production. Her first book, *Out of the Basement: Youth Cultural Production in Practice and in Policy*, mapped the changing realities of youth self-employment in creative fields in the twenty-first century and was shortlisted for the Donner Prize for the best public policy book by a Canadian. Dr. Campbell's involvement with creative communities includes coordination and board of director roles with Rock Camp for Girls Montreal, a summer camp dedicated to empowerment for girls through music education, and with Whippersnapper Gallery, an artist-run center focusing on emerging artists in Toronto.

www.ingramcontent.com/pod-product-compliance
Lightning Source LLC
Chambersburg PA
CBHW070332270326
41926CB00017B/3849
9781538145050